The Men Who Lost Singapore
1938–1942

The Men Who
Lost Singapore
1938–1942

RONALD MCCRUM

NUS PRESS
SINGAPORE

© 2017 Ronald McCrum

Published by:
NUS Press
National University of Singapore
AS3-01-02, 3 Arts Link
Singapore 117569

Fax: (65) 6774-0652
E-mail: nusbooks@nus.edu.sg
Website: http://nuspress.nus.edu.sg

ISBN 978-981-4722-39-1

National Library Board, Singapore Cataloguing-in-Publication Data

McCrum, Ronald, author
    The men who lost Singapore, 1938-1942 / Ronald McCrum. – Singapore:
    NUS Press, [2017]
    Includes bibliographical references and index.
    ISBN 978-981-4722-39-1 (paperback)
    LCSH: Great Britain—Colonies—Asia—Administration. | Great Britain—
    Colonies—Officials and employees. | Governors—Singapore—History—20th
    century. | Singapore—History—Siege, 1942. | World War, 1939-1945—Campaigns—
    Singapore.
    DDC
    940.5425957 — dc23   OCN959875701

Cover photo: Reproduced from photograph courtesy Imperial War Museum, London—ACM Sir Robert Brooke-Popham, Duff-Cooper, Sir Shenton Thomas and Vice-Admiral Geoffrey Layton

Typeset by: Jojy Philip
Printed by: Markono Print Media Pte Ltd

CONTENTS

ACKNOWLEDGEMENTS

I am most grateful to the many authors whose inspirational and learned works I have drawn upon during my research. Their contributions are listed in the Bibliography. I am also hugely indebted to the various people who found time to talk with me and offer advice, particularly veterans of the period whose reminisces and nostalgic tales brought alive the prevailing conditions. Among numerous others whose advice and guidance was pivotal are Dr Mike Charney, Professor Brian P. Farrell, Dr Malcolm Murfett, Emeritus Professor Nicholas Tarling, Major General Clifford Kinvig, Dr Philip Towle, Peter Elphick, Brigadier James Percival, Dr Paul H. Kratoska, Sibylla Flower, Merilyn Hewel-Jones, Colonel Christopher Myers, Andrew Barber, Captain Richard Channon RN, Datuk Henry Barlow, John Evans, Mako Yoshiura Haro Fujio, Prabhakaran S. Nair, Sylvia Yap, Lucy McCann, Professor Susan Lim, Jonathan Moffatt, Francis Kennett, Tim Bishop and Eliza McCrum. I am especially indebted to the very helpful and always cheerful archive staff at the Imperial War Museum, London; Rhodes House Library, Oxford University; Liddell Hart Centre, King's College London; Churchill College Archive Centre, University of Cambridge; Arkib Negara, Kuala Lumpur, Malaysia; the National Archives, Singapore; Australian War Memorial; and Secker & Warburg.

PROLOGUE

The Japanese invasion of Malaya, and their later conquest of Singapore in 1942, was an event of significantly more political consequence than was its strategic impact on the course of the war in the Far East. The defeat of a sizeable British imperial military force and the speed and humiliation with which it was inflicted, destroyed forever the icon of British invincibility and prestige. This fateful affair, most historians agree, was the catalyst that signalled the demise of the British Empire. The loss of the "island fortress" to an Asian military invader demolished the cultivated, centuries-old image of British infallibility.

Following the ravages of the First World War, Britain was impoverished, economically and militarily. An increasing inability to meet the disparate demands of a worldwide empire became grievously exposed. One manifestation of this bankruptcy was the failure to provide Singapore with the tools to meet an invasion. The paucity of military support from London for the Far East theatre was abysmal and it shrank even more when the Second World War erupted in Europe.

The shocking military failure of this campaign is a well-documented and closely examined affair. And while most analyses focus on the performance of the military, scant attention has been given to the role of the Colonial Governor and his staff during this period. Their participation has not been subjected to the same rigorous scrutiny. Quite evidently, they had a vital role to play in conjunction with the military to prepare the people and the country for a possible war. The colonial administration's contribution to this duty bordered on negligence. By pursuing different priorities, often demanded by Whitehall, the civil authorities needlessly created distraction and serious confusion to an already harassed military. The shamefully poor, even hostile, relations that developed between the local government and the military hierarchy hampered a joint approach to the growing threat and shaped the course of the campaign. In addition, the apathetic management of civil defence matters led to a scandalous and unnecessary loss of civilian life.

In this book, I examine in detail the role and the responsibilities of the colonial government both in the lead-up to the war and during it. My research has left me with the conviction that the British administration responsible for the affairs of Singapore and Malaya at this crucial time, was a seriously flawed establishment. It was composed of mediocre bureaucrats unable and, more seriously, unwilling to confront the enormity of the challenge about to engulf them and the people for whose protection they were responsible.

LIST OF ABBREVIATIONS

ABDACOM	American–British–Dutch–Australian Command
ADM	Admiralty (British)
AFHQ	Allied Forces Headquarters
AIR	Air Ministry (British)
AOC	Air Officer Commanding
ARP	Air Raid Precautions
AWM	Australian War Memorial
BAM	British Association of Malaya
BEF	British Expeditionary Force
BP	Bletchley Park
CAS	Chief of Air Staff
CBS	Columbia Broadcasting System
CIBM	Combined Intelligence Bureau, Malaya
CID	Committee of Imperial Defence
C-in-C	Commander-in-chief
CIGS	Chief of Imperial General Staff
CO	Colonial Office
COS	Chief of Staff
COIS	Chief of Intelligence Staff
CU	Cambridge University
DGCD	Director General of Civil Defence
DMI	Director of Military Intelligence
DMO	Directorate of Military Operations
Enigma	German rotor cryptograph

FE	Far East
FECB	Far East Combined Bureau, Singapore
FESS	Far Eastern Security Service, Singapore
FEW	Far East Weekly (Intelligence Summary)
FMS	Federated Malay States
FO	Foreign Office
FORCE 136	SOE in the Far East
GHQ	General Headquarters
GOC	General Officer Commanding
HK	Hong Kong
ICS	Indian Civil Service
IISS	International Institute for Strategic Studies
IJA	Imperial Japanese Army
IIL	Indian Independence League
INA	Indian National Army
JIC	Joint Intelligence Committee
JPS	Joint Planning Staff
KL	Kuala Lumpur (capital of FMS)
KMM	Kesatuan Melayu Muda (League of Malay Youth)
KMT	Kuomintang (Chinese Nationalist Party)
Magic	Decrypts of Japanese diplomatic material
MCP	Malayan Communist Party
MCS	Malayan Civil Service
MPAJA	Malayan People's Anti-Japanese Army
NCO	Non-Commissioned Officer
NUS	National University of Singapore
OAG	Officer Administering the Government
POW	Prisoner of War
Purple	American name for the Japanese Type B cryptograph
PWD	Public Works Department
RAF	Royal Air Force
RCS	Royal Commonwealth Society
RN	Royal Navy
SAC	Strategic Appreciation Committee
SEAC	South East Asia Command
SOE	Special Operations Executive
S of S	Secretary of State

SS	Straits Settlements
UK	United Kingdom
Ultra	British classification for signals intelligence
UMS	Unfederated Malay States
USA	United States of America
WO	War Office

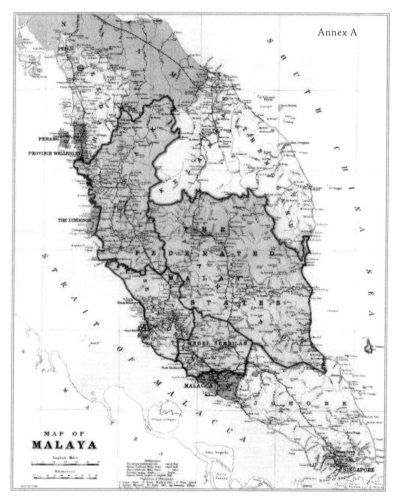

Annex A

Map of Malaya
(Courtesy SOAS Library, SOAS, University of London)

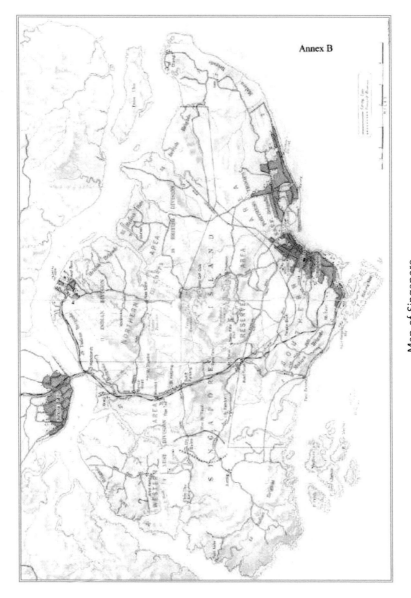

Annex B

Map of Singapore
(Courtesy SOAS Library, SOAS, University of London)

1

INTRODUCTION

At 5.15 pm on 15 February 1942, the British and Japanese delegations met to agree the terms of surrender of the British Forces. They assembled at the relatively undamaged, bare and austere works offices of the Ford Motor Factory in the centre of Singapore Island. The tall, spare and unprepossessing figure of the British commander, Lieutenant General Arthur Percival, led the delegation of senior staff officers, all looking disconsolate. The distressing photograph recording this event shows the group arriving, looking incongruous in steel helmets and shorts, towering over their Japanese captors. The triumphant, short, pugnacious Japanese army commander, Lieutenant General Tomoyuki Yamashita, was waiting for them. The Governor, Sir Shenton Thomas, refused to attend this ceremony. He regarded the loss of Singapore as an ignominious military disaster and the military alone, therefore, should face the indignity of laying down their arms. He was not surrendering the Crown Colony.[1] His resolve—to disassociate his government from the military failure— was symptomatic of the poor civil-military relationship which had so dominated the campaign and inhibited a united war effort. His pretentious stand, however, was a mere technical statement of no political significance. Thomas was a colonial officer of the old school and of limited ability. He

---

[1] Brian Montgomery, *Shenton of Singapore: Governor and Prisoner of War* (London: Leo Cooper in association with Secker & Warburg, 1984), p. 138. It is interesting to contrast this standpoint with that taken by the Governor of Hong Kong, Sir Mark Young, who resisted military advice to surrender the colony to the Japanese until it was clearly impossible to carry on and then insisted that he as Governor would surrender the colony.

was on his final posting before retirement and had wanted a quiet and uneventful conclusion. His bailiwick included Peninsula Malaya as well as Singapore and some outlying islands. Throughout the campaign, he sought the least contentious solutions to serious issues of war preparation. He frequently ignored military advice, lacked resolve and equivocated. The demands of his colonial masters for ever-increasing production of the vital war commodities, rubber and tin, obsessed him. He never seems to have thought to warn London of his quandary: he could not simultaneously prepare the country for invasion and increase production.

The fall of Singapore was the end of an era; British authority would never be the same again. The effect on world opinion of the loss of Singapore proved to be more serious than its effect upon the course of the war.[2] Western power and authority was no longer secure and the relationship between the European and Asian peoples changed forever. Doubts arose in the minds of the indigenous peoples of Malaya and Singapore, for whose protection Britain was responsible. The first flaws appeared as early as ten days after the Japanese landings when the British hastily abandoned the island of Penang. Only the Europeans on the island had warning of the impending withdrawal and arrangements made for their departure. The Asian population was not told of the danger. The later reaction from the local people was one of disbelief and astonishment. They were shocked at the apparent inability of the civilian administration to deal with the emergencies of war, and of their display of racial selectivity and the failure to tell them, honestly, what was happening.[3] It also cast the European civilian population as a whole in a bewildering and damaging image, and diminished the existing relationship.

Many have claimed that the population of Malaya was neither psychologically nor physically prepared for the ordeal that descended upon it and, importantly, despite endless pleadings from the military authorities for support, Britain proved powerless to avert it.[4] The

[2] Virginia Thompson, *Postmortem on Malay* (New York: The Macmillan Company, 1943), p. vii.

3 Ernest C.T. Chew and Edwin Lee, eds, *A History of Singapore* (New York: Oxford University Press, 1991), p. 117.

[4] See, for example, the case made by Sir George Sansom in the Foreword to *Postmortem on Malay*.

revisionist theory is that the colonial power should have either sent adequate forces from outside to avoid the disaster or given the indigenous population enough of a stake in the colony to make it worth its while to help defend British rule. Contemporary journalist Virginia Thompson suggested that "the root of the evil lay in the purely economic form of imperialism which developed and which failed to weld the peoples of the country into a Malayan nation".[5]

It is true that the colonial governance of Malaya focused on the exploitation of the country's natural resources rather than on preparing the nation for self-government. On the other hand, there was no compelling reason to change the status quo. The administration was working perfectly satisfactorily and created many benefits for the people. There was not a restless population demanding change and scant evidence of any nationalist desire. A little-known Malay organization, Kesatuan Muda Melayu (League of Malay Youth), tried to arouse interest but had limited success.[6] Moreover, at no point throughout the period of British rule had there been even a hint of an external threat to the country's security, a condition which might have forced the authorities to attempt to create a unified nation. Even so, in the light of subsequent events, it is doubtful that a united Malayan nation would have had any noticeable impact on the course of the campaign.

Both the local inhabitants and the Colonial Office (CO) in London regarded this corner of Southeast Asia as a successful and peaceful backwater. That is not to say, however, that the question of self-determination did not arise. The authorities both in the country and in London debated the issue on a number of occasions, sometimes heatedly. The matter of governance was complex in that Britain's piecemeal expansion into Peninsular Malaya meant that, by the 1930s, the country consisted of autonomous and semi-autonomous states. Before the late

---

[5] Ibid. See also Christopher Bayly and Tim Harper, *Forgotten Wars* (London: Allen Lane, 2007), p. 10.

[6] John Sturgus Bastin and Robin W. Winks, *Malaysia: Selected Historical Readings* (Kuala Lumpur and New York: Oxford University Press, 1966), p. 294; Thomas Silcock and Ungku Abdul Aziz, "Nationalism in Malaya", in *Asian Nationalism and the West: A Symposium Based on Documents and Reports of the Eleventh Conference Institute of Pacific Relations*, ed. William Holland (New York: Octogon, 1953).

19th century, Britain largely practised a non-interventionist policy; its primary interest was its trading posts along the west coast, known as the Straits Settlements (Penang, Province Wellesley, Malacca and Singapore). Thereafter, several factors persuaded the British to play a more active role on the mainland, such as fluctuating supplies of raw materials (the Straits Settlements becoming increasingly dependent on the economy of the Malay States) and requests for assistance from state rulers to either resolve disputes or help them suppress internecine troubles. The outcome was a plethora of different agreements and relationships with individual states. Over time, it became clear that some form of rationalization was needed. Each state ruler, however, while accepting British advice, protection, progress and economic growth, showed little enthusiasm for centralized control. By the end of the 19th century, Britain nevertheless persuaded the four contiguous and most lucrative states on the west coast (Selangor, Perak, Negri Sembilan and Pahang) to combine into a federation, the Federated Malay States (FMS), with Kuala Lumpur (KL) as its capital. The remaining states were classified as "Unfederated" (UMS). The important implication of this administrative medley was that the Governor, in 1940, did not have the jurisdiction to impose nationwide commands. In the Straits Settlements he had absolute power; in the FMS limited authority; and in the UMS merely an advisory role. This meant that if matters arose which would clearly be beneficial countrywide, they had to undergo lengthy consultative processes with each state.

Added to this administrative miscellany was the complex racial make-up of the peoples of Malaya. The Malays were the *Bumiputera* (sons of the soil), the rightful indigenous natives of the country. The Chinese, made up of mainland Chinese and Malayan-born Chinese, together with Indians from southern India and local born, comprised the multinational and segregated community. At this point in the country's development these different ethnic groups rarely intermarried, lived separate existences, spoke different languages and had different religions. They were also inclined to confine their employment to specific niches of the economy; Indians, for example, worked mostly as labourers on rubber estates and on the railways and those with some education gravitated towards clerical employment.[7] The Chinese had strong commercial instincts which, combined with their natural hard-work ethic, meant that they dominated the business world. Most of the big trading companies were Chinese-owned and the tin industry was very dependent on Chinese labour. The Malays were inclined towards agriculture and fishing and as yet showed no political or national aspirations, content that their country should be run for them. "A plural society was evolving which would inevitably place heavy emphasis on communal rather than 'national' values."[8]

A consequence of the evolving colonial arrangements, barely noticeable in peacetime, was the variety of government departments that mushroomed to deal with the increasing cultural, social, structural and commercial issues in a materially rich, developing, multicultural country. Many of these departments were independent, answering directly to their authorities in London. Soon after the outbreak of war in Europe, it became evident that:

> The multiplicity of official organs in the Far East was hampering the conduct of affairs. The strain of emergencies revealed weakness in the governmental structure which not only prevented quick and concerted action but also had the serious disadvantage that, because the picture of events in the Far East was presented piecemeal by a variety of organs overseas to a variety of departments in London, the essential unity of the problem of the Far East tended to be obscured. [9]

Later, this autonomy would cause serious confusion and obstruct coordination of action, but even before the onset of war the mass of uncoordinated data from Singapore to London was so bewildering that attempts were made to deal with it. Special organs like the Eastern Group Supply Council were established in London, and the Far Eastern Branch of the Ministry of Information and the Far East Mission of the Ministry of Economic Warfare were established in Singapore. There was also in Singapore the Far East Combined Bureau (FECB) of Intelligence,

---

[7] Bastin and Winks, *Malaysia*, p. 257; Robert Jackson, "Indian Immigration into Malaya", in *Malaysia: Selected Historical Readings*, ed. John Sturgus Bastin and Robin W. Winks (Kuala Lumpur and New York: Oxford University Press, 1966).

[8] Ibid., p. 272.

[9] Thompson, *Postmortem on Malaya*, p. xv.

which collected and collated naval, military and political information, principally for the use of the service commanders. All these mediums provoked the major complaint, which became glaringly obvious, about the lack of a single and authoritative voice in the Far East able to speak in convincing terms to the government in the United Kingdom (UK).[10]

In the military domain, the forces were catastrophically short of vital weapons and armaments of war, for which they had been pleading for years, though this failure to deliver must be judged against the context of Britain's global obligations at that time. Churchill had decided that the needs of the Libyan and the Russian fronts must come first, and Britain was simply not in a position to provide and meet simultaneously several worldwide demands for manpower and equipment. Anything given to Malaya would have been at the expense of the other theatres. In any case, as will be seen, because the strategic assumptions for the defence of Singapore were forever changing, it would have been impossible to assemble, in time, the correct balance of men and equipment to defeat a determined Japanese attack.

The fall of France left Britain without an ally to protect the vital Mediterranean Sea route, a task that Britain now had to take on alone. In turn, this meant that one of the tenets of the defence of Malaya, a deterrent naval fleet sailing quickly to Singapore, was not available. Furthermore, France's capitulation left its Far East possession, Indo-China, virtually defenceless and enabled the Japanese to establish themselves there and in Thailand. Nor did any of the pre-war military "studies" envisage Japan attacking the United States of America (USA) at the same time as assaulting British and Dutch possessions. Indeed, Churchill believed that any thought Japan may have had of advancing down Asia's eastern seaboard would be deterred by the knowledge that its long exposed flank would be vulnerable to the power of America's mighty Pacific Fleet sailing from Hawaii.[11] Fundamentally, strategic military shortcomings can be attributed not so much to misjudgement but to the compelling needs of global warfare.

---

[10] "Report on Lessons from the Point of View of the Colonial Administration in Wartime from the Experience of Hong Kong and Malaya", CO 967/80, 4 Dec. 1942, NA.
[11] CAB 79/6. COS 317th meeting, 19 Sept. 1940, NA.

The strategic concept upon which the Singapore Naval Base was founded was that it was a protected naval harbour from which a powerful fleet could operate. In addition, at the time of its planning and the beginning of construction in the 1920s, the perceived threat was properly assessed to be from the sea because the hinterland of the Malay Peninsula, still covered in dense tropical forest and with a primitive communications network, was regarded as virtually impenetrable. At this stage, nearly all internal transportation was by river craft. The coastal defences were thus built to protect Singapore from a sea approach. The claim made by some that Singapore was lost because the guns faced the wrong way, is inaccurate. This conviction appears to have started with a disaffected civilian government official, C.A. Vlieland, who in his capacity as Secretary of Defence in the Singapore government (1939–41) should have offered a more qualified judgement. After the war, he claimed:

> No one should have been fooled by the legend of the mighty fortress of Singapore. The place had none of the natural characteristics of an old time fortress like Gibraltar; nor was it 'fortified' in any way, though it had been armed with guns which were useless against anything but a sea-borne assault.[12]

The primary task of the installed heavy artillery was to fire armour-piercing shells at warships at sea, though some of the guns were capable of pointing at the mainland and were later actually so used.

During the naval base's 12 years of construction, weapons of war and armaments became more sophisticated and technologically, spectacularly advanced. Added to this many areas of mainland Malaya opened up, particularly on the west coast, with the building of roads and railways and the laying down of larger areas for rubber estates. The most important factor in developing the west coast was the tin industry. The first roads and railways were built to connect tin mines to the ports and towns.[13] Plans for the defence of the naval base had to be constantly

---

[12] Vlieland Papers, King's College London, LHCMA.

[13] Siew Nim Chee, "The Tin Mining Industry in Malaya" as quoted in John Sturgus Bastin and Robin W. Winks, *Malaysia: Selected Historical Readings* (Kuala Lumpur and New York: Oxford University Press, 1966), p. 281.

revised in the light of these developments and as the strategic outlook in
the Far East changed in regard to Japan's restless aggressive behaviour.
Then, with the outbreak of war in Europe, it became abundantly clear
that the main strength of the Royal Navy was needed in the Atlantic and
the Mediterranean and there would be precious few warships available to
rush to the aid of Singapore.

It was one thing to identify the changing threat and reassess the
manpower and equipment needed to meet it, and quite another to be
given the wherewithal for the task. After much debate, and mindful of
their meagre resources, the services eventually agreed that the weight
of responsibility for the defence of the naval base lay with the air force,
the premise being that a strong air arm would destroy an invading
force well out to sea. Consequently, the Royal Air Force (RAF) asked
for a substantial increase in number and quality of aircraft. The Chiefs
of Staff in London promised them a significant enhancement, albeit
short of their ideal. On this basis deployment plans were drawn up and
airfields constructed. Unfortunately, the choice of airfield locations was
taken without consulting the army whose task it was to protect them.
The upshot was that a significant proportion of already under strength
ground forces were dispersed to defend airfields in remote locations
over a vast area and, because of the nature of the terrain, there was little
chance of swiftly redeploying or reinforcing them. Some airfields were
built on the exposed east coast, in places next to long and excellent
beaches, which were difficult to defend and of which the Japanese were
later to take full advantage.[14]

The promised modern aircraft never came and the Royal Navy's late
and inconsequential contribution, without air support, meant that the
outcome of the campaign became evident within days of the Japanese
landings. After 48 hours of battle, the RAF had only ten serviceable,
obsolete aircraft remaining in the area. They were compelled to withdraw
from northern Malaya. Due to a serious miscalculation, the Royal Navy's
only two capital ships in the Far East were sunk. While no historian
has argued that with the existing conditions at the time of the invasion

---

[14] Dennis Richards and Hilary St George Saunders, *Royal Air Force 1939–1945:
Volume II: The Fight Avails* (London: Her Majesty's Stationer's Office, 1954), p. 7.

Singapore could have been saved, there is nevertheless a strong case made that a more aggressive and determined defence could perhaps have created time to enable reinforcements to arrive, which might have turned the tide of events,[15] and that perhaps a more proactive administration could have helped the military install better defences to delay the enemy for longer. Unquestionably, it would have been invaluable to have a country forewarned of the ordeals ahead and told how its citizens could help and how they could contribute to preparations.

The many diagnoses of the campaign have thus far not considered explicitly the place of the civilian administration in Singapore's failed defence. It is self-evident that the Governor and his team of civil servants had a crucial part to play in this momentous historical event, but their role has not, to my knowledge, been subjected to the same close analysis as has the military.

Official and severe criticism has been levelled at the government of Shenton Thomas for the tardy and casual approach it took about alerting the peoples of Malaya to the danger ahead, and its failure to put in place a properly organized civil defence infrastructure. Probably more importantly, Thomas and his staff had not compiled emergency plans for the evacuation of civilians or designed a system for the continued administration of the Malayan states during hostilities. A prime example was the lack of civil management during the loss of the island of Penang, which revealed serious weaknesses in local civil administration and military control. After it was heavily bombed on 11 December and for three days afterwards, the destruction and casualties were dreadful. Nearly all the essential services broke down and most of the local population fled to Penang Hill. However, it was the hasty evacuation of the European population, on the misguided orders of a confused civil-military command, which caused the greatest offence. This evacuation became a *cause célèbre* and a huge embarrassment to the government

---

[15] The view of Colonel (later General) Jacob, a member of the War Cabinet Secretariat was that, with conditions existing at the time of the invasion, Singapore was "hopeless from the start" and that the fall of Singapore and Malaya was a foregone conclusion from the time of the first landings at Singora and Patani. Quoted in Clifford Kinvig, *Scapegoat: General Percival of Singapore* (London and Washington, DC: Brassey's, 1996), p. 223.

in Singapore because of its effect on Asian opinion.[16] Had a number of British civil servants remained in place they might have been able to arrange for an orderly evacuation of the Asian population who, aware of Japanese gratuitous cruelty, stood in particular danger from the invaders.

Governor Thomas had a strong belief, not wholly shared by the military, that the Japanese would not invade Malaya or if they did, would be driven back into the sea. The colonial authorities in London, urging political caution in any estimation of Japanese intentions, may have heavily influenced his conviction.[17] Nevertheless, he was privy to all the immediate regional military and political intelligence information, which increasingly and accurately predicted Japanese activities. He maintained that his major concern was to meet the directive from the CO to increase the production of vital war commodities. Determined that nothing should interfere with the task, he objected to the military preparing overt defensive sites and would not release labour to help the army with this work. Thomas passionately believed that the construction of trenches and the laying of minefields were bad for the morale of the population. They would convey a defeatist image, which in turn would infect the motivation to work.[18] The General Officer Commanding (GOC), General Percival, was of a similar opinion about the effect on morale, though specifically on soldiers' morale, of rearward defences. It seems that this mindset of the Governor also pervaded his control of information given to the country before and during the war. He imposed such severe restrictions on the release of details about the progress of the invasion that much of the population was quite unaware of the advancing Imperial Japanese Army until it was upon them. Even when the Japanese were

---

[16] Raymond Callahan, *The Worst Disaster: The Fall of Singapore* (London: Associated University Press, 1977), p. 242.

[17] See ODC Paper No: 19, 20 Mar. 1940, NA. When Thomas attended a joint planning sub-committee in London during his 1940 leave, a committee member (Air Commander Slessor) also informed him "that at the present it was not intended that we should go to war with Japan even if they advanced into Indo-China or Thailand"(CO967/75). Also, in the opinion of Churchill, as late as 28 Apr. 1941, Japan was unlikely to enter the war if it feared the United States would join the allied cause. PREM 3/156/6 reprinted in James Ramsay Montagu Butler, *Grand Strategy. Vol. 2, September 1939–June 1941* (London HMSO, 1957), pp. 577–8.

[18] Peter Thompson, *The Battle for Singapore* (London: Portrait Books, 2005), p. 42.

in Johor Bahru, looking across the 1-kilometre causeway at Singapore Island and preparing to attack, the scale of the imminent catastrophe was barely raised. A chaotic evacuation arrangement for women and children was underway, but so ambiguous was the war news that others were still partying and dining in the hotels and clubs of Singapore city. The press was not allowed to use the word "siege".[19]

By late 1940, the British Government was becoming more than a little concerned by evident aggressive Japanese behaviour in the Far East. It was also troubled that the politico-military relations and arrangements in Singapore, to meet the worrying development, were less than satisfactory. In a half-hearted attempt to remedy the discord, it appointed an elderly and retired Air Chief Marshal, Sir Robert Brooke-Popham, as Commander-in-Chief (C-in-C), and later, in 1941, Alfred Duff Cooper, a senior government minister in need of employment, to coordinate the military strategy and improve the relations between the military and the administration. Neither appointment was entirely successful. The elderly, pedestrian C-in-C, recalled to service but with restricted powers, only added another layer to an already cumbersome structure. The minister, an arrogant, failed Cabinet Officer, after too brief a review, recommended swinging changes, which included the sacking of senior civil servants and even a proposal to replace the Governor. Instead of being helpful, the new incumbents were not only resentful of the others' authority but also disagreed with each other.

The focus of this book is an examination of the behaviour of the civil authorities in this crisis. In retrospect, their behaviour was ranked as irresponsible and incompetent. Their failure to manage an emergency exposed a gross failure of duty to the people for whom they were responsible. From the Governor down, a languid, nonchalant approach to the danger was engendered and propagated. And even when the enemy arrived, there was still a pedestrian scepticism about the gravity of the state of affairs. Why did this happen, and why, when it became obvious that confusion and disagreement reigned, did the British government allow it to continue? These are issues I address.

---

[19] Noel Barber, *Sinister Twilight: The Fall and Rise again of Singapore* (London: Collins, 1969), p. 133.

2

HARBINGERS OF WAR

The warning indicators of Japan's desire for the lands of Southeast Asia were, in the light of Britain's later pitiful response, distressingly obvious. By the middle of 1941, Japan had greatly expanded its territorial possessions: it aggressively occupied Hainan, Formosa and took possession of Indo-China (Vietnam) and openly declared its intention of forming a Greater East Asia Co-Prosperity Sphere, by force if necessary,[1] all this while at the same time performing a charade of engaging in talks in Washington aimed at having an economic embargo removed and resuming normal relations with the western powers. Allied intelligence sources reported an increase in Japanese agents in southern Thailand and a build-up of military forces, resources and aircraft in southern Indo-China. Moreover, the British ambassador to Tokyo, Sir Robert Craigie, cabled his strong belief that the behaviour of the Japanese authorities and other information he acquired, indicated a pre-emptive southern assault.

> It would be unsafe to assume too confidently that Japan does not want a campaign in the south .... Should Washington conversations break down, immediate move southwards cannot be excluded, despite weather conditions.[2]

---

[1] Intelligence information from many sources was compiled by the Joint Intelligence Committee (JIC), London and sent to Singapore, keeping them informed of Japanese movement. In addition, the Far Eastern Combined Bureau (FECB) had regional agents providing information. The acting consul's generals were also important informers.

[2] FO Cable No. 2079. Craigie to FO, 22 Oct. 1941. Repeated to Singapore as No. 367 on 23 Oct. 1941, NA.

By this time, Japan had increased significantly the size of its armed forces. The great majority of them were well-equipped and battle-hardened. By 1941, in addition to its army in China and with bases in the southern reaches of East Asia, Japan was poised to fulfil its brazenly declared expansionist designs. Malaya, and in particular Singapore, was a crucial objective in the Japanese strategic plan for the conquest of Southeast Asia.[3]

In this twilight period preceding the Singapore debacle, the civilian authorities were barely bothered by the belligerent Japanese behaviour intensifying throughout Southeast Asia. The Governor and his staff, while not contemptuous, took scant notice of the rising potency of military indicators. Japanese conduct in far-off China and French Indo-China caused little anxiety to the colonial government. The conflagration erupting in western Europe received more attention. But, apart from acknowledging London's demand for increased supply of rubber and tin, it did not inspire an appraisal of the likely implications for the Straits Settlements and Malaya. And it certainly did not prevent the Governor from preparing for his mid-term leave in England.

It was Japan's grand strategy for territorial expansion in East Asia, particularly after the First World War, that forced Britain to re-examine its capability to defend its Eastern Dominions and colonial responsibilities. Japan had already won two important wars: against China in 1894 and Russia in 1905, when it had established rights in the Chinese province of South Manchuria and claimed a right to Korea. It also fought on the side of the Western Allies against Germany in 1914–18 and at the end of the war, in return for this support, sought an extension of its rights on the Chinese mainland in what was the former German sphere of the Shantung Peninsula, as well as in Manchuria and Fukien. The Versailles Conference in 1919 confirmed these gains and it emerged from this conference with an enhanced status and a place among the major world powers. Its success and authority in these adventures increased its desire for territorial supremacy,[4] added to which the Japanese people had, for some time, believed it was their natural destiny

---

[3] Masanobu Tsuji, *Singapore: The Japanese Version* (New York: St Martin's Press, 1960), p. 216.

[4] John Keegan, *The Second World War* (New York: Viking, 1990 [1989]), pp. 240–5.

to control and lead the nations of East Asia. "The Japanese people came to believe that the extension of their control over this vast region was both natural and destined."[5] Further, by 1936, there was the pragmatic and serious economic consideration of a need for an accessible empire rich in natural wealth. At this point, the Japanese nation was suffering a severe financial crises compounded by not having fully recovered from the world depression of 1929 and, more than most, was heavily affected by the disintegration of the world trading markets. Japan was no longer self-sufficient in food. It relied heavily on imported raw material such as non-ferrous metals, rubber and, above all, oil to sustain its industry and manufacture armaments for its armed forces. The solution to the economic crises lay in the mineral and agriculturally rich lands of its East Asian neighbours. "There in the crumbling British, Dutch and French Empires lay the oil, rubber, bauxite and other vital resources Japan needed so badly."[6]

A further significant and pressing problem was population growth and the demand for more food and basic commodities. In 1868, the population of Japan stood at 32 million, and the area under rice cultivation was 6 million acres with a total yield of 125 million bushels. The average consumption per head of population, per annum was about 4 bushels, so at this time there was enough rice to feed the country. By 1940, however, the population was 73 million, while the cultivated area had risen only marginally to 8 million acres, yielding 325 million bushels. Consumption had risen to over 5 bushels per head, so there was a rice shortage of approximately 65 million bushels.[7] Anticipating the mounting problem an eminent Japanese banker, Hirozo Mori, stated in October 1937:

> Our population is increasing, and this increase can be supported only by expansion of trade and industry, for which the nearest market is China and the Asiatic mainland. Herein lies our economic future. There

---

[5] Herbert Feis, *The Road to Pearl Harbor: The Coming of the War between the United States and Japan* (Princeton, NJ: Princeton University Press, 1971 [1967]), p. 3.

[6] Louis Morton, *Japan's Decision for War. United States Army in World War II: The War in the Pacific*, US Naval Institute Proceedings, vol. 80 (Dec. 1954) (Washington, DC: Office of the Chief of Military History).

[7] David H. James, *The Rise and Fall of the Japanese Empire* (London: Allen & Unwin, 1951), p. 16. See also Feis, *The Road to Pearl Harbor*, p. 234, fn.

is no gainsaying the fact. We want the world and the Chinese people to understand and recognise it.[8]

During this time the Japanese military increasingly determined government policies. Since 1900, the government appointments of Minister of War and Navy Minister were, by Imperial Ordinance, held only by serving army and navy officers. By 1918, the army was already showing a willingness to act independently of civil control, noticeably in operations against Soviet Russia in Siberia. By the mid-1930s, Japan's political development and strategy was dominated by senior officers of the armed forces. Its national policy shifted inexorably towards military power and imperial expansion.[9] By 1936, the Imperial Japanese Army, in particular, had gained a predominant influence in the political life of the nation and openly proclaimed the need to establish a firm position on the Asian mainland, which was its way of saying that China must be conquered. The overture to establishing authority in the region was the promotion of a proposal that the nations on the Pacific Rim should form a "Greater East Asia Co-Prosperity Sphere" under the direction and authority of Japan. The intention was that such a cooperative should first be attempted by peaceful and persuasive means. If that failed, military action in both China and Southeast Asia must follow. To prepare for that contingency the Japanese Government now turned its efforts to war production.

Japan first approached China with the Co-Prosperity Sphere proposal because it coveted China's agricultural regions. However, with little regard for diplomatic refinement and displaying the disdain in which it held China, the talks were unsuccessful. Under the leadership of Chiang Kai-shek and actively supported by the USA and other powers with special interests in the region, such as Britain and France, China refused to acquiesce to Japan's advances. The political atmosphere between the two countries became precarious and, with Japan's foreign policy blatantly and aggressively militaristic, even minor incidents between Chinese and Japanese troops became potentially explosive. In July 1937, skirmishes began near Peking and quickly erupted into full-scale war. The Chinese

---

[8] Morton, *Japan's Decision for War*, loc. cit, p. 23.
[9] Keegan, *The Second World War*, pp. 242–3 and passim.

army performed poorly and, in December, China's capital, Nanking, was ravaged by the Japanese army; Chiang Kai-shek's government fled to the interior. Within the next year, Japan completed its conquest of eastern and central China and proclaimed a New Order in which the western powers were to be driven out from eastern Asia.

The USA and the UK were affronted particularly by Japan's occupation of the southern Chinese seaboard, which prevented them from sending supplies directly to China by sea. In response, both countries resorted to sending aid overland through Burma on a highway known as the Burma Road. It ran from Rangoon to Lashio, northeast Burma and onto Chungking, the new centre of Chiang Kai-shek's government. This vital support stiffened Chiang's resolve not to capitulate. In reply, in February 1939, Japan occupied Hainan Island and, five months later, blockaded British and French concessions in Tientsin. In a confrontational retaliation, the USA renounced its treaty of commerce with Japan. This was a most serious commercial and economic setback. The Japanese Government concluded that its destiny now depended on the acquisition of the natural resources which were abundant in the Philippines, Burma, Malaya and the Dutch East Indies. There was another motive behind this reasoning. At this time, 1939, a major war had erupted in the west between Nazi Germany and the nations of western Europe and the allies urgently needed these very resources that Japan sought to control. Furthermore, witnessing the overwhelming success of the German blitzkrieg in Europe, Japan saw this as an opportunity to identify with the Axis powers and persuade them to endorse its own expansionist plans in the East. Most importantly, Japan noted that Germany's defeat of France left the way open for the acquisition of the French possession of Indo-China—an important foothold from which to launch imperialist expansion and, as Japan claimed, a bulwark to protect its own national security.[10] It also gave Japan the opportunity to consolidate its position in Peking and the treaty ports of Shanghai and Tientsin.

Japan demanded that the British withdraw their token forces from China's northern cities. Reflecting on the vulnerability of these small, isolated garrisons and the glaring fact that they were of little military

---

[10] Feis, *The Road to Pearl Harbor*, p. 104, fn. 8.

significance, Britain conceded and its troops were eventually withdrawn to bolster the forces in Singapore and Malaya. In September 1940, Japan also decided that the moment was right to join Germany and Italy to form a western Tripartite Alliance. Crucially, Japan then secured the others' endorsement for its New Order in East Asia.

By 1940, with a population over 73 million, Japan's experienced army consisted of 3 million men and a modern, equipped air force. In early 1941, adding the trained reserves under the age of 40, the total grew to reach 6 million under arms. The number of army divisions rose from 20 to 50, air squadrons from 50 to 150 (5,300 aircraft). And significantly, the naval combat tonnage shot up to over 1 million tons, which then gave Japan a navy more powerful than the combined fleets of America and Britain.[11]

Again, in 1941, on the pretext of intervening in a conflict which arose between the French Vichy forces and Thailand over a long-running border dispute, Japan realized its goal and established a military garrison in Indo-China. This brought the Japanese military into Southeast Asia for the first time.[12] This garrison, later in the year, increased in number to 40,000 troops and the occupation extended to cover the whole of Indo-China. Vichy, France, as Japan had anticipated, was in no position to resist. Thus, by the middle of 1941, Japan had greatly expanded its territorial possessions: its armed forces had significantly increased and, of these, the great majority was well-equipped and battle-experienced. In addition to its army in China, it had strategically located air and naval bases in the southern reaches of East Asia—Formosa, Hainan and now Indo-China—and was poised to fulfil its declared imperial expansionist designs in the region.

Even though Singapore was only one aspect in Japan's grand strategic design for the region, its location and thus its possession was a critical factor for the overall success of the Greater East Asia Co-Prosperity Sphere. Singapore lay at the junction of the Pacific and Indian oceans; from here, Japan could control the East-West sea routes and dominate the movement of shipping. Possessing it would give added security to

---

[11] Morton, *Japan's Decision for War*, loc. cit, p. 101.
[12] Feis, *The Road to Pearl Harbor*, passim.

Japan's line of communication to the south and deprive the Allies of a base from which to launch counter-attacks. Moreover, Singapore had recently completed the construction of a modern naval base capable of harbouring and servicing most of the Japanese fleet; additionally, the lucrative Malayan hinterland was rich in important minerals and rubber.

It was the change in the balance of power after the end of the First World War and Japan's expansionist aspirations that convinced Britain it needed to maintain a naval force in the Far East. It became obvious that the British government had to look at ways to guard the nation's trading sea routes to China and India. Britain also had a responsibility for the maritime protection of Australia and New Zealand, both of which were particularly alarmed about the growing Japanese naval strength and belligerent posturing.[13] The USA was also gravely concerned at Japan's naval growth. In an attempt to curtail what was becoming an arms race in the Pacific region and at the same time contain Japanese expansionist designs, the USA convened an international conference in Washington in 1921.

After much argument, the conference managed to impose universal limits and control on naval strength and naval bases relating to the maritime powers around the Pacific Rim. Following the Washington Naval Treaty agreements, the Committee of Imperial Defence (CID) in London sat in 1922 to both assess the effect of these changing political circumstances in the Far East and the proposed naval strengths in the region. The deliberations confirmed that a major naval base capable of accommodating and supporting a substantial part of the British Fleet was needed. "This was particularly important because of the change-over of the Fleet from coal to oil-firing; for there were not enough oil tankers in the world to fuel the Fleet on a voyage to the East and maintain it there at sea."[14] After an exhaustive study about possible locations, the Admiralty decided that Singapore was best suited both geographically and strategically as the location for the base. Until this point, Hong Kong was where Britain's China fleet harboured, but it was both too small for the anticipated deployment and too close to the Japanese presence on mainland China.

---

[13] Paul Haggie, *Britannia at Bay: The Defence of the British Empire against Japan 1931–1941* (Oxford: Clarendon Press and New York: Oxford University Press, 1981), p. 1.
[14] Feis, *The Road to Pearl Harbor*, p. 278.

In 1824 when the Sultan of Johor ceded Singapore to Sir Stamford Raffles, acting on behalf of the East India Company, it was almost uninhabited; now it was a prosperous city port but its only defence was a few guns protecting Keppel Harbour.[15] The selection of Singapore was not universally popular and, before work could begin, lengthy and fiery government financial debates took place about whether the whole project was necessary.[16] The uncertainty was further exacerbated by a change of government, which imposed new parameters on the plan and indeed at one point considered abandoning it. In an effort to reduce the proposed budget, a thorough examination of the intended facilities— size, dockyard capacity, fuelling services, arsenal and defensive arrangements—were all subject to intense scrutiny. After a number of false starts and compromises, the project finally got underway in 1926.[17]

There was, nevertheless, still disagreement about the important matter of how to defend this expensive new base. The Admiralty and the Air Ministry had strongly divergent opinions about its protection. In the mid-1920s, the perceived threat was likely to be an approach from the sea; the Admiralty favoured 15-inch guns and the air force torpedo bombers. At that time, there simply were not enough funds to have both. This dispute over which service—air or navy—should have predominance of responsibility for the defence of the base continued until 1931. A less than convincing case was made that the air force should prevail, but with the qualification that the aircraft and the entire infrastructure needed to support them should be permanent fixtures and not a transient group rushed there in time of tension.

The RAF then argued that, in the prevailing conditions, they needed to extend the radius of both their reconnaissance and offensive capability against seaborne enemy forces approaching from the Gulf of Thailand and the South China Sea. But the only airfields in Malaya in early 1930 were

---

[15] Louis Allen, *Singapore 1941–1942* (New Jersey: Associated University Press, 1977), p. 38.

[16] The CID declared "in existing circumstances aggressive action against the British Empire on the part of Japan within the next ten years is not a contingency seriously to be apprehended". Butler, *Grand Strategy*, quoted in N. H. Gibbs, Vol. I: *Rearmament Policy* (London: HMSO, 1976), p. 51.

[17] Haggie, *Britannia at Bay*, p. 3.

commercial and on the west coast. The conclusion was that three new airfields were required on the east coast of Malaya. A government report (Baldwin Committee)[18] nonetheless recommended that the first stage of gun emplacements should also go ahead and take precedence. It added that before the second stage began, the relative merits of both naval guns or aircraft were again to be explored. In July 1935 the government relented and, with funding contributions from Malaya, Hong Kong and New Zealand, authorized work to begin on additional heavy gun emplacements and two airfields, as part of the second stage.[19] Thus, from the very outset, there was no outright agreement on the necessity for a large naval base and there was certainly no consensus about how best to defend it.

The Governor, Sir Shenton Thomas, formally opened the naval base, which cost £63 million, in February 1938. In addition, work had begun on a group of three airfields on the east coast of Peninsular Malaya—one near Kota Bharu in the State of Kelantan, one at Kuantan and a landing ground at Kahang in eastern Johor. The army was barely consulted during the defence discussions, not even about the site selection for the east coast airfields and, as later transpired, defending them would be their responsibility.

By the mid-1930s, it became apparent that the defensive measures needed for the protection of the base called for a radical review. The scale of the likely threat had changed dramatically; not only had the terrain of mainland Malaya opened up and the transport network improved, but major advances in the weapons of war had given the attackers a greater range of options and locations for invasion. The capacity, range and power of evolving weaponry of the three armed services had changed the circumstances of defence and called for a fundamental and fresh assessment of the perceived threat. It was becoming apparent to both the army and the air commanders that the defence of the naval base also meant preventing an assault from Peninsular Malaya. A year before the base was completed in 1937, the then GOC Malaya, Major General W.G.S. Dobbie, instigated a fresh study of the likely changing dangers facing the naval base and the forces and deployment needed to defend it.

---

[18] CAB 27/407, CP173 (30), Enclosure No 2, NA.
[19] Haggie, *Britannia at Bay*, p. 34.

His Chief Staff Officer Colonel Percival, later ominously promoted and appointed GOC at the time of the invasion, conducted the Appreciation. The conclusions of the research were radical in that for the first time they unequivocally determined that the defence of the naval base involved the defence of the whole of the Malay Peninsula, enemy landings were quite feasible on the east coast of Malaya and, indeed, an enemy force could approach Singapore from the mainland. To reinforce his supposition, the GOC tested the practicability of landings from the sea on the east coast during the monsoon period and not only were they perfectly possible but he also found that, conversely, poor visibility could seriously restrict allied air reconnaissance. He also prophetically identified Singora and Patani in Thailand and Kota Bharu in Malaya as highly suitable landing beaches.[20] The narrow Kra Isthmus joining Thailand to Malaya like an "umbilical cord", no more than 35 miles wide, suddenly assumed significant importance because the two countries were so close to these sites. In 1939, the British ambassador to Thailand, Sir Josiah Crosby, also reported that the Thai government officers asserted that if the Japanese decided to strike at Singapore they would first land their forces at Singora.[21]

Until this point, the Government of Malaya was not directly involved in the defensive discussions because talks were inconclusive and in any case based on hypothetical conditions. The Governor was, nevertheless, aware of these new developments and his administration negotiated the securing of land for the proposed east coast airfields. The governance of Singapore and Malaya before the Second World War, as mentioned, was complex and diverse. The Governor's authority and administration across the Malay States was variable, each state having its own distinctive arrangements. In turn, these arrangements differed from the authority he exercised in the Straits Settlements. His relationship with the Malay rulers was a subtle arrangement of guidance through his representative,

---

[20] Stanley Woodburn Kirby, *History of the Second World War: Vol. I: The War Against Japan* (London: HMSO, 1957), p. 15.

[21] Crosby, Bangkok to FO, No. 28, 9 Apr. 1939.

*Collectively known after 1867 as the Crown Colony of Straits Settlements when jurisdiction for them transferred from the government of India to the Colonial Office (CO) in London.

the British adviser. The sultans, while safeguarding their sovereignty, accepted advice on how to improve and manage their parochial affairs. They did not, however, welcome interference in their direct authority or in religious matters. The inevitable outcome was that administrative proposals from the central government followed a recognized eastern process of ponderous discussions and subtle persuasion. The part played by the adviser was therefore critical. He had to be fluent in the Malay language, and it was helpful if he had more than a passing understanding of Chinese and Tamil, but, crucially, he had to have the patience of Job. It is important to note, therefore, that with this labyrinthine arrangement all countrywide government schemes had to be processed by way of this ponderous arrangement, even matters of national emergency. Singapore, on the other hand, was, and had been since 1826, a British colony and part of the Straits Settlements. The colonial administration in Singapore therefore was responsible to the British government, through the CO, for the administration, foreign affairs and protection of the Straits Settlements and the FMS and the UMS. Shenton Thomas thus inherited a clutch of titles—Governor of the Straits Settlements, High Commissioner to the Federated and Unfederated States and Commander-in-Chief.

The capital of the Federated States was Kuala Lumpur (KL) and the head civil servant the Federal Secretary, domiciled in KL, represented the high commissioner in everyday affairs. The FMS had its own assembly. The remaining states, the UMS, had less formal assemblies with the "British adviser" accountable to the Federal Secretary in Kuala Lumpur. In effect, there were 11 different authorities running the affairs of Malaya and Singapore, all of whom had to be consulted before the enactment of any major legislative edict. The High Commissioner could not give orders to any of the sultans. The "protected" states were not possessions of the British Crown. The inhabitants were "protected" but were not British subjects. Sovereign power rested with the Malay rulers.[22]

The British personnel running all these administrative affairs came from the Malayan Civil Service (MCS). The MCS, although not as well-

---

[22] Sir Richard Winstedt, *Malaya and its History* (London: Anchor Press, 1950), p. 89. Also Montgomery, *Shenton of Singapore*, op. cit., p. 42.

known as the Indian Civil Service (ICS), nonetheless regarded itself as an elite service, administering a very rich country with a complex multiracial social structure.[23] In 1940, the population of Malaya was about 5 million, of which 2 million were Malay, 2 million Chinese and 1 million Indian (mostly Tamil) and other races. At the southern tip of the Malay peninsula lay Singapore Island, with the naval base and its city of half a million inhabitants.

Governor Thomas was a long-serving civil servant, a Colonial Governor of the "old school", very much a man conscious of the dignity and the authority of his appointment. In 1941 he was 62 years of age and had, by then, held office for seven years. He had joined the colonial service in 1909 and, after a quarter of a century in Africa, rose to the governorship of Nyasaland and then of the Gold Coast (Ghana). He was surprised, in 1934, to be appointed to Singapore. He was regarded as a competent peacetime administrator. When war broke out in Europe in 1939, he was close to retirement as he had reached the official retirement age of 60 in October of that year. However, the CO considered that a change was undesirable and asked Thomas to remain in his post.[24] It is worth noting that the staff of the CO London were all home civil servants who themselves did not serve overseas. They had no experience of life in the colonies though they were solely responsible for the selection of officers for appointments throughout the British Empire.

During the First World War, Thomas was serving in Kenya. He asked to be released from his appointment to enlist in the services but his request was refused because his government work was vital. As Governor of Singapore he held the honorific title of C-in-C but, until this point in his career, he had never been involved with or exposed to military affairs. To further compound his inexperience, there was a scarcity of military understanding among his civil staff; very few of them had any experience of military service. Consequently, when danger threatened, none among them had any comprehension of the enormity of the menace, nor did they grasp the extent of planning and preparation needed to protect a

---

[23] Raymond Callahan, *The Worst Disaster: The Fall of Singapore* (London: Associated University Press, 1977), p. 63.

[24] Montgomery, *Shenton of Singapore*, loc. cit, p. 65.

country from the inevitable destruction and death that accompanied an armed invasion.

This lack of imagination and myopic view was later reflected in the administration's casual approach to civil defence measures. Their world, in what they regarded as a remote corner of Southeast Asia, seemed isolated and safe. In mitigation and unlike western Europe, there was no war on their doorstep. The nearest conflict was the Japanese war in China, nearly 3,000 miles distant. The annual cycle of living in the comfort and well-ordered routine of a prosperous country focused on expansion of trade and optimizing the country's natural resources, was the height of their concern. Even so, it has been argued that in matters of civil defence where the civil authorities lacked knowledge and energy, the military authorities had a responsibility to insist and galvanize the civil government in a vigorous manner, both to educate the people in civil defence matters and to supervise the necessary preparations.[25] This, however, would have needed dedicated military personnel and they were simply not available. Besides, the Governor was against any overt measures which, he believed, would upset the population and, importantly, hinder the incentive to increase the production of rubber and tin.

In early 1940, the Governor left Singapore for his due entitlement of home leave: indeed, when asked to extend his tour beyond retirement age he had secured an agreement with the Colonial Secretary to do so. In the meantime, the international situation had deteriorated dramatically with western Europe under attack by a rampant Nazi Germany, and Japan's volatile behaviour in the East displaying all the symptoms of a nation set upon war. Thomas' departure at this moment has been harshly criticized as irresponsible. He left his post from April to December and, with all the uncertainty and danger attached to international travel, there was not, even then, any guarantee he would either arrive home or indeed get back. In the event, 1940 proved to be a year when many major decisions about Malaya's defensive posture, and the inevitable implications these posed for its trade, industry and economy, had to be taken. Thomas' deputy, Stanley Jones, the Officer Administering the Government (OAG) in

---

[25] Letter from F.M. Archibald Wavell to Sir Shenton Thomas, 1 Jan. 1948, Thomas private papers, Mss.Ind.Ocn. S341. RHL (hereafter referred to as Thomas Papers).

his absence, was not a man of strong character and, whenever possible, avoided taking any controversial decisions and was quite out of his depth in discussions of military strategy. To add uncertainty, it was a time of significant change among senior appointments, both civil and military. There was growing and anxious concern in London that the management of military and civil affairs in Singapore was dangerously astray. The War Office (WO) appointed a C-in-C, Brooke-Popham, while the Governor was on leave, and later the home government appointed Duff Cooper as minister resident.

Shortly after the outbreak of war in the West, and before he went on leave, the Governor decided to form a defence committee, later called the war committee, of which Thomas was Chairman. Its everyday affairs were handled by a secretariat, created for the purpose under a Defence Secretary. Thomas appointed C.A. Vlieland, a Malayan civil servant, as Defence Secretary. Vlielend had 26 years of service in Malaya and, like the Governor, had no military experience at all. He was given the broad task of coordinating the defence activities of all government departments. There was no written directive for either him or the committee, nor was there any precise agenda during its formative meetings. It would seem that Thomas thought it no more than a good idea to have some type of forum in which to air views about general war precautions, but without a clear idea of its purpose. It was, in other words, an amateurish affair.

The armed forces were represented on this committee by their respective service heads. The war committee was empowered to discuss questions affecting the services and the civil defence departments, but had no executive functions.[26] In matters relating to defence in the Malay States, Vlieland was authorized to deal directly with the British resident or adviser in each of the States who, in turn, and taking account of Vlieland's guidance, had the authority to make decisions on behalf of the state. But with no agenda and no minutes it was chaotic. When Brooke-Popham arrived in Singapore in October 1940, one of his first steps was to attend a meeting of the war committee. Afterwards he wrote a letter to General Ismay, then Chief of the Imperial General Staff (CIGS):

---

[26] Stanley Woodburn Kirby, *History of the Second World War*, p. 157. See also Montgomery, *Shenton of Singapore*, p. 64.

[A]s you may know there is a War committee in Singapore .... I attended the only meeting that there has been since I arrived. I was surprised to find that not only do they not have an agenda but that no minutes are kept; individuals make notes on scraps of paper on any point in which they are particularly interested. On expressing my views I found to my surprise a certain amount of opposition on the part of the govt officials to keeping any record.[27]

The date of this meeting was 4 December 1940; almost exactly a year later the country was invaded. While of course the officials assembled at that time had no way of knowing what the future held, there were the beginnings of concern at Japan's irrational behaviour. Certainly, there were enough sinister indications to have encouraged them to engage in serious and recorded discussion. In the absence of any such documentation there is scant evidence of the early functions of this committee, but passing reference to its deliberations convey a gathering that seemed to feed mainly on personality clashes, and that hampered rather than improved Malaya's preparedness for war. In a further letter to the CIGS, Brooke-Popham had this to say:

[Y]ou have doubtless heard of Vlieland, the Secretary for Defence. I have seldom met anyone who is, so universally distrusted by government officials, by the Services and as far as I can judge by the civilian community. He also seems to have established procrastination as a fine art ... he is however trusted by the Governor, Sir Shenton Thomas.[28]

In spite of these disparaging remarks—and there were similar ones from others—Vlieland drew up, in July 1940, a most accurate and prescient "Appreciation" for the defence of Malaya. He uncannily predicted almost exactly the Japanese strategic plan for their assault on the Peninsula. The Appreciation was his own unprompted initiative and the military hierarchy was grossly affronted that a civil servant without military experience should enter the realm of military strategy without even consulting them.

In those days, before joint services headquarters, the three military arms had their own separate command arrangements and three separate

---

[27] Sir Robert Brooke-Popham Papers, 6/2/3 of 5 Dec. 1940. IWM.
[28] Ibid.

headquarters locations on the island of Singapore. The overall naval commander of the Far East, Admiral Layton, C-in-C China Station, had recently transferred his flag from Hong Kong to the naval base in the northeast corner of the island; he had, under his command, Rear Admiral Spooner, directly responsible for the seas around Malaya. The army was under the command of a Lieutenant General, GOC Malaya, whose headquarters was located at Fort Canning in southwest Singapore. The Air Officer Commanding (AOC), an Air Vice Marshal, was based at the RAF airfield, Seletar in the north of the island. The Governor and his staff conducted their business from Government House on the outskirts of the city; the other civil authorities and government departments were in various locations dispersed around Singapore. It is self-evident that when the three services established their command arrangements on the island there was no necessity, in the early 20th century, to co-locate. Nor indeed would the civil authorities have considered it necessary to be near the heads of services. It is interesting to note, though, that even when the military outlook was worsening, the idea of a joint headquarters did not arise. Throughout the campaign, there was no combined headquarters. Commanders got together periodically in the war committee but their staff worked from separate locations across the island.

In October 1940, the innovative appointment of the C-in-C for the Far East region took effect. Air Chief Marshal Sir Robert Brooke-Popham was given the directive of coordinating the activities of the air and land forces. The GOCs (land and air) would be subordinate to him, but control of naval operations was to remain directly under the C-in-C, China. His area of responsibility stretched from Hong Kong to Singapore, including Borneo, Burma, the Bay of Bengal and the operations of the British air forces in Ceylon (Sri Lanka). This was an absurdly large responsibility and area to cover, especially as radio communications in this region were notoriously poor and travel was fraught with danger. Moreover, a commander, to have any impact on strategic planning, would need an intimate knowledge of the countries in his domain. Brooke-Popham had no practical knowledge of this region.

In practice, his task was to deal primarily with matters of major military policy and strategy. He was instructed not to relieve his subordinate commanders of any of their administrative, financial or other normal command functions. By this untidy arrangement the army and air commanders continued to correspond and be instructed by their respective branches in the WO London, and the navy remained quite independent of the other two.[29] It was obviously a command arrangement intended to mollify the vanity of commanders than improve inter-service collaboration. A confusing and disjointed chain of command was set up that would prove incapable of meeting the challenges ahead.

The character of Air Chief Marshal Sir Robert Brooke-Popham was nevertheless to have considerable influence on affairs from this point. He had retired from active service in 1937, after a distinguished career. He then accepted the appointment of Governor of Kenya from 1937–39, incidentally, a country and appointment well-known to Thomas who served the then Governor for nearly ten years. When war broke out in Europe, he was recalled to active service. Robert Menzies, the Australian prime minister who met Brooke-Popham, wrote that he had borne the "white man's burden in many places and this had left his shoulders a little stooped".[30] Raymond Callahan also described him, in his highly critical account of these events, as being "like his aircraft, Sir Robert was something less than modern".[31] Brooke-Popham established his General Headquarters (GHQ), after a period of uncertainty, in the naval base close to the naval C-in-C. As Stanley Woodburn Kirby commented in his official history: "The appointment of a Commander-in-Chief Far East, although it was designed to solve the problem of co-ordinating the defence of that area, did little more than add another cog to an already somewhat complex machine."[32]

In consequence, the military structure in place by the end of 1940 meant there were two Cs-in-C answering to two different authorities in London. This was patently an illogical arrangement. To add further complications, the important intelligence analysis division, the FECB, which reported directly to the naval C-in-C, was under the charge of a naval captain and located in the naval base. The FECB was responsible for

[29] Kirby, *History of the Second World War*, loc. cit, p. 50.

[30] Ong Chit Chung, *Operation Matador: Britain's War Plans against the Japanese, 1918–1941* (Singapore: Times Academic Press, 1997), quoted on p. 128.

[31] Callahan, *The Worst Disaster*, loc. cit, p. 134.

[32] Kirby, *History of the Second World War*, loc. cit, p. 51.

the compilation and dissemination of significant intelligence information not only for the military but also for the clandestine civilian world. Recruited local agents, political staff in embassies and consuls general and many others contributed invaluable information to the FECB. Located in the naval base, however, it was remote from the other services and the naval C-in-C was seen as regarding it almost as his personal preserve.

In September 1941, Alfred Duff Cooper, a minister of cabinet rank, took up his appointment as Minister Resident Singapore. His task was to appraise and advise on the state of the relationship between the services and the civil authorities. At that time, he held the sinecure appointment of Chancellor of the Duchy of Lancaster, an undemanding job from which he could be released for this important mission. A month after his arrival he filed his first report. Among a number of recommendations, he highlighted the anomalous situation:

> [T]wo Commanders-in-Chief, one for the Far East and one for China, live side by side at the Naval Base at Singapore, [this] does not appear to be a sound one in theory and in practice led to considerable inconvenience. There are also a General Officer Commanding, Malaya, and an Air Officer Commanding, Far East, at the other end of the island.[33]

His most disapproving comments, however, were reserved for the colonial administration. He was taken aback by the pedestrian and lengthy processes of consultation among the various colonial government departments in Singapore and between these departments and their ministries in London over the most urgent affairs of state. The laborious peacetime procedure of seeking departmental agreement on all affairs was distressing, he maintained, but on matters of grave importance, the process bordered on a dereliction of duty.[34]

What his report conveys is that the higher direction of government affairs, in a country faced with threats no more serious than occasional piracy, had descended into a torpor from which only a persistent visionary could arouse it. Such a leader did not exist in Malaya or Singapore, neither among colonial officers nor military leaders. The organization

---

[33] CAB/66/20/9, para 58. Sir Alfred Duff Cooper, "Report by Chancellor of the Duchy of Lancaster", NA.

[34] Ibid., para. 28.

and proposals for civil defence lacked urgency and decisiveness; there was such desultory talk in Legislative Council meetings but little action. The incentive for planning civil defence was, in any case, undermined by a Governor who, on his return from leave, insisted that no visible defence precautions should be constructed because it would undermine morale and distress the population. Nor would he agree to reassign civil labour from industries and estates to help the army build defences and new bases for the air force. His myopic defence was the demand to maintain a high level of industrial productivity as an "absolute priority".[35]

The outbreak of war in Europe, and the salutary lessons from the blitz of Britain, prompted some members of the legislature to press the authorities to consider the question of protection against air raids. In council, proposals for an air raid warning system and air raid shelters were tabled and considered. However, the protective measures proposed applied officially only to the Straits Settlements. The FMS and the UMS were prompted to consider similar arrangements. Not surprisingly, this caused an outcry from expatriates. How was it possible, they questioned, to protect some and not others, particularly if such protection had direct consequences for the safety of the tin and rubber industries and the important employees who maintained these industries?[36] The furore generated by this subject brought up the more fundamental issue of the best way of organizing civil defence. Most of the state authorities believed that control of civil defence measures should be in the hands of the armed forces. The colonial authorities in Singapore disagreed. They did concur, however, that the whole of Malaya should be included in all future civil defence measures, and although they were unable to insist that the FMS and the UMS comply, the latter were strongly encouraged to do so.

By the autumn of 1941, the total military force in Malaya had increased to approximately 88,600. It consisted predominantly of Indian troops but

---

[35] Montgomery, *Shenton of Singapore*, p. 68. Montgomery quotes from a Thomas despatch to the CO of 27 Jan. 1940.

[36] Kirby, *History of the Second World War*, p. 159. According to Kirby, the FMS Chamber of Mines and the United Planters Association strongly condemned the government for failing to take adequate measures for the defence and safety of the civil population of the Malay States and the security of the tin and rubber industries.

with a sizeable minority of British, Australian and Malay troops. The breakdown by nationality was 19,600 British, 15,200 Australian, 37,000 Indian and about 16,800 locally enlisted Asians. These numbers were well below the fighting strength previously asked for and approved by the WO. In terms of fighting infantry units, they constituted 31 infantry battalions and their supporting elements. The units were organized into one Australian and two Indian divisions, with some in reserve. Singapore had its own garrison of two brigades, dedicated to the defence of the "Fortress". In addition, Penang had a garrison of one battalion plus some support units. There were also fixed coastal defence and anti-aircraft batteries for Singapore, some airfield defence battalions and local volunteer units. There were, however, no armoured forces.[37] Many of the troops had received only basic training and some had not been long enough in station to get used to the enervating climate before hostilities began. Of the 37,000 Indian troops, many were scarcely better than raw recruits and a number were only 17 years of age. Importantly, they were bereft of trained officers and non-commissioned officers. With the urgent expansion of the Indian army, many quality units were "milked" of experienced officers and senior non-commissioned officers (NCOs) who were sent to form new battalions. It was a euphemism to classify those arriving in Singapore as infantry "combat" divisions. The 15,200 Australians also lacked experienced leaders and, although slightly better trained, had no knowledge of jungle warfare. The same applied to the British element. The remaining 16,800 local forces were equivalent to a militia or, in modern parlance, a territorial army. The members of these units were part-time soldiers whose primary employment covered the spectrum of Malayan business and industry; they had only rudimentary military skills acquired in brief periods of weekend training. However, they had valuable local knowledge of terrain and spoke native languages—Malay, Tamil and Chinese.

There were no British divisions in Malaya at the beginning of the campaign. Later, and much too late to have any impact on the outcome of the battle, the British 18th Division, then at sea en route to Persia

---

[37] Stanley L. Falk, *Seventy Days to Singapore: The Malayan Campaign, 1941–1942* (London: Hale, 1975), p. 54. See also Kirby, *History of the Second World War*, p. 163.

(Iran), was redirected to Singapore. Of the six British infantry battalions, three were in Singapore and the others assigned to the Indian brigades. Indian units, while a separate force within the British military system, were trained and organized along the same lines as the British army. Equipment, however, tended to be somewhat lighter: there was less artillery, and fewer anti-tank and anti-aircraft weapons. Officers were both British and Indian. Incredibly, some young Indian soldiers arriving in Malaya had never seen a tank.[38]

The commander of the army from May 1941 was Lieutenant General Arthur Percival (GOC Malaya). He was described as the "eternal staff officer", an opinion reinforced by his appearance and personal manner. He was tall, angular, raw-boned, somewhat stooped and had protruding front teeth. His manner was low-key and he was a poor public speaker with the suspicion of a lisp. He was, however, unquestionably brave, remarkably fit and active and, by general agreement, very bright, determined and quite unflappable.[39]

The only non-Indian division in Malaya at this time was the Australian 8th Division. While subject to Percival's operational control, it occupied a unique position. Its commander, Major General Gordon Bennett, was under instructions from his government to ensure that the division remained a unified force and was not split or used piecemeal by Malaya Command without his approval. Moreover, if Bennett was unhappy with any tactical deployment that infringed this arrangement, he was authorized to have direct communication with Australia. In effect, it gave him a right to go over Percival's head on tactical matters or indeed or any other reason. This autonomy, in the pressure of combat, severely restricted Percival's tactical options. Outspoken to the point of rudeness, sarcastic and impatient, he did not get along well with British regular officers and, for that matter, with anyone else with whom he disagreed, including many of his own staff. His rasping personality did nothing to improve command relationships, and under the test of battle his

---

[38] Kirby, *History of the Second World War*, p. 164 and passim.

[39] Brian P. Farrell and Sandy Hunter, *A Great Betrayal: The Fall of Singapore Revisited* (Singapore: Marshall Cavendish, 2000), p. 199. See also Kinvig, *Scapegoat*, passim, for a very balanced judgement of Percival as GOC. Kinvig concedes that while Percival was very capable and intelligent, he was not a dynamic leader.

leadership was found wanting.[40] An official report compiled after the war commented:

> It was well known in Malaya before the operations and it was amply borne out during operations, that the Australian GOC was incapable of subordinating himself to Malaya Command or of co-operating wholeheartedly with other commanders.[41]

A point of importance worth repeating, because it imposed additional problems on command and control, is that the composition of the Allied forces was from places as far apart as the UK, Australia, Malaya, Burma and British India, and they fought under leaders divided by differences of nationality, outlook, background, political allegiance and language. Neither were they equipped nor trained for operations in the close country of Malaya. As a force they were overburdened with a road-bound logistics tail: endless columns of motor transport moved men, equipment and stores. A glaring omission in the military organization, however, was the failure to enlist the local community for their language skills and knowledge of the terrain and, above all, to assist the combat troops prepare military sites and defensive positions. A compelling reason for this omission, apart from the Governor's obstinacy, was that the WO, London would only pay a derisory labourer's daily rate for those so enlisted.

From the mid-1930s, Japan's increasingly erratic and aggressive behaviour in the Far East created apprehension among the western powers, and gave Britain's Pacific Dominions serious cause for concern.[42] Every political move or direct action by Japan, already closely monitored, came under more intense scrutiny from this point. Of particular interest was the expansion and deployment of its armed forces. Japan's war with China was closely observed and battlefield skills in this campaign were studied and analysed. Japan's undisguised intention to extend its empire now gave the West's intelligence agencies the weighty challenge of determining the direction from which Japan would strike, and when.

---

[40] Falk, loc. cit, p. 55. Also A.B. Lodge, *The Fall of General Gordon Bennett* (Sydney and Boston: Allen & Unwin, 1986), pp. 6–20 and passim.

[41] CAB 106/162, report on operations of 8th Australian Division in Malaya, NA.

[42] Feis, *The Road to Pearl Harbor*, pp. 3–5. Also Keegan, *The Second World War*, pp. 241–3.

During 1940, when a growing number of intelligence precursors were detected, indicating an unusual pattern of movement by Japanese military and naval forces throughout Southeast Asia—reports substantiated by a variety of diplomatic and civilian sources—raised serious concern at the WO, London. Adding impetus to their fears, on 1 August 1940, the Japanese government proclaimed the "construction of a new order in Greater Asia". Following this disquieting proclamation, the Chiefs of Staff (COS) called for a comprehensive review of Singapore's defence plans. The three service commanders then in post—C-in-C China (Layton) AOC (Babington) and GOC (Bond)—compiled an Appreciation. On 16 October 1940, they presented their findings to a defence conference in Singapore.[43] The discussion and conclusions of this conference confirmed, and added substance to, the growing awareness of Japan's intentions, the weakness of the allied preparations, and the serious shortage of vital war *materiel*. Among its major conclusions was that the arrival of a relieving fleet would only partially safeguard against a Japanese overland threat to Malaya through Thailand. Second, it was necessary to hold all Malaya rather than concentrate on the defence of Singapore Island. Third, it would now be the responsibility of the air and land forces to prevent the Japanese from establishing advanced air bases on the mainland and to stop any overland advance. Overall, they assumed that the Japanese had unhindered use of the ports and air bases in Indo-China and the railways of Thailand, that the Thais would maintain "forced neutrality" and that "before the opening of hostilities the Japanese would have established themselves in South Thailand".[44]

The tactical Appreciation also concluded that the Japanese had sufficient forces for simultaneously launching an overland attack from Thailand and a seaborne attack on Malaya. These invading forces would be strongly supported by shore-based Japanese aircraft. Singapore was within range

---

[43] The three commanders were joined by the GOC Burma, the COS of the Dutch East Indies Station, the DMO (Director Military Operations) India and the Secretary for Defence in Malaya (Vlieland). In attendance were DCOS (Deputy Chief of Staff) Australia, COS New Zealand and Commander A. Thomas USN attaché Bangkok, as an observer. CAB/80/24, NA.

[44] Nicholas Tarling, *A Sudden Rampage: The Japanese Occupation of Southeast Asia, 1941–1945* (London: Hurst, 2001), pp. 82–5.

of heavy bombers operating from Thailand. Further, northern Malaya was within range of heavy bombers and reconnaissance aircraft operating from Indo-China, and from light bombers and fighters operating from Thailand.

Facing the urgent realities of the situation, the conference moved on and prophetically considered that the Japanese were likely to attack Hong Kong, Malaya, Burma, British Borneo, Netherlands East Indies, Timor and communications in the Pacific and Indian oceans, either separately or all at the same time. There could also be attacks on American bases in the Philippines and Guam.[45]

> Our first immediate consideration must be to ensure the security of Malaya against direct attack. The Tactical Appreciation shows that the army and air forces in Malaya (including reinforcements now being provided) are, both in numbers and equipment, far below those required in view of the inadequacy of the naval forces available. *This deficiency must obviously be remedied immediately* and we recommend that the further co-operation of India, Australia and New Zealand be sought without delay.[46]

The conference considered that a minimum of 566 aircraft were needed for the defence of Malaya and Burma.[47] The harsh reality was that there were then only 88 aircraft in the area, of which 40 were obsolete; therefore there should be a reinforcement of 534 modern aircraft. In terms of army strength, Malaya was deficient by 12 regular battalions, 6 field artillery regiments, 8 anti-tank batteries, 6 anti-tank companies, 3 light tank companies and other units.

These important and prescient findings went to the COS in London. The COS replied that they hoped to accelerate the dispatch of land reinforcements to Malaya and pledged to send 170 Buffalo aircraft, 40 Glen Martin aircraft, one squadron of flying boats and one squadron of Beauforts by June 1941. They also approved the expansion of air base facilities in the north to allow for a concentration of two-thirds of the aircraft in either the north or south of Malaya.[48]

At this same time (October 1940), by the direction of the C-in-Cs, the

---

[45] Ong, *Operation Matador*, loc. cit, p. 123.

[46] Ibid., p. 125, with original emphasis.

[47] Richards and St George Saunders, *Royal Air Force 1939–1945*, p. 4. Tactical Appreciation, 16 Oct. 1940.

[48] COS Paper No: 33, para. 6, 24 Dec. 1940, NA.

FECB compiled a weekly intelligence summary—"The Far East Weekly" or "FEW". It was sent to the Admiralty, Australian Naval Board, New Zealand Naval Board, Naval Intelligence in Ottawa and New Delhi, British command in East Asia and British representatives in Washington, Tokyo and Chungking and, of course, to the Governor's office in Singapore. Thus every important department, national and international, concerned with the worrying developments in the Far East region, received it. By the time Brooke-Popham took up his appointment in October 1940, there were, in place, sound arrangements to disseminate a steady flow of intelligence information from a variety of sources to the Western Allies. All the main diplomatic posts and trained military officials throughout East Asia were watching and reporting important intelligence clues. However, as always in the case of intelligence gathering processes, there was, inevitably, some conflicting or inaccurate information, leading sometimes to incorrect conclusions but, taken altogether, there was unmistakable and mounting evidence of Japan's preparation for imminent action. The most obvious indicator of Japanese intention was the level of mobilization and distribution of its forces; these movements were closely monitored by FECB and other British agencies.

On 2 July 1941, at an imperial conference in Tokyo, which the Emperor himself attended, government ministers put before him their combined agreement that the nation's future lay in the dominance of the mineral-rich southern states of Southeast Asia.[49] Even at this point, however, there was still a dispute, mainly between the army and the navy, on whether to focus expansion north against Russia or south against the western powers. Hitler was pressing Japan to follow his lead and strike north, taking advantage of Russia's dilemma. Certainly, this scheme appealed to a number of senior army officers but the more pragmatic among them felt such a move would do little to assuage Japan's economic problems.[50]

---

[49] Douglas Ford, *The Pacific War: Clash of Empires in World War II* (London and New York: Continuum, 2012), p. 43.

[50] Anthony Best, *Britain, Japan and Pearl Harbor: Avoiding War in East Asia, 1936–41* (London and New York: Routledge, 1995). Brooke-Popham, in his post-war despatch (No: 38183 of Jan. 1948), declared: "As the Japanese spread south into Cambodia and Cochin China, the potential danger to Burma, Malaya, the South China Sea and even the Philippines increased; this danger had been realised from the start ..."

Regardless of the north-south outcome, military preparations for either contingency were well underway and had been since 1940. Even while it was conducting torturous political negotiations—with America in particular—over the harsh economic embargo, the Japanese army and navy were actively preparing for a general war.[51]

The political dialogue between Japan's embassy in Washington and the government in Tokyo had, for a number of years, been intercepted and deciphered, as had the diplomatic telegrams sent from its embassy in Berlin.[52] Both the USA and Britain were fully aware of the convoluted procrastinating negotiations that Japan was conducting. The purpose, they realized, was to enable Japan to strengthen its hold on its recent territorial acquisitions in East Asia as well as gain time to enlarge its military arsenal. The aid to China by the two western powers via the Burma Road was, in part, a response to these manoeuvrings and it was an effective irritant to the Japanese, indeed, a concern they continuously raised during the negotiations. From the point of view of both the USA and Britain, supplying China with armaments to enable it to continue the war with Japan meant that a significant part of the Imperial Japanese Army was committed to the Chinese campaign and unavailable for other military adventures. The USA Secretary of State, Cordell Hull, recognizing the harmful effect these important supplies to China were having on Japan, declared that, "in order to deter Japan and place obstacles in the way of Japan's programme of conquest", he proposed giving large credits to China to aid its resistance to the Japanese.[53]

Even though the interceptions via the US decipher system called "Magic" revealed the intentions of the Japanese government that "the

[51] Eric Robertson, *The Japanese File: Pre-War Japanese Penetration in Southeast Asia* (Hong Kong: Heinemann Asia, 1979), pp. 1–8 and passim. Also Feis, *The Road to Pearl Harbor*, p. 215.

[52] The United States' decipher facility was known as "Magic" and the Japanese cipher system was called "Purple". Bletchley Park in England also successfully read Japanese signals traffic and both nations exchanged important information. See Jonathan Marshall, *To Have and Have Not: Southeast Asian Raw Materials and the Origins of the Pacific War* (Berkeley, CA: University of California Press, 1995), passim and Best, *Britain, Japan and Pearl Harbor*, passim.

[53] Quoted in Marshall, *To Have and Have Not*, p. 131.

Japanese Empire, to save its very life, must take measures to secure the raw materials of the South Seas",[54] it still was not clear whether Japan's next move would be north or south. What was not in question was its determination to continue acquiring Asian territory. Military intelligence assessments in the final months before its assault on Malaya showed that, regardless of the north-south debate in Tokyo, preparations for further conquests to the south continued. The army was especially concerned that the loss of Thailand would clearly undermine any future expansion into Malaya and Singapore.[55] However, there were other interpretations of these same indicators. Lord Halifax, the British ambassador in Washington, learnt that the Americans believed the likely attack would indeed be southwards but judged that the Japanese aim was to cut the Burma Road. By the end of October Whitehall had also adopted this analysis; it had further support from Chiang Kai-shek and Brook-Popham, both of whom, separately, believed the Burma Road was the likely target.[56] One of the factors mentioned in support of the move south was that the flat country of Cambodia/central Thailand, which baked hard during the dry season, meant that runways there could be easily improvised. Shenton Thomas, who travelled through this area in February 1939, confirmed this in a telegram to the CO in November 1941.[57]

The stockpiling of vital war materials was also well underway and, in late October, a Japanese Total War Research Institute was established with the task of drawing up a comprehensive plan for the intended deployments. Three divisions from south China were ordered to begin training for operations in tropical regions. They were despatched to Indo-China (where, as mentioned, Japan had already established a sizeable garrison). Special studies began of the geography, terrain and climate of Malaya, the Netherlands East Indies, Thailand and Burma. By early 1941, Japanese pilots were flying reconnaissance missions and taking illegal photographs over the Malayan coast and the Philippines. At the same

---

[54] Ibid., p. 133.
[55] Ibid., p. 135.
[56] FO 371/27986 and CAB 96/2, NA.
[57] FO 371/28126 of 3 Nov. 1941 and WO 208/1898.

time, the Ministry of War and Foreign Office (FO) was printing military currency for use in the southern area.[58] It was at this time, signalling his service's autonomy and disregard of government restraint, that Admiral Yamamoto Commander of the Combined Fleet conceived the idea of a carrier-based air attack on Pearl Harbour and ordered his staff to work out the problems posed by such an operation.[59]

In mid-September 1941, E.W. Meiklereid, the acting consul-general in Saigon, reported that there were 25,000 Japanese troops and 70 aircraft in Indo-China, while Ambassador Crosby reported from Bangkok that his information gave the numbers as 23,000 troops and 51 aircraft. By the end of September, Brooke-Popham stated that his sources gave slightly different figures: 25,000 troops and 50 aircraft. These were not significant discrepancies although strangely he remained convinced that the Japanese were not yet ready to launch an attack on Thailand or Malaya.[60] To add some conviction to his premise, he said that there were no signs of the upgrading of facilities at the air bases or the presence of long-range fighters or heavy bombers, which he considered essential for such an attack.[61] In any case, he announced, he remained of the opinion that any Japanese excursion would be northwards.

On 22 October 1941, the British ambassador in Tokyo, Sir Robert Craigie, sent a very stiff critique to the FO in London of Brooke-Popham's assertion of 30 September. Craigie was, by now, most suspicious of Japanese intentions and placed more emphasis on a Japanese move to the south. In a pointed criticism of Brooke-Popham's theory of "northern attack", Craigie, referring to the talks then underway between Japan and Washington about the economic embargo, said:

> [S]hould Washington conversations [between Japan and USA about the economic sanctions] break down, [an] immediate move southwards cannot be excluded despite weather conditions ... Much of course depends on the outcome of the Washington talks, but even now, with

---

[58] Tsuji, *Singapore*, passim.

[59] Ong, *Operation Matador*, loc. cit, p. 216.

[60] Brooke-Popham to WO for COS No, 492/4, 2 Sept. 1941 and GHQ Far East Report, "Possibilities of the Japanese Attacking in the South", 8 Sept. 1941, NA.

[61] Ibid., p. 220.

tension as high as it is, and increasing economic distress caused by freezing measures it would take very little further pressure to drive Japan to rash enterprise.[62]

During the latter period of 1941, the number of intelligence reports grew in volume and detail. Many reliable sources noted the increased movement of Japanese troops, shipping and aircraft. By the end of October, it was believed that the number of troops in Indo-China had reached 50,000 and that considerable quantities of equipment and stores were being landed in both northern and southern areas of the country, including tanks (estimated at 100), transport vehicles, oil tankers, railway equipment and ammunition. The Japanese had also taken over another two air bases in Cambodia and were giving top priority to the extension of air facilities in Saigon, Phnom Penh and two other air bases in southern Indo-China.[63]

On 17 October 1941, Captain D. Tufnell, the British naval attaché in Tokyo, reported that all units of the Japanese navy had been mobilized and were now on a complete war footing. The Chinese ambassador to Singapore, from his sources, subsequently confirmed this. In addition, and significantly, in the early months of 1941 the average number of Japanese merchant ships outside Japanese-controlled waters had stood at 162. This rapidly declined from 79 in September to 50 at the end of the month, dropping again to 25 by late October. It was obvious that there was some haste in getting Japanese shipping back to Japanese territories. Craigie again reported from Tokyo that there were indications that more reservists were being mobilized.[64]

In this feverish pre-war period, diplomatic relations between Japan and the western powers, particularly the USA, were at breaking point. The Imperial Japanese Armed Forces were displaying unambiguous signs of war and indicating preparation for a pre-emptive assault. Even these alarms, however, did not dispel the reservations in some minds, both military and civil, that Singapore Island was a Japanese objective and that

---

[62] Ibid, p. 222. See also p. 242, n. 74. Craigie, Tokyo to FO. No: 2079, 22 Oct 41. Repeated by FO to Singapore as No. 367 on 23 Oct. 1941.

[63] Ibid., p. 221.

[64] Ibid.

danger was imminent. A defence committee had been formed and now that a C-in-C and Minister Resident were in station, the committee met more regularly and conducted its business more formally but not with noticeable urgency. Life in Singapore and in Peninsula Malaya remained leisurely and comfortable. No senior figure urged haste or proposed that the country be alerted and prepared for conflict. The Governor was not distracted from his unchanging secure routine of managing the political and commercial affairs of his domain.

3

THE COLONIAL RULERS

The governance of the Straits Settlements and individual states in Peninsula Malaya, which Sir Shenton Thomas inherited, was a system developed by trial and error during the 150 years of colonial rule. The varied provisions for guiding the affairs of each group was labyrinthine but workable. By careful control, and under the direction of experienced British civil servants sensitive to the ethnic distinctions of the multicultural population, it worked perfectly well. But what became increasingly obvious was that the consultative and management procedures that worked in a measured, indeed leisurely manner, were unsuited to a crisis. Had the Governor the foresight to put the country on a war footing at the first signs of trouble, he would undoubtedly have met resistance from a number of the Malay rulers. Thomas' first obstacle would have been to convince the sultans that there was a threat. Certainly, the remoter and poorer parts of east Malaya (where fatefully the actual landings took place) would not have understood the alarm. At this stage in its progress Malaya was not a unified nation, communications were embryonic and the British, while seen as benevolent colonial masters, were nevertheless regarded as firm rulers. If the Japanese came, most people would greet their arrival as simply a matter of one ruler replacing another. In addition, they would almost certainly have objected to the disruption and cost entailed in preparations for defence. Under these conditions, galvanizing the country and demanding war measures would have been a huge challenge for even the most determined of leaders.

The manner by which administrative control developed also

meant that many government departments acted independently of central authority. This led to poor coordination and even poorer inter-department communications. As previously explained, the Governor residing in Singapore was President of the Straits Settlements Council, which sat in Singapore, and President of the FMS Federal Council which sat in KL. The FMS assembly met about six times a year. Apart from this bi-monthly commute to KL for meetings, there is no mention of Thomas visiting the countryside outside the capital or meeting with the sultans of the UMS. The existence of two legislative councils also meant duplication of many administrative issues, not to mention the expense of running two similar large legislative chambers.

Both the CO, London and a succession of governors recognized the untidy, fragmented and unsatisfactory governance in this area. What they did not agree upon was a solution to the problem. There were those who favoured tighter central control and those who championed devolvement—passing governmental responsibility to the indigenous inhabitants. The issue was unresolved when Shenton Thomas took up his appointment as Governor; indeed, his predecessor had been removed from the post because of the indignation he provoked by promoting the idea of devolvement.[1] Thomas was told to defuse the furore, play down the whole debate about governance and live with the status quo. It meant, of course, that when war loomed, he was technically unable to insist (unless he declared martial law) that the nine Malay States conform to coordinated and countrywide preparations for a conflict: he simply did not have the legal authority (there is no evidence, however, that he ever thought to do so). It also placed him on a collision course with the military when their intended plans ran roughshod across state boundaries. The military failed to understand the subtleties of dissimilar state governments or the constraints this imposed on Thomas' power, nor did they grasp the delicate sensibilities of the separate state rulers. It is worth remembering that, until 1909, the northern part of the Peninsula was claimed by Siam (Thailand). Perlis, Kedah, Kelantan and Terengganu,

---

[1] Robert Heussler, *British Rule in Malaya: The Malayan Civil Service and its Predecessors, 1867–1942* (Oxford: Clio Press, 1981), p. 265. See also S.W. Jones, *Public Administration in Malaya* (New York and London: Royal Institute of International Affairs, 1953), pp. 83–90.

whose populations are predominantly Malay and Muslim, were governed by hereditary Malay rulers who sent tribute to Bangkok triennially in the form of *Bunga Mas* (gold and silver flowers). Their foreign relations were handled by Bangkok and their rulers had to be confirmed in office by the Siamese authorities. In return, these vassal states were entitled to Siamese protection and were allowed to live separately under their own laws, customs and rulers.

To not only integrate these states within Malaya but also require them to surrender their authoritarianism would have called for lengthy and torturous diplomacy. Asking them, in addition, to accept British governance would have entailed compromise and measureable persuasion. While the military saw its task in simple, unequivocal countrywide terms, the civilian officials, on the other hand, had to manage the affairs of the country according to existing fragile rules. In any case, in 1940, it was hard for them to conceive of any such grave and immediate threat to the colony's existence that would call for high handed disregard of well-rehearsed regulations. Besides, there was the country's welfare and economy to consider.

The political and military conditions that prevailed in Malaya and Singapore in 1940 were quite different from those in other parts of the British Empire. After many years of directing and guiding the country's development, the administration took a patriarchal approach to governing. The colony was an acknowledged success enjoying a healthy economy, development and expansion of trade, the introduction of a modern communications infrastructure and significant improvement in health and education. Importantly, though, what the British failed to address, and what was later to prove a serious shortcoming, was the creation of national unity, in other words, a short-sighted acceptance of the local rulers' various autonomies. As already mentioned Malaya was a country of different nationalities, on the surface living a contented existence. However, as the war later exposed, it was a country with little loyalty to its British masters. Indeed, as predicted, the majority of the working-class people simply regarded the Japanese as a replacement for the British masters. Even when the danger was obvious, there was little display of either panic or an urge to rush to arms to protect their legacy of security and quality of life. Pragmatists say that this behaviour was a clear manifestation of the significant failure to foster loyalty and national identity. "There was no personal friendliness, no sympathy or understanding, no participation in common ideas or purposes. On the surface there was complete indifference toward one another."[2]

This situation was typified by events in Penang. It was the earliest British foothold in the area, first occupied in 1786, and remained the sole British enterprise in the Peninsula until the end of the 1800s. By the early 19th century, however, the major islands of Southeast Asia, collectively then known as the East Indies, were within the "sphere of influence" of either the Dutch or the British. At the time, the British used this concept to limit the commercial or political ambitions of rival powers while avoiding the expense of establishing additional outposts of empire.[3] In 1824, in a move to prevent other western powers—notably, the French—from establishing commercial links in the Malay Archipelago, an Anglo-Dutch treaty was negotiated with the Netherlands. By the terms of the treaty Britain relinquished all interests in the islands south of Singapore, notably Java and, in particular, Bencoolen in Sumatra, in return for the Dutch colony of Malacca. Britain now had exclusive influence in the Peninsula. To consolidate further its own commercial dominance over the important west coast trading ports, in 1826 Britain decided to create a single administrative unit out of Singapore, Malacca, Penang and Province Wellesley—collectively known as the Straits Settlements. It remained under the control of the British authorities in India until 1867, when it was transferred to the CO, London. It was to become the base from whence the British influence was gradually extended throughout the Peninsula.

Relations with the remaining nine Malay States evolved gradually in a different manner, each case determined by the commercial value of individual state's natural resources. At this stage, London was reluctant to absorb further territorial responsibility within the Archipelago if

---

[2] Barbara Watson Andaya and Leonard Y. Andaya, *A History of Malaysia* (New York: St Martin's Press, 1982), p. 176 and passim. Also Jones, *Public Administration in Malaya*, p. 99, who explains: "There was no personal friendliness, no sympathy or understanding, no participation in common ideas or purposes. On the surface there was complete indifference toward one another."

[3] Ibid., p. 125. See also Isabella L. Bird, *The Golden Chersonese* (Singapore: Monsoon Books, 2010 [1884]), pp. 147–52 and passim.

there was little profit to be gained, even though some of the Malay States actively sought protection. Persistent internecine disputes amongst a number of the Malay rulers sometimes led to open warfare. Conflicting Chinese factions threatened to involve the Straits Settlements, forcing Britain into some restraining action.[4] In 1874, when the State of Perak asked for help to secure the shaky authority of its Sultan, the Governor of the Straits Settlements signed the Pangkor Treaty in return for British protection. The Sultan had to accept a British resident whose advice had to be sought and acted upon on all questions other than those touching on Malay custom and religion.[5]

The Pangkor Treaty was a turning point in political and commercial relations with the remaining states. Malay rulers began to recognize the potential benefits of such an agreement: there was security, prospective economic development and, in a number of particular cases, the likely curtailment of aggressive Chinese commercial exploitation, chiefly in tin mining. Following the example of Perak, three other states—Selangor, Negri Sembilan and Pahang—signed agreements with the British authorities seeking "protected" status, and accepted the installation of a "Resident". In 1896, these four Protected States were unified as the Federated Malay States (FMS), with the capital in KL, the heart of the tin-mining region. A secretariat was established in KL with a Resident-General at its head. It had jurisdiction over the "residents" in the four FMS and authority to represent the federation's interests to the Singapore Governor, who also became High Commissioner of the Federation. Departments of police, public works, post and telegraph, railways and agriculture were now under a single director; a unified civil service was set up and proposals were made for a common treasury. To assure uniformity, all laws except those of a purely local nature, and all financial measures were decreed in KL.[6] Over the next ten years, further moves

---

[4] John Michael Gullick, *Indigenous Political Systems of Western Malaya* (London: The Athlone Press, 1958), pp. 11–8 and passim. See also Frank Athelstane Swettenham, *British Malaya: An Account of the Origin and Progress of British Influence in Malaya* (London: John Lane, 1929 [1907]), passim. C.D. Cowan, *Nineteenth Century Malaya: The Origins of British Political Control* (London: Oxford University Press, 1961), pp. 169–75.

[5] Andaya and Andaya, *A History of Malaysia*, p. 158.

[6] Ibid., p. 186.

were made towards uniformity and centralization and, by 1909, a Federal Council was created with the Governor at its head. The role of Resident-General was renamed "Chief Secretary". In the process, the four FMS sultans lost their power of veto and the council was enlarged to include senior and influential businessmen from the tin and rubber industries, both European and Chinese. The Chief Secretary became subordinate to the High Commissioner rather than an independent defender of the Federated States' rights, which he previously exercised in his role as Resident-General.[7]

By 1909, Thailand agreed to transfer responsibility for the four northern states (Terengganu, Kedah, Kelantan and Perlis) to Britain.[8] The state of Johor was acquired in 1914. Thus direct and indirect control of all the Malay States and Singapore was in the hands of the British government. British authority, either in the form of a Governor, High Commissioner, agent, resident or adviser, exercised control throughout Malaya and Singapore—now labelled British Malaya. It was a political arrangement that would remain almost unchanged until the Japanese invasion of 1941. However, the four northern states (above) and Johor remained un-federated; their sultans refused to join the FMS because they would not accept any erosion of their traditional royal powers. They had observed this decline in the sultans within the FMS. Peninsular Malaya was therefore made up administratively of the Straits Settlements (Crown Colony), FMS and UMS.

In practice, this development meant that the political, economic and administrative control of the three categories of suzerainty within Malaya and Singapore was in the hands of 11 different authorities. This arrangement was the source of heated debate between the colonial office and officials in post. In the 1920s and 1930s, the situation led to the long-running centralized or decentralized political argument.[9] The colonial authorities felt that a large degree of centralized direction was necessary in a peninsula of such ill-defined state boundaries, uneven

---

[7] Jones, *Public Administration in Malaya*, p. 87.

[8] Bastin and Winks, *Malaysia*. E. Thio, "The British Forward Movement in Malaya, 1880-9", p. 227.

[9] Jones, *Public Administration in Malaya*, pp. 78–80, 83–90. Also Swettenham, *British Malaya*, pp. 273–5 and passim.

geographical distribution of natural wealth and growing ethnic immigrant conurbations. Some officials, however, worried that central control would lead to a lessening of respect for the rulers in certain circles; even so, until the outbreak of war, it was still evident that the prestige of sultans within their own states and their hold over rural Malays was still strong.[10]

In theory, the Legislative Council of the Straits Settlements and the Federal Council of the FMS were independent of each other although much of the legislation enacted by the Straits Settlements was endorsed by the FMS. The UMS, on the other hand, could and did resist rulings from the High Commissioner. The colonial goal of creating an administrative unity for British Malaya was still unfulfilled by 1941.[11] Despite general agreement that a union for Malaya was ultimately desirable, established political and commercial interests distrusted any change.[12] With a system of consultative dialogue rather than pronouncements from the centre, even important matters such as the deployment of military units needed the agreement of the state into whose area they planned to move. In his book *Speaking Generally*, written after the war, General (later Field Marshal) Wavell gave an example of this cumbersome process: "... about a week after war had broken out an important movement of troops was delayed by the police enforcing the customs barrier between two states and insisting on taking particulars of each lorry as it passed".[13]

In addition to the nine Legislative Council meetings in Singapore and the six Federal meetings in KL, there were six residents' conferences, each followed by a durbar. These meetings were the forums for discussion and approval of major acts of legislation and the ratification of government expenditure. Sub-committees undertook preparatory and investigative stages of important legislation before presentation to the council for endorsement. The system of government was entirely transparent and democratic, closely following British parliamentary procedures. The GOC Malaya was ex-officio a member of both the executive and legislative councils of the Straits Settlements. A reading of the council proceedings suggests a ponderous and pedantic process

[10] Ibid.
[11] Ibid.
[12] Andaya and Andaya, *A History of Malaya*, p. 252.
[13] Archibald Percial Wavell, *Speaking Generally* (London: Macmillan, 1946), p. 114.

with procedural dialogue heavy in Victorian preciseness and spoken with laboured, careful etiquette. Business was not conducted swiftly and purposefully.

British civil servants, following a well-trodden and well-defined path forged in the growth of an empire, were determining the management of the country's affairs. "By the late thirties their instrument of rule—the MCS—was one of the most seasoned and self-confident in the empire, secure in its local acceptance and in its reputation at home."[14] In the later stages, the MCS attained an image as an elite service. During the inter-war years, however, it had suffered a drop in the quality of recruitment and was regarded as less desirable than entry into the ICS. Only a conscious recruiting effort and redesigned selection procedure restored the quality of entrants.[15] Thus, by 1940, the MCS was a highly efficient service comprising able, intelligent and dedicated officers skilled in their respective fields of administration. The arrangement of government departments and distribution of powers among the officers of the MCS followed closely the successful pattern practised in India.

When he retired as Chief Secretary, FMS, Sir George Maxwell informed a London newspaper (*Daily Telegraph*, April 1942):

> I could not have wished to have a finer body of men under me. The district officer made a point of establishing that direct personal contact which means everything in any difficulty or emergency, and the understanding and sympathy on the one side met with confidence and respect from the other. Not only in the administrative branches, but in all the professional departments, the men were devoted, heart and soul, to their work for the country, and all were deeply attached to the peoples of Malaya. In mutual understanding between the people of the country and the administration, Malaya has been unsurpassed in the Colonial Empire.[16]

---

[14] Heussler, *British Rule in Malaya*, p. 280.

[15] Ibid., pp. 263–7.

[16] Heussler Papers, Mss. Brit. Emp. s.480.8/1.RHL. Quoted in a letter of 2 July 1982 from Paul H. Kratoska to Heussler in which he added: "As a resident in the FMS at the time he speaks of, and not being a civil servant myself but the editor of a newspaper whose motto was certainly not one of uncritical subservience to authority local or otherwise, and furthermore having lived and worked in other tropical Colonies so that I am well able to draw the necessary comparisons, I can testify to the accuracy of the tribute."

Their training and preparation was just as thorough as that of their Indian counterparts. All of them had to learn the Malay language and many had a working knowledge of other local languages.[17] In general, everyone served at one time or another in both the secretariat and rural posts, the intention being that every officer should understand both the central processes of administration and, at a distance, its impact on the community. Inevitably, there were those who preferred to retain the freedom and responsibilities of remote districts than return to the oppressive routine of the central bureaucracy.[18]

The system worked perfectly well, but with one unforeseen weakness. On the outbreak of war in December 1941, the affairs of this important region were being conducted by a corps of proficient officers abiding by a diplomatic process which had changed little from the days of Queen Victoria. As noted earlier, the impracticability of the system was that many different Malayan government departments answered independently to their separate authorities in London. During an emergency, this revealed a serious flaw in the management of information. These independent departments sent, without consultation or verification, their view of events to their London bosses. Inevitably, this led to a serious loss of coordinated endeavour and presented the London authorities with a confused and fragmented picture of events, sometimes even conflicting data. Shortly after he arrived in post, Duff Cooper remarked on this duplication of effort:

> I was distressed to learn that the representative of my former Department, the Ministry of Information, was engaged on precisely similar work to that of a representative of the Ministry of Economic Warfare. Two officials in fact engaged on the same task were reporting to two different departments in London.[19]

One of the major tasks of the colonial administration was to keep the economy growing and running efficiently. The two major commodities

---

[17] A.H.M. Kirk-Green, *Britain's Imperial Administrators, 1858–1966* (Basingstoke: Macmillan Press and Oxford St Antony's College, 2000), pp. 129–31. From the early 1930s the Colonial Administrative Service (CAS) became a single colonial service and recruits were allocated to various overseas territories according to demand and ability.

[18] Heussler, *British Rule in Malaya*, p. 271.

[19] Viscount Norwich Duff Cooper, *Old Men Forget: The Autobiography of Duff Cooper (Viscount Norwich)* (London: Hart Davis, 1953), p. 293.

that gave Malaya its prominence in Southeast Asia in the early 20th century were rich and extensive deposits of high-grade tin ore and an abundance of cultivated rubber. Rice was also a major crop grown mainly in north Malaya, as was palm oil throughout the peninsula. The First World War generated a huge demand for tin and rubber and, by 1920, Malaya was exporting more than half of the world's total rubber production (196,000 tons). The demand for both commodities fell off during the economic slump of 1929 but afterwards picked up again, with the emergent American car industry being a major consumer. On the eve of the Second World War, European companies owned 74 per cent of the rubber estates in Malaya. Of the remainder, 17 per cent were owned by Chinese, 5 per cent by Indians and 4 per cent by other Asians, mainly Japanese.[20] British companies owned the majority of the European estates.

The tin-mining industry came to be dominated by the Europeans who, in the inter-war years, acquired abandoned mines from the Chinese. With revolutionary new methods of dredging, these ore deposits still yielded high-grade tin. European capital was heavily invested in the industry and, in time, control passed from the Chinese to the British. Chinese men continued to be the industry's labour force. Production of tin in the years preceding the war was about 90,000 tons per year. In 1941, it was 82,188 tons. Rubber cultivation covered some 3,250,000 acres and, in 1940, produced 505,749 tons while in 1941, to 31 October (last record before the invasion), 500,982 tons. The sale of these commodities, mainly to the USA, was invaluable in terms of foreign exchange, particularly at this critical period. In 1939, Malayan sales to the USA stood at Straits $235 million and exceeded the country's import expenditure by more than US$12 million a month. No other colony matched these figures.[21]

The colonial civil administration had to contend with the demographic changes encouraged by a thriving colonial economy. The major concern of indigenous Malays was the high proportion and distribution of non-Malays in the country. By 1931, the population of 4.5 million in Malaya

---

[20] Thompson, *Postmortem on Malaya*, p. 89. See also Winstedt, *Malaya and its History*, p. 117.

[21] Sir Shenton Thomas, unpublished private paper, "What Malaya Did", Mss. Ind. Ocn. S34, RHL (hereafter referred to as Thomas Papers).

included 1.7 million Chinese and 1.6 million Malays, with the remainder including Indians and others.[22] The 1931 census report also showed that geographical factors were an important feature in the distribution of Malaya's varied population. The indigenous Malays were predominantly concentrated in areas of agricultural smallholdings; there were also a number of mainly Malay fishing communities along the east and west littoral coasts. The northern states of Perlis, Kedah, Kelantan and Terengganu were almost wholly Malay.

The great variety of the population would produce its own negative consequences in the final events of the region. Some understanding of their differences is an essential part of an understanding of the outcome. Different races and peoples worked in distinct industries but had no motive or desire to enter into a multifaceted society. The Chinese community in Malaya, arriving mainly as traders from southern mainland China and settling along the western seaboard, was long established. The Chinese were largely an urban society and, in time, whole communities moved into the hinterland where they came to dominate the lucrative tin industry. Chinese immigration further swelled in the early 20th century, drawn by the economic opportunities of the increasing world demand for this commodity. However, the varied Chinese factions were accompanied by Chinese secret societies and criminal organizations, which thrived and took control of important industries like the large import/export trading houses. In particular, the secret societies tended to dominate the labourers who worked in the tin mines with great ruthlessness, even when control of the business moved to western management. The bulk of the Indian population, on the other hand, worked on the rubber and tea estates where there were only a few Chinese and almost no Malays. The Indians, mainly Tamils from southern India, in large part, were imported in increasing numbers to meet the needs of the expanding rubber industry.[23] The Tamils were also attracted to the growing railway network and the ancillary work associated with it.

---

[22] C. Vlieland, "Report on 1931 Singapore & Malaya Census" (Singapore: Government Printing Office, Feb. 1932).

[23] Bastin and Winks, *Malaysia*, pp. 257–66. Robert Nicholas Jackson, *Immigrant Labour and the Development of Malaya, 1786–1920: A Historical Monograph* (Kuala Lumpur: Government Press, 1961).

At first the Chinese and Indians were seen as a transient population but, by the 1930s, significant numbers had either decided to settle or lacked the ability to return to their homelands. Over time the three groups—Chinese, Malay and Indian—retreated into their own communities. Their ethnic and cultural differences were deepened by British perceptions and policies. Stereotyped attitudes meant that the Malays were effectively excluded from the modernizing economy as lacking the requisite drive and work ethic. Their upper class was encouraged to think about an English public school-style education and a career within the branch of government which administered the Malays.[24] The indigenous Malays were regarded as rice farmers and fisherfolk, and their vernacular education was tailored to such modest aspirations. The growing towns and cities of British Malaya, predominantly populated by Chinese, became unfamiliar places to most Malays. The Chinese were now a mixture of Straits-born Chinese, who took pride in calling themselves "the King's Chinese", and immigrants from mainland China. They differed from each other not only in language but also in their diverse ethnic groupings. Nevertheless, all had a traditional inclination to organize themselves into fraternal societies or triads to which they gave their primary loyalty. Administering this diverse Chinese population required a separate department of government, known as the "Chinese Protectorate". The head of this department, "Secretary for Chinese Affairs", an MCS official, sat on the executive and legislative councils of both the colony and the Federal Council. At first the Chinese were allowed to manage their own educational system in Chinese languages or English but this came to be seen to be a flawed policy, enabling the Chinese leaders to control the content of the curriculum for their own propaganda.[25] Much later, it was realized that some of these schools had become breeding grounds for the promotion of communist ideology. The Chinese Protectorate department claimed that it "needed every scrap of advice and assistance it could get, for not only did Chinese affairs frequently assume all aspects of an empire within an empire but also of anarchy within that empire".[26]

---

[24] Heussler, *British Rule in Malaya*, p. 278. In 1921, the administration began to recruit Malay candidates direct from leading colleges in Malaya.

[25] Jones, *Public Administration in Malaya*, p. 103.

[26] Ibid.

Conversely, most Indians were, effectively, subjects of the rubber estates on which they laboured; their children received Indian-language education untainted by any such political motives.

Thus with most Malays in villages, Chinese in towns and Indians on plantations, the various ethnic groups basically lived in their own neighbourhoods, followed different occupations, practised their own religions, spoke their own languages and operated their own schools. Such separation of the communities made the emergence of nationalism, in the sense of a pan-ethnic movement, highly unlikely. The racial divisions, intentional or not, almost entirely avoided the rise of a united anti-colonial sentiment which many other western colonies in Asia endured before the Second World War.[27]

In summary, most Malays tended to be loyal to their particular state and sultan. Clan, dialect and a growing commitment to either the Kuomintang or the communists of China divided the Chinese. The Indians maintained their allegiance with their homeland and saw their existence in Malaya purely in terms of work opportunity. Nevertheless, relations between the races were generally good. The Malays welcomed the protecting presence of the British partly because they had a concealed but increasing anxiety about the growing Chinese presence. However, this multinational arrangement, while superficially satisfactory, had a fundamental and important flaw. There was no common bond of love of country uniting these disparate communities.

On the eve of the Second World War, Malaya was rich both financially and in mineral wealth, a colony efficiently run and with the brightest prospects. The profits from its successful exports were reinvested in the country's infrastructure. Malaya had a better road network than any other country in the empire, and a railway system that was extensive and expanding.[28] All the services necessary for the

---

[27] Sir William George Maxwell, *The Civil Defence of Malaya: A Narrative of the Part Taken in it by the Civilian Population of the Country in the Japanese Invasion* (New York: Hutchinson & Co., 1944), pp. 83–7.

[28] By 1941 Malaya had 6,500 to 8,000 kilometres of metalled roads, "generally admitted to be among the best in the world", and 1,600 kilometres of railway which linked Malaya with Siam. The causeway linking Singapore with Johor was built in 1923. "China Station Colonial Intelligence Report", June 1941, vol. 3, pp. 11–2. Also see WO 33/1834, NA.

country's health and efficient management were in place—hospitals, schools, telecommunications, banking, post, transport, judiciary, police, agricultural, fisheries and forestry commissions. During the pre-war period, the administration of British Malaya allied with the healthy economy made for a generally contented people. There was no discernible evidence of a pan-Malayan movement focusing on constitutional change. The British authorities were confident in declaring that, in Malaya, "good government was preferred to self-government".[29] Even so, the nature of the colonial economy and its mixed society meant that the administration always had to be alert for potential domestic strife. Strikes by workers for better working conditions and higher wages were not unusual. More worrying, however, was the rise of discontented Chinese who believed that communism was a better form of government than democracy. There was also the problem of their engaging in habitual gang war. While not unduly threatening, these activities caused occasional disturbances that disrupted the country's economy.

Labour unrest had existed in varying degrees since the depression of the early 1930s. Beforehand, from 1911–31, the government encouraged unrestricted immigration from India, China and the Netherlands East Indies to provide much needed workers for the booming tin and rubber industries. When world prices in these commodities fell during the depression, the government favoured the repatriation of alien labour. A restricted immigration law came into force from 1931. The new law left them vulnerable to the corruption of ruthless Chinese gang bosses able to prey not only on their desperation for work, but also in avoiding returning to the starvation and population pressure in the provinces of Kwangtung, Fukien and Kwangsi from which many labourers came. These same provinces, however, were also the stronghold of the Kuomintang and the scene of anti-British boycotts; the immigrants brought their political values with them to Malaya. So concerned was the government that, in 1927, it was forced to introduce an ordinance which provided for the deportation of undesirables; later, in 1931, the Kuomintang party was banned.[30]

---

[29] Ibid., pp. 78–80.

[30] Victor Purcell, *The Chinese in Malaya* (London and New York: Oxford University Press, 1948), pp. 216–7.

The first disturbances occurred among the Chinese labourers: as the depression began to recede, commodity prices began to rise and they felt they were not sharing in the returning prosperity. In 1936 there was a serious strike among the tin miners from the Hong Fatt mine in Selangor, which prevented operations for several days. Then both the Indian and Chinese employees of the Singapore Traction Company struck for higher wages and shorter working hours. This event turned out to be the longest and most serious strike in Malaya's history. In 1937, the largest known strikes in Malaya involving thousands of Chinese rubber tappers took place in Selangor and, in 1938 and 1939, a further series of serious strikes occurred. In late 1940, the Indian rubber tappers demonstrated their sympathy for the Chinese labourers and also came out on strike, even though they were better paid and had considerably better working conditions.[31]

British officials in Malaya were becoming increasingly concerned at the growth of radical ideas, especially those that threatened the socio-economic framework on which the colonial government rested. Their primary focus was on the Chinese community where the government's abandonment of responsibility for the education of the Chinese labour force was a major contribution to the propagation of left-wing ideas. These developments, strikes and anti-colonial May Day rallies in 1940 provoked a strong reaction from the authorities and, in July, more than 200 communist leaders in Singapore and Malaya were arrested. The colonial authorities in London were so concerned at the effect of the strikes on the vital production of rubber and tin that they suggested sending out a trained union official to examine the situation and advise on the introduction of the procedures of negotiation and arbitration. Perhaps inevitably, the "Government shied off this radical experiment and unwisely rejected this suggestion from the Colonial Office ..."[32]

---

[31] Ibid.

[32] CO 273/662/10. See also Jones, *Public Administration in Malaya*, p. 72. It is of interest to note that this proposal in 1940 was made at the time when the author Stanley Jones was the Acting Governor (AOG) and presumably had some influence on the decision to refuse. The matter of labour unrest was also raised with Shenton Thomas when he visited the CO during his leave and in a file note of his visit it records: "S Thomas expressed himself as very much in favour of Trade Union experts visiting Malaya unofficially and informally" (CO/273/662/10, NA).

An important aspect of this period of civil and industrial unrest was the successful employment of the police force to meet and contain many of the more violent demonstrations. The ordinary police officers were mainly Malays and Sikhs; the detective branch was largely Chinese with a few Indians. They were well-trained and led by predominantly European officers. The containment of some volatile and potentially explosive incidents earned them general admiration from not only the public but also the approval of the strikers themselves. In the process, they accumulated considerable intelligence about the subversive elements, mainly among the Chinese community, who were using the industrial disputes to foment and spread communist doctrine. In summary, the internal industrial unrest and the nascent attempt to spread communist doctrine were no more than symptoms of disaffection; they did not indicate an attempt to create a subversive fifth column. They were, however, a worrying and inconvenient distraction at this time.

Sir Shenton Thomas had replaced Sir Cecil Clementi, the previous Governor, who was a notable sinologist and a former Governor of Hong Kong (HK). Clementi had not been popular because of his reforming zeal. He was of the school that advocated devolution, aiming to unify the country with Malays taking greater responsibility for government. He proposed a pan-Malayan union. "Opposition was vehement. The Colony objected strongly to a proposal which swept away its foundation of free trade; the Unfederated refused to lie down with the Federated States."[33] His consistent and inflexible preferment of this ideal was to be his downfall and, in 1934, after only four years in post, he was replaced by Thomas; the CO, "confident of their ability to rule well, they also felt that self-government for a society so obviously divided on ethnic lines would be a disservice to the Malayan peoples".[34]

Thoroughly briefed by the CO, Thomas stayed well away from questions of self-government; the initial impression he gave was that he was there to learn and that he would take his time before making any comment. The business community found him approachable, friendly

---

[33] Jones, *Public Administration in Malaya*, p. 89.

[34] Anthony J. Stockwell, "British Imperial Policy and Decolonisation in Malaya 1942-52", *Journal of Imperial and Commonwealth History* 13 (Oct. 1984).

and sound.[35] When he assumed the appointment in 1934, he was 55 and supposed it to be his last career appointment before retiring at 60. However, he was surprised and pleased when asked in 1939 to extend his service. Britain then at war with Nazi Germany, the CO decided that a change at that point was not appropriate. When Japan invaded Malaya in late 1941, Thomas was nearly 63. Many observers have described him as an affable, sociable person, solid, imperturbable and unimaginative, who rose to the position he held not through outstanding ability but because of long and conscientious service.[36] Later, Thomas drew censure for what was described as less than total commitment to the country. He showed little apparent personal incentive to plant deep roots for himself in Malaya or to gain a profound understanding of the local terrain. Early in the job, he made a visible effort to visit and acquaint himself with the region, the country, its people and their rulers. He travelled in great style and comfort, but he never took the trouble to learn Malay, recognizably not a difficult language. He thus lost some of his standing with senior Malays by always having to rely on interpreters and perhaps, in a way, indicating that he had no more than a superficial and temporary commitment to the country. It was also noticed that, after his initial foray, he rarely made the effort to visit outlying rulers. He was, however, comfortable with his staff of civil servants who held many senior administrative appointments.

In a little known and rarely mentioned episode, he showed a disconcerting lack of judgement, which exposed a surprising lack of integrity. In 1938, he was confronted with a serious accusation of corruption within the magistracy of the FMS. One of his colleagues, Sir Roger Hall, after a brief time in the position of Chief Justice to the FMS, asked to resign because he could not serve as the head of a legal system that was so venal, incompetent and extensively corrupt. Thomas persuaded him not to resign but instead to examine and report on the whole system of justice in the FMS. Hall's account, "Report of the Chief Justice into Allegations of Incompetency and Corruption in the Magistracy of the FMS",[37] was a damning indictment of a legal system not only riddled

[35] Heussler, *British Rule in Malaya*, pp. 252–3.
[36] Ian Morrison, *Malayan Postscript* (London: Faber and Faber, 1942), p. 157. Morrison was the accredited *London Times* reporter in Singapore throughout the campaign.
[37] CO 967/73, NA.

with corruption but also presided over by many unqualified magistrates. So shocking was the report that Thomas suppressed it. A year later, the CO heard of its existence because Hall—who had, anyway, resigned from Malaya—brought up the subject, while visiting London, in a conversation with the legal department at the CO. Sir Grattan Bushe, the head legal adviser, then challenged Thomas about the existence of the report. The Governor disparaged the document and claimed that, in any case, "it was a secret report for the Governor's information and was strictly confidential".[38] Bushe was astonished at this comment and rebuked Thomas, reminding him that nothing in colonial territories should be withheld from the CO. Further, in an internal memo Bushe said, "[I]n my view a Governor who hides from the Secretary of State such grave events as these, is doing the Colonial Office a gross disservice".[39] Thomas' withholding information and dismissing bad news was a character defect that was to manifest itself again in the more serious circumstances of wartime Malaya.

As noted, the business of administration in Malaya was a slow and indirect process that characterized Thomas' administration even after the outbreak of war in Europe. At a meeting of the Legislative Council in Singapore on 16 October 1939, Shenton Thomas made a lengthy address to the chamber and, among other things, said:

> When I addressed you at the Budget Meeting of last year I was able to give expression to the relief we all felt at being spared the horrors of war and the hope that we might be blessed with real enduring peace. That hope has not been fulfilled. Great Britain is once again at war, fighting for the freedom of the world from Nazi domination. In this, she has the full support of the British Empire which, as in 1914, has placed its whole resources at the disposal of the Mother Country in her hour of need. We know that victory will be ours ...
>
> Here in Malaya our duty is clear. Last year this country set an example to the Colonial Empire in its contributions to Imperial defence. The Colony of the Straits Settlements alone made a free-will offering of one million pounds, and decided to increase its annual contribution by $2 million for a period of five years. Most of the Malay States gave according

---

[38] Ibid.
[39] Ibid.

to their means and I felt very proud that I should be [the] channel through which these voluntary tokens of loyalty were communicated to the Secretary of State ...[40]

This comment and others throughout his speech underlines the difference between his authority over the Straits Settlements and his lesser influence in the "Malay States". In the same address, he took the opportunity to raise a number of civil defence matters and warn about likely future food controls and the possibility of increased training for military volunteers. Further demonstrating the separation of thought and deed between the administrations, he explained that a system of broadcasts had been arranged for keeping the people informed by means of loud speakers. They would be placed in the most thickly populated areas of Singapore. Pointedly, he spoke only of Singapore, not even the other members of the Straits Settlements, let alone the FMS and the UMS.[41]

All military matters and particularly those relating to the defence of Singapore and Malaya during the inter-war years was the domain of the armed services. Although the government was not involved in the minutiae of tactical details, the Governor was fully informed of the detailed strategy and military intentions. Until the possibility of war loomed, the civil authorities were content to leave to the GOC the established arrangements for frequent scrutiny of the nation's defensive plans. He controlled these reviews through a number of sub-committees, which assumed responsibility for various aspects of the scheme. Representatives of the other two services and civil servants were appointed where it was appropriate. One body dealt with the supply of food for the population of Malaya during war. In August 1938, Thomas, uncharacteristically and prompted by his staff, decided that emergency food supplies should be the subject of a separate study. He nominated a senior civil servant, C.A. Vlieland, a man with 26 years of service in Malaya, to undertake this task. Vlieland had never served in the armed forces but he took a keen interest in military affairs and military strategy. Quite rightly, as part of his investigation, he examined the extant defensive plan. He concluded,

[40] Proceedings of Legislative Council meeting, 16 Oct. 1939 (Singapore: Government Printing Office, 1940).
[41] Ibid.

first, that the defence plan was deficient in its scope and second, that the existing defence committee should be reconstituted to include greater civilian representation. In a memoir he wrote after he left Singapore, he recorded:

> Up to the end of 1938 the defence organisation in Malaya consisted of a Defence Committee with a set of sub-committees for various aspects of planning preparedness—food supply, transport, medical, A.R.P. Manpower etc. The Army was overwhelmingly represented on all of these and exercised practically the sole initiative. The GSO 3 [junior staff officer] at Fort Canning was the secretary of the Committee and a member of most of the sub-committees and his office was the only centre resembling a defence secretariat. No one with experience of committee organisations will need telling how such an organisation would work. It would I think not be unfair to say that the naval representatives were not much interested, the RAF was disgusted with the whole setup and busy civilian administrators, engineers, doctors and policemen regarded their duties on the various committees as a tiresome and time wasting chore.[42]

In response to Vlieland's report, at the end of 1938, Thomas brought together a number of the un-coordinated sub-committees under the direction and control of the Secretary for Defence, Malaya, a new office to which Vlieland was appointed. As Thomas described it, the job "was, in effect, the defence branch of the Colonial and Federal Secretariats and the High Commissioners Office, and focused and co-ordinated civil defence policy and practice throughout Malaya".[43] The Governor, as C-in-C, decided it was appropriate that he should be Chairman of this new defence committee and defined his task as that of considering questions affecting the fighting services and the civil defence departments, although, as noted, nothing in his previous career had prepared him to preside over such a committee. The heads of the three services were all now members, which was a sensible adaptation; previously the navy and RAF commanders relied on briefings from their subordinate representatives on the various sub-committees. In the case of the Air Commander, he positively welcomed the change as it gave him and his service a much greater say in the formulation of policy. In due course, the committee

---

[42] C. Vlieland, unpublished memoir "Disaster in the Far East", Vlieland 3.2.5.LHCMA.
[43] Thomas Papers.

was increased to include three unofficial members of the legislative and federal councils. The C-in-C, Far East and the C-in-C, Far East Fleet, at their own request, were not substantive members but had an open invitation to attend, which they invariably did. When war broke out in Europe, the Governor changed the title "defence" to "war committee". It met at irregular intervals at the discretion of the Chairman when he believed or was persuaded that there were enough serious matters calling for attention. However, while the committee was empowered to discuss questions affecting the services and the civil defence departments, it had no executive function. In matters relating to defence in the Malay states, the Defence Secretary was authorized to deal directly with the British resident or adviser in each of the states who, in turn, and taking account of Vlieland's guidance, had the authority to make decisions on behalf of the state. The war committee had no agenda and kept no minutes.

As noted in Chapter 1, this unusual and unprofessional arrangement astonished Brooke-Popham and provoked him to insist that records be kept, much to the irritation of the civil servants. Because earlier meetings were not documented there is no record of matters discussed or decisions taken. The gatherings were fractious and unproductive. To add to Brooke-Popham's exasperation, he found Vlieland's unhurried response to implementing committee decisions maddening.

In April 1940, Thomas left Singapore for England for his due entitlement of home leave. This decision was, at the time and subsequently, strongly criticized as bordering on irresponsible in view of the escalating war in the West and the growing Japanese threat in East Asia. He left the affairs of government in the hands of his deputy Stanley Jones, the Colonial Secretary, who became in situ the OAG. Jones, a long-serving officer in the MCS, was described by a colleague, Hugh Bryson, as "a dour type who found it hard to admit himself wrong; blunt and plain spoken .... Jones was either complacent at best or defeatist at worst".[44] In the event, 1940 proved to be a critical year both on the domestic scene and in terms of military and civil defence preparations. Decisions and resolutions made during this period had not only far-reaching effects on later events

---

[44] Hugh Bryson, private papers, Royal Commonwealth Society Library, Cambridge University Library.

but also subsequent commanders could only change with great difficulty. In general, those in charge had to live with them.

The senior figures in both the civil and military organizations (the military commanders at this time were Major General (later Lieutenant General) Lionel Bond, Air Vice-Marshall Babington and Admiral Sir Percy Noble) were ill-assorted, frequently disagreed with each other and, on a number of major issues, were quite incompatible. Vlieland's relationship with the military was especially abrasive. It is claimed by some that his elevation to the appointment of Secretary for Defence with direct and unfiltered access to the Governor bred, in Vlieland, a touch of megalomania.[45] He treated most senior military officers with disdain and believed that he was their intellectual superior. Thomas, on his departure, did not help matters by saying to his Secretary for Defence: "Remember Vlieland, I rely on you to hold the fort while I am away and not let Bond get away with it. Jones knows very little of the defence side, and you'll have to keep him straight."[46]

Not long after Thomas left, Vlieland took it upon himself to compose an "Appreciation of the Defence of Malaya" in July 1940.[47] It was a well-presented, prescient and accurate forecast of how he anticipated the Japanese would invade Malaya, even to the extent of identifying the very beaches on which they, in fact, landed. (There is, however, a strong suspicion among academics that he could only have produced this piece by plagiarizing the Dobbie Appreciation).[48] The GOC regarded it as a gross intrusion into military affairs that were not his concern. And, in any case, the Vlieland Appreciation did not accord with his recent WO briefings. He was extremely offended by this interference. Their

---

[45] Louis Allen, *Singapore 1941–1942* (Newark: University of Delaware Press, 1977), pp. 225–46. See also Kirby, *Singapore*, p. 52 and passim.

[46] Vlieland, *Disaster*, op. cit., p. 26. (Jones, by virtue of his appointment as OAG, was chairman of the War Committee, arguably a position that required an intimate knowledge of the military situation).

[47] Vlieland Papers. 3.3. LHCMA. It is, in fact, so accurate in its predictions that Ong Chit Chung, in his book *Operation Matador*, disputes the validity of it being an original document. Ong considers it has the appearance of having been amended after the event and before he passed his personal papers to the Liddell Hart Centre at King's College, London.

[48] Ibid.

professional relationship started badly and did not recover. In addition, what soon became apparent to Bond was that the Appreciation was supportive of the air commander's views of the defence of Malaya and this, in turn, led to the most fundamental disagreement between the two commanders over the core concept of the defence plan. In his memoir, Vlieland records:[49]

> It was clear from the first that General Bond's briefing by the War Office, no less than his own point of view, were going to make things very difficult .... He clearly thought that my functions should be strictly confined to "civil defence" and that defence policy and military strategy were no concern of mine, or even the Governor. But worse than all this was that he told me specifically, at his first interview with me, that his orders were to defend Singapore and did not permit him to concern himself with the peninsula. All this was more than tiresome. ... Until Sir Shenton went on leave in April 1940 the balance of power in defence councils was secure. The Naval C-in-C was still in Hong Kong and the senior naval officer in Singapore gave no trouble. The Air C-in-C was wholeheartedly on the side of the Governor and myself, and determined upon the defence of all Malaya; and I had Sir Shenton behind and with me all the way.

This outburst, written in 1944, when Vlieland had been removed from his appointment and was back in England, conveys the passion and conviction with which he saw his role as Secretary for Defence. It is a greatly inflated image of the task that he had described in the *Straits Times* newspaper of 30 December 1938 announcing his appointment. He detailed his duties as:

- Wartime censorship arrangements.
- Passive Air Raid precautions.
- Maintenance of Food Supplies.
- Emergency transport organisations.
- Mobilisation of manpower for maintenance of essential services.
- Other social, economic and administrative readjustments, which are necessary in time of war.[50]

---

[49] Ibid.
[50] *The Straits Times*, Friday, 30 Dec. 1938.

In 1940, while the Governor was on leave, the question of imposing martial law was raised in the war committee as a means of imposing countrywide compliance to civil defence measures and thus overcoming the current lengthy consultative processes among the FMS and UMS. There was no majority agreement and they rejected it as incompatible with the need to portray an image of confidence and reassurance. Even later, when the country was on the verge of being overwhelmed, the British authorities could not agree among themselves regarding the imposition of martial law.[51]

In 1941, nearly a year after Brooke-Popham was appointed C-in-C, it was becoming clear that the conduct and coordination of government-military affairs in Singapore were still not running smoothly. The next step, London decided, was that a minister of cabinet rank should go to Singapore to assess and give advice on the situation. Alfred Duff Cooper was chosen. He had previously been Minister for Information in Churchill's wartime cabinet, an appointment at which he did not perform well and had to resign. He was then employed as Chancellor of the Duchy of Lancaster, an undemanding sinecure from which he could be released without consequence. He arrived in Singapore in September 1941, and filed his first report the following month. As mentioned earlier, he was astonished that two Cs-in-C lived side by side at the naval base at Singapore, which he considered neither practical nor convenient, and he was particularly vituperative about the pedantic, leisurely attitude and lack of urgency that permeated government business.[52]

Thomas resented the arrival of Duff Cooper and was offended that the London authorities felt it necessary to appoint a Cabinet Minister Resident, Singapore.[53] He wrote:

---

[51] It was the opinion of Percival that martial law should only be introduced when the government was no longer capable of maintaining law and order and had to turn to the military to restore it. And as this did not apply in Malaya it was unnecessary. Moreover, he had no suitable senior officer available to take on the appointment of Military Governor. See his *The War in Malaya*, p. 180.

[52] NA, CAB/66/20/9 para. 58. Duff Cooper, "Report by Chancellor of the Duchy of Lancaster".

[53] Sir Winston Churchill, *The Second World War: Volume 3: The Grand Alliance* (London: Cassell, 1950), p. 544.

The news of Duff Cooper's appointment to the Far East had been received with little enthusiasm. He had not been successful as a Minister of Information and had been demoted to be Chancellor of the Duchy of Lancaster. We felt we were being landed with a failure. We remembered Sir Stafford Cripps' description of him as a "petulant little pipsqueak".[54]

It is probably fair to say, based on many written comments, that Duff Cooper did not relish his time in Singapore. He resented being away from London, by then the centre of international attention, and felt remote from his friends and his colleague Churchill. By his own admission, he missed the social scene where he was renowned as a serial philanderer.[55] He was not in a frame of mind to confront the parochial, insular and, to his mind, petty bureaucracy clogging the machinery of government. Nevertheless, at this time of serious concern about Japan, brutally frank honesty was called for together with major political surgery to jolt the inertia of the colonial government. Duff Cooper did not get on with Thomas, and thought Brooke-Popham too old and out of his depth for the growing military threat facing Singapore and Malaya. His first report to London after a month of observation and regional visits was comprehensive and perceptive. His major observation was that the complex and varied London offices of state administering British interests in Southeast Asia led to confusion and territorial conflict. He pointed out that the diplomatic or consular representatives in Tokyo, Chungking, Bangkok, Manila, Saigon and Batavia reported to the FO, while the governors of the Straits Settlements and HK reported to the CO. Further, the Governor of Burma referred to the Burma Office, while high commissioners in Australia and New Zealand represented the Dominions Office but usually had a diplomatic officer on their staff who was appointed by the FO. To add to the complexity, he added,

> The Governor of the Straits Settlements was also High Commissioner for Malaya, and Malaya was composed of a Crown Colony, of a Federation of Malay States and of group of Unfederated States, each of these three elements differing from the others in method of government and in other important respects. Here existed a system under which four different

[54] Quoted in Montgomery, *Shenton of Singapore*, p. 77.
[55] Duff Cooper, *Old Men Forget*, passim.

types of official reported to and received orders from four different departments of State ... and no effort was made to co-ordinate the activities of the officials or the policies of the departments concerned.[56]

With prescience, looking at the future of the region, he foresaw it developing into a major world producer of industrial goods and an important provider of natural resources. To coordinate Britain's interests he recommended the creation of a Secretary of State for the Far East. In a separate private letter to Churchill, he suggested the former Prime Minister of Australia, Sir Robert Menzies, for this role. Churchill minuted at the bottom of the letter: "I am against Menzies; I think DC [Duff Cooper] should be told to stay there and do it himself."[57] Duff Cooper's wife Diana, who was with him in Singapore, anticipated this response believing that, "Winston will think Duff comfortably out of the way and offer him the post."[58] In the event, the proposal was made redundant by the Japanese invasion. When the war began, he nevertheless volunteered to perform the coordinating duties suggested in his report "pending the appointment of a successor". In a reply from London, he was appointed Resident Minister in Singapore for far eastern affairs.[59]

In addition to pointing out the anomaly of having two Cs-in-C, Duff Cooper remarked on the unsatisfactory intelligence gathering and dissemination arrangements. The Far Eastern Combined Intelligence Bureau (FECB) which, while performing most useful work, had a serious flaw in that it lacked a civilian branch; there was a danger of the political, diplomatic and economic value of information not being correctly estimated. And because the bureau had individuals reporting to different government departments "working independently of one another and sometimes in ignorance of each other's action, [it] could not be expected to produce entirely satisfactorily results". Further, on duplication of effort, Duff Cooper reported,

I was distressed to learn that the representative of my former Department, the Ministry of Information, was engaged on precisely similar work

[56] CAB/66/20/0. 29 Oct. 1941. Duff Cooper report.
[57] Prem. 3/155. fol. 94 WSC note, 29 Nov. 1941, NA.
[58] John Charmley, *Duff Cooper* (London: Weidenfeld & Nicolson, 1986), p. 159.
[59] Ibid.

to that of a representative of the Ministry of Economic Warfare. Two officials in fact engaged on the same task were reporting to two different departments in London.[60]

He was also scornful that a useful and important services public relations office, which was sensibly set up at the behest of Brooke-Popham, was placed in the hands of a retired naval commander who had spent the previous 20 years as a magistrate in Fiji. The press correspondents found him obstinate and quite out of his depth. One of his female staff, Anne Kennaway, remarked in her book *Journey by Candlelight*: "The Commander was right when he said he had no experience of Public Relations ... He was totally unsuited to the job, knowing little of the press world and the correspondents were indignant at his lack of understanding."[61] They complained of the severe censorship of their reports and of information being withheld from them. They were also contemptuous of material issued from GHQ, dismissing it as propaganda.

To allay fears among senior figures, Duff Cooper explained that the purpose of his new appointment was to give the Cs-in-C political guidance and relieve them, as far as possible, of extraneous responsibilities so that they could give their full attention to the conduct of the campaign. Importantly, he was given the power to settle emergency matters on the spot when there was no time to refer to London and he could delegate to departmental officers authority to incur expenditure when he believed urgent action was necessary. In this role, he assumed chairmanship of a newly formed War Council, replacing Shenton Thomas' local war committee; while it was ostensibly a forum for the whole of the Far East theatre, the majority of its agenda addressed only the immediate local problems. He also took control of the affairs of civil defence, forming a civil defence committee. Membership of the new War Council was extended to include Sir George Sansom (Director of Publicity), V.G. Bowden, who represented the Australian government and, if he wished to attend, Major General Gordon Bennett, the Commander of the 8th Australian Division.

---

[60] CAB/66/20/0.29 Oct. 1941, NA.

[61] Anne Kennaway, *Journey by Candlelight: A Memoir* (Edinburgh: Pentland, 1999), p. 48.

The formation of the War Council was not unanimously welcomed; Brooke-Popham fought hard against its creation. In a secret and personal letter to Prime Minister Churchill, Duff Cooper said:

> The Governor, Sir Shenton Thomas, is one of those people who find it quite impossible to adjust their minds to war conditions. He is also the mouthpiece of the last person he speaks to. When I informed him of my appointment he professed himself delighted, welcomed the idea of a War Council and was most helpful at the first meeting which we held the same afternoon. That evening he dined with Sir Robert Brooke-Popham and at the meeting next morning he supported the latter's attitude in contesting the need for a War Council, and produced stronger arguments against it than Sir R. Brooke-Popham could produce himself.[62]

In this same letter, Duff Cooper took the opportunity to give vent to his personal jaundiced opinions of the leading figures in Singapore; he claimed that Brooke-Popham "is a very much older man than his years warrant and sometimes seems on the verge of collapse". Regarding Thomas, "the Governor is very much influenced by his Colonial Secretary, a sinister figure called Stanley Jones who is universally detested in the Colony, where he is accused of having been defeatist since the beginning of the war". Regarding General Percival, the GOC "is a nice good man who began life as a schoolmaster. I am sometimes tempted to wish he had remained one."[63] He then asked for Churchill's permission to sack Stanley Jones and replace him with the "admirable" Federal Secretary from KL, Hugh Fraser.

During this deceptive interlude, there was not only a cumbersome bureaucratic system of governance but also serious dissension and debilitating jealousy among and between both the leading civil and military figures responsible for the safety of the country. The discord inexorably led to a fundamental dispute about preparations, to meet the growing menace. By December 1940, there was a Secretary for Defence, Vlieland, who disagreed to the point of obstruction with the army commander about the basic concept of the defensive plans. The Air

---

[62] CAB 967/77. 18 Dec. 1941, NA.

[63] Percival was never a schoolmaster. Before joining the army in the First World War he worked in the city of London. However, Shenton Thomas was a schoolmaster before joining the colonial service. See Montgomery, *Shenton of Singapore*, p. 18.

Commander agreed with Vlieland and was barely on speaking terms with the Army Commander. There was an acting head of government, Jones (OAG), quite remote and almost disinterested in military affairs, an elderly C-in-C, Brooke-Popham, burdened with an impossibly large parish and with an old-fashioned, unsure touch towards its military problems and an ethnically divided population, not fully aware of the threat to its existence and quite unprepared for the rigours of war. To an outside observer there was no noticeable difference to the pace and quality of life throughout the country. People went about their work, domestic affairs and leisure, unchanged and unaffected by far-off international turmoil. Workers in the major industries were more concerned about their wage levels and prepared to demonstrate their disaffection by striking, rather than increasing the quota of vital resources.

By the middle of 1941, Vlieland, the Army Commander (Bond) and the Air Commander (Babington) were all replaced. A Resident Minister for Singapore was appointed and the C-in-C told he was to be relieved of his appointment. In addition, on Duff Cooper's recommendation, Stanley Jones was removed from the important and senior appointment of Colonial Secretary. Hugh Fraser, the Federal Secretary from KL, replaced him.

4

THE AMBIGUOUS STRATEGY

To understand the state of affairs prevailing in Singapore during the war with which the civil administration had to contend, it is important to set governmental activities against the overall military strategic situation. It is also necessary to be aware of how the developing strategy engaged the civil authorities—not only what contribution they made in military discussions, but also where military demands conflicted with their civil objectives and responsibilities. There were, in fact, some rudimentary disagreements about the gravity of the growing Japanese threat, and this in turn reflected the attitude each side took towards dealing with it. At the core of the dissent was a fundamental difference of priorities, the colonial authorities overriding order to the Governor about the production of rubber and tin—two commodities not only vital for the pursuit of war but also for the foreign exchange they generated. The military, on the other hand, was there to defend Singapore against a possible Japanese attack and, to this end, needed not only all practical civil support possible, but also the country to be made both fully aware of the lurking danger and be put on a war footing, with all the manpower, preparations and training this entailed. The Governor saw such a course as alarmist and almost certainly counterproductive because, he said, it would affect the morale of the people, which in turn would prejudice the country's industrial effort. The defensive plan, which the military staff attempted to create, was drawn up against this background. Their complex deliberations were compounded by the serious deficiency of a shortage of vital military manpower and equipment. As the naval base in Singapore was the focus of British strategic military planning in the Far East and the island was also the seat of the Governor and his administration, its protection was paramount.

Singapore rose to strategic prominence when Great Britain examined its global commitments in relation to its military capabilities in the wake of the debilitating First World War. A perceptible change in the international balance of naval power had taken place: no longer was the UK the supreme global naval force, the USA now matched the tonnage of Britain's High Seas' Fleet and Japan was not far behind. The devastating financial wartime expenditure meant that Britain was in no position to embark on a ship-building programme to retain its supremacy. America was, in any case, concerned about Britain's continuing desire for naval dominance and most uneasy at the rise of Japanese naval power particularly in the Pacific region. To address these concerns, the USA called a conference in November 1921 in Washington to discuss the position. The result was the Washington Naval Treaty signed in February 1922 by Great Britain, USA, Japan, France and Italy. Its main feature was a restriction on the size of the three major powers' capital ships—USA, Britain and Japan—and the proposal was for a 5:5:3 ratios in capital ships with a total tonnage of 500,000 each for America and Britain and 300,000 for Japan; Italy and France agreed to 175,000 tons each. Also incorporated into the treaty was the agreement that the three major powers would not build any new fortifications or naval bases in the Pacific area east of longitude 110 degrees, a restriction that excluded Singapore.

In 1922, the Committee of Imperial Defence (CID) agreed, in the light of the limitations of the Washington Treaty and of the changing political Far East scene, that Britain still needed a sizeable naval deterrent in Pacific waters. It recognized, however, that there were no funds to build and maintain a fleet in both home waters and the Far East. The answer was a naval base in Southeast Asia to which the fleet could sail and harbour if the need arose. But even at this point there were some who saw the frailty of this solution, especially if there were simultaneous threats at home and abroad. Following an exhaustive and wide study about possible locations for such a base, including extending the HK naval base, the Admiralty decided that Singapore was best suited both geographically and strategically. After a number of false starts, due mainly to the anticipated expensive cost and the vacillating opinion of the changing UK government, the project finally got underway in 1926. A vignette that portended future civil military relations arose when a visiting war office committee in 1927 visited the site and learnt that the government of the Straits Settlements was unwilling to make the land available for military purposes without first obtaining an assurance that no part of the cost would fall on the local civil community.[1]

In conjunction with the construction of the base was the important matter of how to defend it. This led to lengthy, acrimonious and opposing strategic views. The obvious fact on which they all agreed was that to protect the naval base meant defending Singapore Island. The base in isolation could not be defended like some ancient citadel. If Singapore fell, the base fell. The debate therefore revolved around how best to defend Singapore. The earliest plans in the 1920s concluded that the most likely danger would be an assault from the seas around Singapore; to counter such an attempt, large, expensive 15-inch naval guns were installed that could engage an enemy fleet at a range of 20 miles. During the next decade, this likely scenario diminished because of the changing face of battle. Weapons, tanks, aircraft, ships, landing craft—all the paraphernalia of war made giant technological advances that changed the ground rules. This required a reappraisal of the defensive plan. The topography (and climate) of the Malay Peninsula now acquired a prominent status in all planning. It was also to have a significant bearing on both the changing emphasis of the defensive plan and the likely nature and conduct of a campaign.

The long, narrow and rugged Malay Peninsula was nearly 500 miles long, north to south, and across the bulge in the middle it was about 250 miles wide. It was some 50,000 square miles in area and often compared in size to England and Wales, with the Isle of Wight equating to Singapore at its southern end. In 1940, the east coast was underdeveloped and sparsely populated except in the extreme north, and had no continuous road along its length. There was a road from Johor Bahru, the most southern town, along the southeast coast to Endau, a distance of 104 miles, but here the road ended. And while there were motorable tracks in the dry season

---

[1] Kirby, *History of the Second World War*, p. 8.

which could be used to continue north, it was not until Kuala Terengganu, two-thirds up the east coast, that another road was laid that ran for 103 miles northwards to the most northeastern town of Kota Bharu, capital of the state of Kelantan. The only unbroken communication between Johor Bahru and Kelantan was the railway, which wound its way through the central massif.

On the west coast lay the main road communications; there were 585 miles of good motorable road running from Johor Bahru to the Thai frontier in northwest Malaya, and this western strip intensely developed both agriculturally and commercially. There was also a good railway network on the western plain that ran all the way to Bangkok in Thailand. In addition, a network of feeder roads covered the area. The road surfaces were of first-class tar-macadam and the network of roads altogether covered several thousand miles.[2] The railways were efficient and sophisticated with restaurant cars and air-conditioned coaches. British engineers built the railways initially for the haulage of heavy mining material and the transport of tin ore to cargo ships for export. The network used the same gauge track width as in Britain. Its rolling stock, predominantly manufactured in Britain, increased in scope to include versatile cargo wagons.[3]

Central Malaya consists of a mountainous range of densely covered jungle rising, at its highest, to over 7,000 feet. Lateral communication was confined to three roads across this range. Rivers abound in Malaya but they are usually short and rapid and, since the introduction of intensive tin mining, many of them had silted up. The largest of the Peninsula's rivers are the Perak and the Pahang with their many tributaries. The importance of rivers to Malaya, especially on the west coast, is shown by the fact that the boundary lines of most Malay states follow the river systems and, in many cases, give their names to the states. The bulk of Malaya's tin was located in the western river valleys. Many of the rivers on the west coast were navigable to small steamers and their waters ran into the Straits of Malacca whereas, on the long open east coast, sandbanks barred the mouth of every river and the heavy breakers from

---

[2] Thomas Papers, "Malay's War Effort". Mss. Ind. Ocn. s. 341.3/4. RHL.
[3] Ibid. See also Maxwell, *The Civil Defence of Malaya*, p. 7.

the northeast monsoon were an obstacle for those approaching the beaches from the sea.

Malaya's climate, as described by the Europeans who lived there, was enervating by its monotony rather than actually unhealthy. The weather was consistently hot, between 88 and 92 degrees, and all times of the year were rainy. While seasonal variations in the rest of the country were negligible, the east coast differed from the centre and the west in that the monsoons brought a distinct stormy season from November to March. The absence of bracing winds and the prevalence of great humidity tended to have a depressing effect, especially on Occidentals.[4] In the days before air-conditioning, this was an important factor. Major General Playfair, who became Chief of Staff to the C-in-C, remarked:

> I have been to Malaya twice before and knew it to be a place where, for various reasons, the tempers of busy people become easily frayed; where it seemed more natural to take offence than "to laugh it off"; and where criticism was more common than discretion.[5]

The abundance of rain promoted the luxuriant growth of dense rain forests. Apart from the coastal strips, which were cleared and cultivated with rubber and rice, and the swamp areas and open tin mines, the remainder of the terrain was dense jungle. While the jungle was penetrable, to attempt travel through it called for physical endurance and exceptional navigational skills, was painstakingly slow and, in military terms, suitable only for small, compact parties. The invading Japanese forces recognized fully the difficulties of jungle movement and confined their manoeuvre to rubber estate tracks, railway lines and motorable roads. Although the east coast consisted almost entirely of open beaches, it had limited communication. The predicted danger spots were Singora and Patani in Thailand, and Kuantan and Mersing in Malay. An added incentive for landing at these places was the bait of aerodromes, the possession of which by the Japanese would greatly accelerate their operations.

Singapore Island itself consisted primarily of mangrove swamps and rubber plantations; the impressive naval base was on the northern shore

---

[4] Thompson, *Postmortem on Malaya*, passim.
[5] WO 106/2620 Apr. 1943. Major General Playfair, "Some Personal Reflections on Malayan Campaign", NA.

facing the Straits of Johor and in the south a huge, teeming metropolis, the city of Singapore. In 1941, the city was a mixture of old and new, of baroque beauty and uncontrolled squalor. Stately white western buildings along broad avenues contrasted sharply with the low native houses in filthy, crowded back streets. Three quarters of a million people lived in Singapore. Nearly 600,000 were Chinese, with Malays, Indians, Europeans and a broad mixture of other races making up a varied minority.[6] The £63,000,000 (1937 prices) naval base covered 21 square miles in area and had the capacity to shelter a British fleet. There were two massive 50,000-ton dry docks and a huge floating dock which, by an outstanding feat of seamanship, was towed out from England. The sea channel separating the base from Malaya (the Johor Straits) was 1,500 metres wide.[7]

The tropical rain forests that covered most of the Malay Peninsula were to have a defining effect on the course of the war in Malaya. Not only did the dense vegetation limit military manoeuvre, it also restricted the options for the escaping civilian refugees. The central massif further hindered movement of people and supplies from one coast to the other. Moreover, for fresh military reinforcements, without time to acclimatize, the debilitating tropical climate was an added handicap.

As we learnt, the Admiralty favoured 15-inch guns and the air force torpedo-bombers to defend the base. The air force argument was that air power was more efficient than traditional fixed defence and cheaper since air squadrons designated for Singapore were available for use elsewhere until the need arose for them. The counter-argument, the navy replied, was that the aircraft might be busy elsewhere at the critical time and that it was much too risky not to have permanent protection in place. This disagreement continued until 1931 when the Admiralty, in the light of the worrying international scene, admitted that it would be unable to have a deterrent size force remain in the area.[8] A relieving fleet would sail from home waters in the event of a threat and, they claimed, this reinforced the need for permanent fixed defences.

---

[6] 1931. *Census Report*, NA. Singapore.

[7] Kirby, *History of the Second World War*, p. 153. Also see WO 252, *Topographical and Economic Surveys, 1941–1946.*

[8] Appreciation of the General Naval Situation in 1931 by First Sea Lord, CP 100 (31), 10 Apr. 1931, CAB 24/219. Quoted in Haggie, *Britannia at Bay*, p. 9.

The "period before relief" was the term used to describe the time estimated for the relieving fleet to arrive. It was first calculated that it would take 42 days. Based on this estimate, a less than convincing compromise was reached whereby the RAF would have primary responsibility for the defence of the base until the fleet arrived, but with the qualification that the aircraft and the infrastructure to support them should be permanent features and not transient groups rushed there in time of tension.[9]

The only airfields in Malaya in the early 1930s were commercial and on the west coast. On Singapore Island at that time, three RAF stations were under construction at Seletar, Sembawang and Tengah. To fulfil this new task, the RAF needed to extend the radius of both their reconnaissance and offensive capability against seaborne enemy forces approaching from the Gulf of Thailand and the South China Sea and concluded that they required three new airfields on the east coast of Malaya. A British government report (Baldwin Committee Report)[10] considered the demand and was not entirely convinced of the validity of the Air Ministry's logic; it suggested that the relative merits of both services' defensive plans should again be explored but that, in the meantime, the first stage of gun emplacement should go ahead.[11] In July 1935, the government, following a further review, relented and authorized work to begin on additional heavy gun emplacements and two airfields as part of the next phase of the construction. The base, opened in February 1938, was protected with five 15-inch guns, six 9.2-inch guns and eighteen 6-inch guns as well as secondary armament;[12] all the guns were to be manned by the army. The gun emplacements were not in the base itself but covered all the sea approaches to the island east and west including some located on neighbouring islets; two 6-inch guns were on the tip of southern Johor at Penggerang. All the fixed defences were provided with armour-piercing shell for use against ships although a small proportion of shells, suitable for use against land targets, were provided for the 9.2-inch

---

[9] Ibid., p. 15.

[10] Sub-committee of the Committee of Imperial Defence presided over by Stanley Baldwin.

[11] CAB 23/75 Cabinet Minutes 27(33) 5, 12 Apr. 1933, NA.

[12] Kirby, *History of the Second World War*, p. 21.

and some of the 6-inch batteries. Many of the 6-inch guns, though, had a limited field of fire.[13]

On completion there was still no definitive and unambiguous agreement among the services about the best means of protecting it. As time passed, the initial premises about an invasion force most likely approaching from the seas around Singapore was beginning to look less probable. In addition, even though in the growing arguments there was an element of self-serving promotion of their own arm, both the navy and the air force recognized that until a fleet arrived, the RAF would need to hold the fort.

To understand the plan that eventually evolved it is necessary to look at its progression. The essential amendments to the plan were dictated largely by the technical advances in projecting military force over greater distances with enhanced military hardware to support them. The effect on defensive thinking was the significant extension from the close defence of Singapore Island to the vastly more challenging task of defending the base by deploying to the northern extremities of Malaya. The Governor and his Defence Secretary were involved in this debate because it affected their relations with the Malay States. The deployment of large numbers of military personnel in rural areas, even as important civil defence measures, such as the selection and guarding of reserve food stores, still called for sensitive negotiations.

Early defence discussions assumed (indeed the notion was firmly dismissed) that a ground force could not possibly approach Singapore from the north through Peninsula Malaya because of the hostile terrain and the undeveloped transportation network.[14] During the lengthy gestation period of construction (12 years) the rail and road infrastructure within Malaya improved remarkably, and now there was the additional dimension of major advances in military technology and hardware. The British authorities watchfully monitored the noticeably improving

---

[13] Kirby, *Singapore*, p. 29.

[14] Lord Strabolgi, *Singapore and After: A Study of the Pacific Campaign* (London: Hutchinson and Co., 1942), p. 50. Writing with hindsight Strabolgi (a naval officer) thought otherwise: "... the utterly false statement that the jungle country on the mainland to the north of the island was impenetrable. How intelligent men could have accepted this argument is a mystery."

military capabilities and strength of Japan. The extant assumptions of the military threat began to change in 1937, when fresh minds believed that a seaborne invasion on the east coast of Malaya should no longer be discounted.[15] The officer who challenged the entrenched perceptions and revolutionized thinking about the defence of the naval base was Major General William George Sheddon Dobbie. A highly respected intellectual officer who held strong religious beliefs, he was commissioned into the Royal Engineers.

In 1937, Dobbie was appointed GOC Malaya. Shortly after taking up his post, he pointed out to the air officer commanding that, with the small peacetime army garrison at his disposal, it was impractical to expect the army to protect the airfields under construction on the east coast of Malaya. He also added that their siting made them highly vulnerable to enemy landings, as they were so close to the coast. Dobbie decided on a total reappraisal of the defence issues. He was particularly concerned at the restricted role intended for the army and the effect of the recently extended "period before relief", now put at 70 days.[16] Moreover, he felt that not enough notice had been taken of the major advances in military technology and the increased range of aircraft. More than any of his predecessors and demonstrating an astute awareness of emerging military technology and the fresh capabilities these developments permitted, he was the first to challenge the perceived view that an assault on Singapore from the Malayan mainland was unlikely. To convince the doubters he arranged testing exercises to prove the validity of his beliefs: he assessed the practicability of landings from the sea on the east coast during the monsoon period, which the sceptics claimed was a most serious handicap for a beach assault. He found that not only was it perfectly possible to do so but also, conversely, poor visibility could prove a major restriction for allied air reconnaissance, with the added problem that it would also reduce the efficiency of air attack on the enemy fleet.[17]

---

[15] WO 106/2441, 8 Feb. 1937, NA.

[16] COS Paper No. 596, 14 June 1937, "Far East Appreciation". Prepared for the Imperial Conference. The COS nevertheless cautioned, even at this point, that 90 days were probably more realistic. COS Paper No. 848, 27 Feb. 1939. By July 1939, the CO warned the Governor that 180 days were more practical. CO to Governor of SS, 22 July 1939, NA.

[17] Kirby, *History of the Second World War*, p. 15.

In view of the fluctuating estimates from London about the "period before relief", Dobbie was sure the figure was, in any case, hypothetical and no sensible plan should be put together on this uncertainty.[18] It would be better to start from an assumption that the period could be indefinite and, consequently, the Japanese would have a much better chance of success with a landward attack. In Dobbie's judgment, the combination of critical factors led him to the inescapable conclusion that the defence of Singapore must mean the defence of the whole of Malaya: road and rail communications on the Malayan mainland had improved; it was possible to land during the northeast monsoon; and the noticeably impressive quality of Japanese military hardware and the possibility of Japanese air attacks from advanced air bases. Moreover, there was ambiguity about Thailand's political position.

This fundamental change of strategy meant that additional troops were required on the mainland which meant, he stated, not only a large increase in air and ground forces but also stockpiles of stores, equipment and food to meet this contingency. His important and prophetic conclusions identified almost exactly the future course the campaign was to take. In his view, the Japanese would first secure advanced air bases in Siam [sic] or Indo-China and would probably then land in Singora and Patani in southern Siam and at Kota Bharu in Malaya, although additional landings might be made subsequently further south at Kuantan and Mersing. The Japanese troops would then cross from east to west across the Kra Isthmus and advance along the main roads and railways on the western side of Malaya to attack Singapore Island from the north. In his opinion, it was perfectly possible for land forces to approach the base from the Peninsula hence its defence needed to be extended to the defence of Johor and particular areas of northern Malaya.

The other two services, with little resistance, endorsed this radical reassessment.[19] What is interesting is that his Chief Staff Officer Colonel Percival, later appointed GOC, conducted the fresh Appreciation. It is also curious to learn of the comment made by Percival, on his return to the UK later in 1937 to take up a new appointment. When asked by

---

[18] Dobbie to Dill, DMO, letter CRMC 32845/G, 16 Nov. 1937. WO106/2441, NA.

[19] COS Paper No 596, 14 June 1937, "Far East Appreciation" and CAB 16/182, NA.

General Sir John Dill, a future CIGS, if Singapore was impregnable, he replied:

> [I]n my opinion, far from being impregnable it would be in imminent danger if war broke out in the Far East unless there was an early realization in high places of the complete change in the problem of its defence which was then taking place.[20]

With this fresh view of the problem of the defence of the naval base there followed a series of searching assessments. The main conclusion was that, to meet this new focus of threat and taking account of the terrain, the primary aim must be to prevent the enemy landing at all. Unquestionably, that required superior air and naval power. The army had the supporting role of defending the airfields and the islands of Singapore and Penang; dealing with airborne landings; driving out any incursions; and protecting the food resources, the rice-growing areas and the main lines of communication. The main responsibility for the defence of Malaya would be in the hands of the air force.[21] Several obvious prerequisites emerged from this appraisal: more frontline aircraft were needed; the overall taskforce commander should be an air force officer; a powerful fleet should sail for the area at the first telltale signs of belligerence; and the existing army garrison was not large enough to perform its new extensive and widely dispersed tasks. General Dobbie, for his part, started to organize defence in the southern area of Johor. This work had to stop, most unfortunately as was later proved, because there were insufficient funds (he was authorized by London the sum of £60,000) for the construction of a series of machine-gun blockhouses.[22] The British government, though, was at least stirred enough by the new assessment to authorize an increase of supplies for the island to withstand, in a worst-case scenario, a siege of 180 days (six months).

Before Dobbie's period as GOC ended in August 1939, he attended an Anglo-French senior military commander's conference in Singapore in June, convened at the request of both governments because of their

---

[20] James Leasor, *Singapore: The Battle that Changed the World* (London: House of Stratus, 2001 [1968]) p. 129.

[21] Kirby, *History of the Second World War*, p. 29.

[22] Ibid., p. 16.

disquiet at Japanese activities. And for the first time, Thailand's political posture in the unfolding turmoil was openly discussed, with the group acknowledging the crucial geographical position it occupied in the Southeast Asian cauldron. Dobbie pointed out the dangers if Japan gained control or even had Thai agreement to the use of the Kra Isthmus. Beside facilitating operations against Burma, the Japanese would be able to launch air attacks against Singapore from air bases within Thailand and threaten Malaya by land operations against Penang on one side, and against the east coast of Malaya in the neighbourhood of Kota Bharu on the other. The delegation declared:

> Every attempt, therefore, by Japan to increase her influence in Thailand must be countered ... any positive action by Japan in peace, such as the dispatch of armed forces and military aircraft to Thailand, could only be regarded as an act of war against the Allies.[23]

In addition, to ensure the security of Singapore, the conference further endorsed the recommendation that British forces in Malaya should be increased and quantified "by two infantry brigades and other units".

An international warning was thus declared about the danger to northern Malaya from the vulnerable region of the Kra Isthmus. The Dominions of Australia and New Zealand followed closely this discussion because Britain had long assured both nations that the Royal Navy would guard the seas around them. They did not become involved in the details of the protective measures; their concern was more that the naval base would, in time, harbour a fleet big enough to guard the southern Pacific. A major conclusion about defence measures on which all were agreed was that more emphasis be given to preventing an invading force ever reaching the coast of Malaya than waiting for it to come ashore.

In this critical 1940 period with Nazi Germany threatening Britain, the Royal Navy then emphatically recognized that it would not be able to send any deterrent-sized fleet to the Far East. And also, whatever the size of the force, it would not be able to send it with any haste (a judgement that alarmed the Dominions). The responsibility for the security of the naval base and the defence of Malaya now clearly rested with the

---

[23] COS Paper No. 941. 11 July 1939, para. 25 and CAB 53/52. Franco-British Conference, Singapore, 1939, NA.

RAF. Discussions turned to the question of the increased numbers of aeroplanes required for this task and the particulars of forward airfields from which to fly, and the army manpower and equipment needed for the defence of those airfields. The RAF combat strength was then 8 squadrons (4 bomber, 4 torpedo-bomber) and 2 flying-boat squadrons; 90 aircraft. There were no fighter aircraft and the torpedo-bombers were obsolescent. In February 1941, a squadron from India brought the total to 158.[24] The AOC calculated that the new defence criteria required at least 566 aircraft. He assumed that, in due course, their demand for additional aircraft would be honoured.

The GOC, who succeeded Dobbie in August 1939, was Major General Francis George Bond, another officer with a Royal Engineers' background. He has been described as: "… although a man of sterling worth and character, was lacking in personality, kept himself aloof and was inclined to exercise control from his office chair. He seldom, if ever, studied his problems on the spot."[25] Straight after his arrival, he reviewed and endorsed the findings of the Dobbie Appreciation and added further refinements of his own. Like his predecessor, he realized that little reliance could be placed upon the timely arrival of a naval task force, added to which the Admiralty now declared it was, in any case, unlikely to be able to spare more than two capital ships for this task.[26] With the period before relief becoming longer and the army under pressure to extend hugely its area of operations, he evidently needed a substantial increase in the army garrison. He submitted to the WO a request for his existing force to be greatly increased.[27] At the same time, he drew its attention to the information from intelligence sources about the unusual Japanese interest in the area of the Kra Isthmus. This raised the first murmurings of possible pre-emptive action into southern Thailand to forestall a Japanese move onto Malaya's northern frontier,

---

[24] Kirby, *History of the Second World War*, p. 41.

[25] Kirby, *Singapore*, p. 41.

[26] SAC Paper No. 4, 28 Feb. 1939, "The Despatch of a Fleet to the Far East" and CAB 16/209, NA.

[27] To at least three divisions, two tank battalions, two machine gun battalions and a pool of 20 per cent replacements. Bond to WO, letter WO 106/2440 and CRMC 37406/G 13 Apr. 1940, NA.

for which task he maintained he would require at least an additional two divisions.[28]

The Governor was fully aware of the changing defence criteria and well-informed of all developments. Indeed, now that the defence of the naval base in Singapore entailed deploying sizeable military formations throughout Peninsula Malaya, it was imperative that he know and assess the impact it would have on the community. He was, however, susceptible to the persuasions of Vlieland, his Defence Secretary, who openly agreed with Babington's view that the safety of the country was almost entirely dependent on the air force and per se the army's task was therefore to protect the airfields. On this matter, Thomas clashed with Bond in September 1939 when the army commander justly claimed that, with his existing numbers, he simply did not have the military strength to both defend Singapore and also airfields in remote locations throughout the peninsula. To reinforce his point and in an attempt to relieve some of the immediate manpower shortage, Bond urged that the Governor should consider mobilizing the volunteer forces. Indeed, after listening to Bond's case, Thomas agreed to mobilize them. When he heard of this decision Vlieland objected, and persuaded the Governor to change his mind. Vlieland's argument was that this was indicative of premature panic and would adversely affect the country's morale, and that the government anyway had a clear economic instruction from London.[29]

Such was Thomas' quandary and reluctance to give decisive leadership, he referred the matter to the CO for a ruling. His despatch of January 1940[30] was not a balanced argument but made the case that while the GOC advocated conscription, he felt that such measures would adversely affect the production of rubber and tin. "I conceive it to be our duty to give absolute priority to the claims of industry." In any case, he pointed out that the very organization of the Volunteer Forces was itself unsound. Many of its members would need to be exempt from duties

---

[28] Ibid. In terms of battalions, the basic demand was an increase from the existing 9 to 32 battalions.

[29] Thomas Papers. Vlieland correspondence. RHL.

[30] The Governor's despatch of 27 Jan. 1940 included as Annex in "Singapore: Defence Policy" ODC Paper No. 13, 28 Feb. 1940. Also CAB 94/3. See also Kirby, *Singapore*, pp. 42–5.

such as civil defence. Their essential role was the nation's economy. He added that, in the absence of a fleet stationed at Singapore, successful defence depended on the action of the RAF aided by any submarines and other naval vessels that might be on station. He therefore advocated a large increase in the RAF garrison, even if this was to be at the expense of the army garrison.[31] The views he aired on defence mirrored exactly those of Vlieland and Babington.

The overseas defence committee considered the Governor's despatch in March 1940 and ruled that the economic contribution of Malaya was of the first importance, and any volunteer training should be of brief duration. Training should be restricted to two periods, each of three weeks' duration, and not more than one-third of the volunteers to be enlisted at any one time.[32] In addition, concerning his request for more aircraft, it replied that "... there was in fact no immediate possibility of affecting such an increase that the Governor had requested, or even of bringing the existing squadrons up to their wartime establishment". The committee then contrarily added that it recognized that the security of Singapore was vital to the safety of the British Commonwealth in the Far East.

The reply was heavily influenced by the FO, which emphatically said that the Governor's priority was trade. In its opinion, Japan, which had been at war for some three years and had not been conspicuously successful against the Chinese, was in no position to embark upon adventures against distant British bases. In addition, Japan was in the throes of an internal political crisis.[33] It now seems surprising that the military members of this committee who would certainly have been privy to the accumulating classified information indicating clearly Japanese expansionist intentions, allowed these comments to pass. In fairness, at this time, it was the British government's policy to avoid, if possible, war with Japan despite its irrational behaviour. In the spring of 1940 British forces were heavily engaged in Europe and in the Atlantic. France was showing all the signs of capitulation to the invading Germans, and Italy was volatile and openly courting Nazi Germany. Previous British strategy

---

[31] Ibid.
[32] CAB 94/3. 8 Mar. 1940, NA.
[33] ODC Paper No: 19. 20 Mar. 1940, NA.

assumed the support of France particularly in containing the Italians in the Mediterranean but, as the clouds darkened, it was becoming obvious that Britain was likely to end up alone in the battles ahead and did not want further war in the Far East.

The ODC ruling added fuel to Bond's wrath and he decided to make his case direct to the WO. In April 1940, he submitted a full Appreciation of the situation as he saw it, to the Chiefs of Staff committee. Far from dismissing Japan's debilitating war with China, he saw it as providing the Japanese with invaluable experience in all the demands of war. Moreover, he called attention to the fact there were now Japanese forces in Hainan, and they had also made economic penetration into Thailand. It was now undisputed that they could, if they chose, land at any time of the year on the east coast of Malaya. In addition, to add to this worrying scenario, the "period before relief" was now officially 180 days. His conclusion was to reiterate what, by this point, was generally acknowledged—that the defence of Singapore meant the defence of the whole of Malaya and that in turn needed a substantial increase in ground forces. Then, diluting his own case, he added that with the war now raging in Europe, military manpower would presumably be a near impossibility. In the short term, the answer was to increase the size and striking power of the air force. With the air force bearing the burden of responsibility, he agreed that the commander in overall charge should be a senior RAF officer.

In June 1940, the Chiefs of Staff met in London to consider Bond's Appreciation and crucially acknowledged: "Owing to the increased range of aircraft and development of aerodromes, particularly in Thailand, we can no longer concentrate on defence of Singapore Island alone but must consider defence of Malaya as a whole, particularly security of up-country landing grounds."[34] It also prompted the COS to call for a fresh review of the strategic situation in the Far East, particularly as the two Dominions were being asked by London for help with additional military forces. The paper's conclusions were frank but discouraging: they recognized that, since 1937,[35] when they last considered the likely threat in the East against the forces available, the rise of Nazi Germany and war in the

---

[34] COS. (40) 493. Paper to War Cabinet. 25 June 1940, NA.

[35] "Far East Appreciation 1937" COS Paper No. 557 dated 14 June 1937 and CAB16/182, NA.

West changed all their calculations dramatically. First, they accepted the assumption that the threat to Britain's eastern interests would be seaborne was no longer tenable and second, they could no longer provide a fleet of sufficient strength within three months to protect the Dominions.[36] And, importantly, it was no longer sufficient to concentrate on the defence of Singapore Island but was now necessary to hold the whole of Malaya. The paper ranged across the threat to all the Far East possessions and the part the neighbouring Dutch in the Netherlands East Indies might play. With particular reference to Malaya, they concluded:

> The more important factors affecting the defence of Malaya in the absence of a fleet are as follows:
>
> - The necessity of preventing the establishment of shore-based aircraft within close range of the base at Singapore.
> - Even if the Japanese had not previously established themselves in Thailand, it is more likely that they would attempt a landing up-country in Malaya and then operate southwards, under cover of shore-based aircraft, than that they would risk a direct assault on Singapore Island.
> - The rice-growing country, on which the native population partly depends and most of the government storage centres are in the north.
> - The necessity of establishing food reserves for the garrison and for the civil population of Malaya as long a period as possible. We have already pointed out that sea communications with Malaya might be precarious, but we consider that it would be extremely difficult for the Japanese to blockade the Malayan peninsula completely, and we would expect to get supplies intermittently to our forces in that country, though not necessarily through the port of Singapore.[37]
>
> These factors all point to the necessity for the holding the whole of Malaya rather than concentrating on the defence of Singapore Island. This clearly involves larger land and air forces than when the problem was one of defending Singapore Island.

With this unequivocal recognition of the situation, the Chiefs of Staff offered the best practical support that current resources would

---

[36] CAB /66/10/33, 5 Aug. 1940, NA.
[37] Annex 1 to COS Paper (40) 592. 31 July 1940, NA.

allow. They undertook to provide 336 first line aircraft but warned that they would not arrive before the end of 1941,[*] and to increase the army garrison to the equivalent of six brigades and ancillary troops. Having recognized the need for this level of manpower and equipment, they confessed they were not then in a position to provide even one division (three brigades) either from the Middle East or from the UK or India. They would turn to the Commonwealth governments and ask them to provide "the rough equivalent of one division and to equip it as far as possible".[38] From this point forward all modus operandi and discussion of the defence of Singapore was inseparably linked with Malaya.

The Chiefs of Staff, in a bleak appraisal for the war cabinet in July about the situation facing the nation, remarked, "Our own commitments in Europe are so great that our policy must be directed towards the avoidance of an open clash with Japan."[39] At this point in the war the British Expeditionary Force (BEF) had recently escaped from Dunkirk, the Battle of Britain was at its height, France had now surrendered and Italy had entered the war on the side of Germany.

At this critical time, Shenton Thomas had taken his entitled leave. He was in England, a decision mentioned earlier and seen by many as reckless. The Acting Governor, Stanley Jones, was the government figure at the centre of the maelstrom of military reports and information now arriving and was not comfortable having to address them. Thomas, though, while in the UK, arranged an appointment with the joint planning sub-committee in August 1940 to reinforce the case he had made in his despatch in February. As he later admitted, while it found itself "generally in full agreement" with his views, it was unable to make any practicable change to policy.[40]

Meanwhile, in Singapore, in June 1940, prompted by the CO, Jones tabled and passed the Compulsory Service (Local Forces) Bill. It was a regulation that would prove to be the source of ceaseless conflict between the civil and military authorities. This legislation directed that every European British subject of the prescribed age in the "Colony"

---

[38] Ibid.

[39] CAB 66/10/33. 31 July 1940, NA.

[40] Montgomery, *Shenton of Singapore*, p. 72.

[*] In Aug. 1940, when this paper was discussed, the Battle of Britain was at its height, France had surrendered and Italy had entered the war on the side of Germany.

was liable to compulsory service. He explained that the conscription of only European British subjects was because this was as much as the administration could handle.[41] At the same time, he introduced an exemption clause that caused some dismay. The exemption stated that: "Exemption would be granted on the grounds of conscience, unusual hardship or that the subject would be more usefully employed in the civilian capacity." Bond and the other commanders, while welcoming the legislation, protested against the exemption because it was to be monitored by the civil authorities only and the military authorities had no right of appeal against the grant of an exemption certificate. This led to friction between the two and, in the end, Jones agreed on an amendment to include a right of appeal against exemption to be exercised by a tribunal of both authorities. Even so, there were still civil/military variances about exemption and Percival, on his arrival in May 1941, became immediately embroiled: "there was always potential friction in these claims for exemption as the military authorities wanted all they could get while the government and business managers were equally disinclined to risk cutting their staff too much".[42] The dispute and challenges continued well into 1941 and, at one point, Malaya Command enlisted the commanding officer of the Straits Settlements Volunteer Forces, Lieutenant Colonel F.R. Grimwood, to convene a volunteer advisory committee "to examine the whole problem and make recommendations".[43]

Jones was inescapably caught up in the differing views of defence strategy between Bond and Babington. Unlike Vlieland, though, his sympathies were more inclined to the Bond concept. General Bond now categorically asserted that the defence of Singapore, with the limited forces available to him, had to be concentrated in the south, in Johor. He was adamant that he had no force available for the defence of airfields in upcountry Malaya with the exception that he would provide a small unit for the protection of the major airfield at Alor Star in northwest Malaya.[44]

---

[41] Proceedings of Legislative Council of the Straits Settlements dated 10 June 1940.

[42] A.E. Percival, *The War in Malaya* (London: Eyre & Spottiswood, 1949), p. 83.

[43] *The Straits Times*, 8 Oct. 1941.

[44] He stressed that, without major reinforcements, he would not deploy regular forces outside Singapore, Johor, Penang and approaches to Alor Star. Bond to WO, No 10566, 18 May 1940, NA.

Air Vice-Marshal Babington was entirely opposed to this and insisted that the security of the airfields was paramount because, he pointed out, it was from these that the air assault on the invaders would be launched and, of course, the protection of Alor Star in particular was vital because it was to this airfield that air reinforcing squadrons from India would arrive. The two commanders failed to resolve this fundamental difference that effectively ruined all attempts at serious joint defence planning during their time in command. Jones was simply out of his depth in trying to resolve this difference and, to avoid making a decision, referred the clash to the Chiefs of Staff, London.

Relations between the two commanders were icy and Bond, in particular, was enraged with Jones' indecisiveness. After the war, Bond, in a letter to Thomas, declared: "The trouble between Babington and me … was that he would never tell us what he was doing or could do; he forbade his staff to collaborate with mine, as they were anxious to do."[45] In time, their irreconcilable differences led to both of them being relieved of their appointments.

The naval C-in-C, Sir Percy Noble, whose HQ until late in 1940 was in HK, attended war committee meetings when he was in Singapore. He became very aware of the antagonism between Bond and Babington and the disruption this imposed on proper cooperation between the services, and the confusion it sowed in the minds of the civil administration. He noted that this fundamental disagreement was replicated at all levels between the military and the civilians. In addition, he expressed some serious doubt about the effectiveness of the arrangements suggested to fit the defence plans. After the war, he declared that although there were faults on both sides, the blame for the situation lay mainly with Air Vice-Marshal Babington.

Noble was also aware of dissatisfaction among a number of unofficial members of the Legislative Council in the way the civil administration was addressing the problem of defence, and was conscious of strong feelings that the Governor should be replaced. He also expressed surprise that even after the fall of France, the Governor did not return quickly to his post from leave because of the certain subsidiary danger this

---

[45] Thomas. Mss. Ind. Ocn. S341. F.96. 29.10.1954.RHL.

would bring to Malaya. Noble returned to England in September 1940 to take up another appointment and took the opportunity to talk about the problems to the Secretary of State for the colonies, Lord Lloyd. He recommended that both Bond and Babington be replaced and, while feelings against the Governor were running high, he did not recommend a change at that point, but that a senior military officer be placed in supreme authority, over the head of both the Governor and the service commanders.[46] It is reasonable to postulate that had Noble's advice been followed and someone like Wavell put in overall charge it might have led to a different outcome. As it happened, Lloyd, who agreed with this idea, unfortunately died of a serious illness before it could be implemented. From Jones' point of view, he got a less than helpful reply from London to his plea for guidance. The authorities justified the differences of opinion between the two commanders as being due principally to a lack of resources. In the meantime, he was ordered to place the defence of Malaya in a state of readiness at five days' warning.

The substance of the difference between the two was that Babington's demand for airfield protection was based on the hypothesis that the additional aircraft he requested would arrive and would need these east coast airfields. Bond's refusal was based on fact; he did not have the forces to meet the demand nor, from warnings by the WO, could he expect extra manpower. And, of course, the whole defence plan was designed to protect a naval base in Singapore which at this point had no battle fleet, only a few elderly ships, and, according to the Admiralty, was unlikely to receive any substantial naval presence. As it was pointedly noted, "it was a sentry box without a sentry".[47]

At the same time as the military commanders were barely on speaking terms, another important matter arose causing further hostility. When Jones received the instruction to put the country on five days' alert, the CO also asked for information on reserve rice stocks. A few days later he was instructed that all possible steps should be taken to increase food stocks to the utmost extent possible and that, regarding rice, the WO advised

---

[46] Kirby, *Singapore*, pp. 38–42, 52–3.

[47] James Neidpath, *The Singapore Naval Base and the Defence of Britain's Eastern Empire, 1919–1942* (Oxford: Clarendon Press and New York: Oxford University Press, 1981), p. 117.

that rice storage and milling capacity should be dispersed throughout the country and that he must agree to the arrangements in close liaison with Bond. The matter of food reserves, rice storage and milling developed into a major altercation between the administration and the military. Jones replied to the CO that, on the advice of his Secretary for Defence, the reserves of rice amounted to two months' supply and that to disperse them would be very difficult, and cost a lot of money and man hours, and that the present arrangements were quite satisfactory. Bond only heard of this reply through the WO, which reported this answer to him and he snapped that it was "fallacious" and made without consulting him. After the war, General Bond replied to an enquiry from Thomas about this matter (the incident arose while Thomas was still on leave) and in his letter Bond included an extract from his diary of that time, which clearly discloses the extent of confrontation and depth of animosity which existed. He told Thomas that he had both talked with Jones and then put in writing his recommendations about building up food reserves, and warned Jones of the danger of accepting, at face value, Vlieland's advice, and that he should satisfy himself personally on these important arrangements. Jones expressed every confidence in Vlieland even when Bond informed him that Vlieland had been making decisions on both the level of food reserves and the location of the storage facilities without consulting him and, as it was the army that would have to guard them, it was essential he was consulted. In itself this was bad enough, but to compound the problem Vlieland did not even discuss it with his civilian colleague directly concerned—the Food Controller. Vlieland made the comment openly that it was "the military reinforcements arriving that was causing food problems" and that "it would be better to have no reinforcements and so avoid the difficulty of feeding them".[48]

The matter became notoriously controversial. It was further aggravated when Bond suggested, at a war committee meeting (at which no minutes were taken), that the joint victualling board should be able to submit their views about food storage in writing to the war committee so that matters were transparent, discussed and resolved. He noted in his diary

---

[48] Thomas Papers. Extracts from General Bond's diary (unpublished) Mss..Ind.. Ocn..s. 341 RHL.

that "the AOC (Babington) and the Secretary for Defence contested this". Bond also objected to the building of rice storage facilities in the vulnerable northern region of Malaya and was incensed to hear that, in spite of his objections, Vlieland had authorized the construction of a second 50,000-ton rice store in this same area.[49] When the new naval C-in-C, Admiral Layton, was drawn into these arguments he telegraphed the Admiralty, pointing out that Jones had failed to consult either him or Bond about this important matter and that he disagreed with the views expressed, and it was strategically unsound to hold reserve food stocks near a possible front line. The CO then instructed Jones to reconsider the position. They told him to examine, in particular, the advisability of locating the largest food store near an important airfield, Alor Star. In a handwritten footnote at the bottom of a copy of Bond's diary, Shenton Thomas made the banal comment:

> It seems clear from these extracts from Gen. Bond's diary that between May and November 1940 there has been, to say the least, differences of opinion between Jones (prompted by Vlieland) and the Service Heads on the question of food supplies.[50]

It was into this unacceptable, divisive, hostile and potentially dangerous civil-military milieu that the Chiefs of Staff, with Churchill's agreement, sent Brooke-Popham as the Far East C-in-C. Regrettably, they did not adopt what Admiral Noble had proposed and give the new commander supreme power. Instead, they arrived at what was soon patently an unsatisfactory compromise, having recalled him to the active list at the age of 62 and appointed him to this post in October 1940 (conspicuously, it was an airman whom they chose). As already noted, his charter was responsibility for the operational control and training only of all British land and air forces in the Far East. It did not include naval forces. The army and the air commanders, while subordinate to him, still retained responsibility for the administrative and financial direction of their own service and corresponded directly with their own branch in the WO. In an insipid attempt not to offend the sensitivities and independent authority of the three services and the civil administration, they ended

---

[49] Ibid.
[50] Ibid.

with a hotchpotch arrangement. Brooke-Popham had no power over the civilian authorities either in Malaya nor any other territory in his area of responsibility. In fact, he had no power to enforce decisions necessary for the defence of any country in his region and effectively became another cog in an already unwieldy organization. In his London briefings before his departure, he was reminded, repeatedly, that British policy was to avoid war with Japan. The COS also ordered a trawl of suitable candidates to replace both Bond and Babington.[51]

Faced with the paucity of fighting formations available for the defence of Malaya, the military planners were not idle but examined a number of possible alternative operational ideas. Among them was the highly sensitive proposal of a pre-emptive advance into Thailand to secure and defend the likely landing beaches at Singora and Patani. This highly secret concept matured over time and, in April 1940, General Bond first articulated the idea in a memo accompanying his Appreciation. He asked openly: "Can the idea of offensive action against the Japanese Forces established in Thailand be excluded?"[52] Increasing intelligence information and obvious indicators such as the growing number of Japanese in the region, ostensibly as businessmen but patently military personnel on reconnaissance missions, added to the certainty. Dobbie's study of the region had already revealed its eminent suitability as a beachhead, and any force landing in the area would have not only excellent road and rail facilities in place for a quick breakout from the bridgehead but, importantly, airfields nearby for air support and a harbour facility at Singora.[53] From these beachheads the enemy had various assault options, either crossing the Kra Isthmus at its narrowest point or dividing its forces to advance on several axes, including going directly south to the nearest Malayan border crossing at Kota Bharu. The clear conclusion from these factors was that containment at the arrival areas, and even better, preventing them landing at all, was the evident

---

[51] Brooke-Popham letter to Ismay, 16 May 1941. V/1/12, Brooke-Popham papers. LHCMA.

[52] Bond to WO. CRMC 37406/G, 13 Apr. 1940, NA. See also Kirby, *Singapore*, pp. 28–30 and Neidpath, *The Singapore Naval Base and the Defence of Britain's Eastern Empire, 1919–1942*, pp. 168–9.

[53] Ibid.

solution. To achieve success, it was calculated that the forces opposing the landings would need to be at least a division and in place early enough for preparations and be ready to fight an aggressive and determined foe. The embryo plan was given the name "Operation Matador".

The idea grew and became an increasingly favoured solution. A number of senior commanders were now predicting, "if we allow the Japanese to gain a foothold in Malaya the battle is lost".[54] It had, however, a number of serious complications. Above all else was the government's clear instruction that war with Japan had to be avoided at all costs, and to violate neutral territory in this highly sensitive region would provide them with a *casus belli*. The British ambassador in Thailand, Sir Josiah Crosby, a colonial officer who had spent too long among the Thais, was adamant that Thailand was a friend and, with a little nurturing, could prove a useful protagonist against Japan. To invade her territory, he proclaimed, would be a gross affront and provide Japan with an excuse to come to the aid of an Asian neighbour.[55] Then there was the question of providing a dedicated division-sized force for the task together with the very considerable volume of defensive stores and equipment needed for the job. Men and equipment would need to move by rail and road across the isthmus and it could not be assumed that an unprovoked invasion of neutral territory would be without hindrance. Calculating the time this operation would take, with its many uncertainties, not least of which was the Thai response, required a most careful and quite separate "time appreciation".[56]

Brooke-Popham, early in his appointment on learning from his staff about the Matador plan, backed it and asked that it be investigated in detail. He also put the proposal, in December 1940, before the Chiefs of Staff in London.[57] It was given cautious support. While recognizing

---

[54] Kirby, *History of the Second World War*. Babington Report to Air Ministry, Jan. 1940, p. 26.

[55] Crosby cable, Bangkok to FO, No. 154, 2 Mar. 1941, NA.

[56] Brooke-Popham to WO, No. 146/5, 21 Sept. 1941, NA. Also Andrew Gilchrist, *Malaya 1941: The Fall of a Fighting Empire* (London: Robet Hale, 1992), pp. 164–8 and Karl Hack and Kevin Blackburn, *Did Singapore have to Fall?: Churchill and the Impregnable Fortress* (London: Routledge, 2005), pp. 41–8.

[57] CAB 106/40, 5 Dec. 1940, NA.

the benefits from such pre-emptive action, the COS stated that they could not provide additional forces for the task. Moreover, as the danger of provoking Japan was so great, they decided that in the event of them endorsing the plan they would retain for themselves the authority to launch such a sensitive operation. They asked about the tactical implications of using some of the existing forces in Malaya for Matador, and how much notice would be required to enable the force to get to the destination and into position in time.[58] The planning staff in Singapore, in response to the limitations imposed on them, arrived at an unsatisfactory compromise which was later to cause untold problems. Not only did they nominate a division already allocated a defensive task in north Malaya, thereby giving it the dual role of "perhaps" defending territory near the northwest border or "possibly" launching a thrust across the Kra Isthmus into eastern Thailand, they also calculated what was later seen as an absurd time estimate, of only 36 hours of warning to embark on this complex operation.[59]

When Shenton Thomas returned from leave in December 1940, he found a quite different environment from that which existed in April. There was, among those close to the centre of government, a feeling of frustration, insecurity and unpreparedness. There was general dissatisfaction at the lack of urgent practical support from the military authorities in London. And, whether or not he recognized it, there was a sense of unreality among the administration, which appeared unable or unwilling to recognize the gravity of the growing threat from Japan. He also found in station a new C-in-C, Air Chief Marshal Sir Robert Brooke-Popham, who had assumed command on 18 November 1940. Also, a modest increase had been added to the military garrison with the arrival of two British battalions withdrawn from Shanghai and a divisional headquarters (11th Indian HQ) and two infantry brigade groups without artillery, and there was also a promise of additional aircraft.

One of the first tasks he had to perform was to dismiss Vlieland. There does not appear to be any written evidence describing the grounds for the decision but convincing speculation presumes that Thomas, before

---

[58] COS to Brooke-Popham No. COS 33, 24 Dec. 1940.See also CAB 79/8, NA.

[59] WO No. 202/7, 6 Aug. 1941, NA. See also Kirby, *Singapore*, p. 110 for a realistic estimate of the time necessary to launch Matador.

his return, was made aware that both Bond and Babington were to go and that Vlieland, a catalyst for the disunity, should also go. Vlieland describes the event signalling his demise. On 13 December 1940, at Thomas' first war committee meeting after his return:

> When I entered the council chamber and took my old seat at his right hand, Sir Shenton did not greet me, or even look at me. He opened the proceedings by inviting B.P. (Brooke-Popham) to speak. The C-in-C then made a savage attack on me .... No one said a word. Bond and Layton nodded their approval and my friend the AOC could not rally to my support in defiance of his Air Chief Marshal. Sir Shenton remained silent with bowed head.[60]

Brooke-Popham charged Vlieland with consistently refusing to cooperate with Bond and deliberately using delaying tactics over the initiation of measures necessary for the defence of the civilian population.[61] The following day, Vlieland tendered his resignation and asked that he be allowed to leave the MCS. Although he did not leave Singapore until February 1941, he took no further part in the administrative affairs of the government. C.W. Dawson, who until then was the British adviser to the State of Perlis, replaced him.

The Governor's early impressions of the new C-in-C were very favourable and, in his handwritten letter to the CO about how he found conditions generally on his return to Singapore, he said: "B-P is an immense tower of strength and knows the difficulties of a civil government as the result of his years in Kenya." His further comments, however, disclosed his mounting frustration with the military and, he claimed, their endless petty grievances. But, he added, he now had someone to whom he could unburden his difficulties with the army and the air force

---

[60] Vlieland, "Disaster in the Far East". In a report Thomas wrote to the CO shortly after returning from leave he said: "I found a very unhappy family on my arrival here. Jones has been worked to death and in addition had to contend with a lot of friction. Vlieland, who as Secretary for Defence had done such excellent work in 1939 and had been welcomed by every Resident had let his ego mania get completely out of hand and was quite impossible, obstruction and offensive criticism was his line. He was really the cause of the telegram from some of the ex-Service men to the S of S and the Prime Minister" (CO 967/75, NA).

[61] Callahan, *The Worst Disaster*, p. 110. Also Allen, *Singapore 1941–1942*, pp. 225–46.

which, he maintained, were no less than before he left. Bond he found pleasant enough but a man of one idea and his staff of little help. The idea was that the army should have what it wanted and everyone else could scramble for what was left. He gave an instance of the army wanting 1,000 beds reserved in civil hospitals in Singapore. Thomas rejected the idea and spoke to Brooke-Popham about it. One word from Brooke-Popham and they came down to 500. He also noted they were discussing with the WO, without telling him, senior staff appointments, which would have affected his immediate associates. However, as he observed, "I don't worry, I just decline and all goes well."[62]

In the early months of 1941, the garrison received some more reinforcements. By the end of 1940, Bond had two brigades in Singapore and a further brigade (12th Indian Brigade) in the area of Mersing on the east coast, and in north Malaya, near the important airfield of Alor Star 11th Indian Division (it consisted of two brigades only—the 6th and the 8th) and two independent battalions, one on the island of Penang and one in Taiping. In February 1941 an Australian divisional headquarters, 8th Australian Division HQ, with one brigade under command (22nd Australian Brigade) arrived in Malaya. The commander of this division was Major General Gordon Bennett. In April the 9th Indian Division, less its artillery, arrived. With the Indian contingent forming the largest part of the ground forces, a corps headquarters arrived from India, with Lieutenant General Sir Lewis Heath in charge. By the end of April, Bond would have 26 battalions which was the minimum he calculated was needed, provided the RAF had it first line strength.

On 24 April, Air Vice-Marshal C.W.H. Pulford succeeded Babington and, on 14 May, Lieutenant General A.E. Percival replaced Bond. In April, before Bond left, he made a rather curious remark later seen as dangerously irresponsible. It occurred during a visit by the British military attaché in Tokyo (Colonel G.T. Ward). While this officer was in Singapore, he gave a lecture to a selected senior audience about the Japanese army, a subject about which he was clearly competent to speak. He expounded, without any exaggeration, the impressive qualities of

---

[62] Letter from Thomas to Parkinson [US of S for the Colonies], 16 Mar. 1941. CO 967/75, NA.

Japanese soldiers, describing their superb physical fitness, ability to move long distances both day and night with a minimum of personal effects, overcome obstacles, fanatical patriotism, ability to be well led by junior sub-unit commanders, *esprit de corps* and refusal to surrender. He also pointed out the highly trained dedicated senior officers of the general staff. In essence, he tried to dispel the dangerous entrenched opinion that they were a poorly motivated, weak, badly led organization which never operated at night, and were poor mechanics, drivers and air pilots. He had seen them fight against the Chinese with astonishing aggression and fierce courage. They were not to be underestimated, and they would prove a formidable foe. Bond, after he had finished, rose and said:

> [W]hile the lecturer has told you that the Japanese army is very efficient and that the Japanese know all about us in Singapore, this is far from the truth .... What the lecturer has told you is his own opinion and is in no way a correct appreciation of the situation. I will now tell you that every morning the telegrams which the Japanese Consul-General sends to his government in Tokyo are placed on my office table and from these I know what the Japanese are up to and just how much or how little they know about us. If this is the best the Japanese can do, I do not think much of them and you can take it from me that we have nothing to fear from them.[63]

If Bond genuinely believed his own words, then his tenacious struggle throughout his period in command for more men and equipment against an enemy for whom he had little regard seems a pointless, costly exercise. On the other hand, if he was trying to moderate the fear which the attaché's talk may have generated, he shifted too far, invoking the military dictum of dangerously underrating the enemy.

At a time of growing tension and indisputable indications that the Japanese were close to committing an act of war against Britain, the Governor was on leave in England. And in spite of changes in the command structure, there was still disharmony both within the government and between it and the military. It was also clear that Britain's struggle in

---

[63] Quoted in Kirby, *Singapore*, p. 75. The earliest intercepted message from the Japanese consul-general at Singapore to the Foreign Ministry at Tokyo is dated 9 Jan. 1935. WO 106/5504, NA. Regardless of the exclusive audience this was nevertheless a very rash public disclosure to make.

Europe, understandably, took priority both in a claim on resources and the home government's attention. This recognition, however, did not motivate a critical revision of the defence of Singapore. It did not provoke the policy makers to reason that a shortage of manpower and equipment and the prospect of a long wait for any of these vital resources must mean a review of existing strategy. Indeed, the disunited military command had still not agreed a common ground about the basic tenets of the defence of Malaya and Singapore. The army had received some (untrained) reinforcements but the vital additional aircraft on which the flawed plan was conceived had not arrived and, in any case, they were warned that any that could be spared would not arrive before December 1941. Probably most serious, there was no planning for civil emergencies except for a confused policy on the location and storage of rice reserves. The lethargy and tempo of the administration, when dealing with crucial civil defence matters, reflected its sceptical approach to the threat of war. It simply did not grasp the urgency of the gathering storm.

The Federal Council, Kuala Lumpur, 1940. Stanley Jones deputizing for the Governor. Hugh Fraser, the Federal Secretary is fifth from the left in the second row (Photograph courtesy Arkib Negara, Kuala Lumpur)

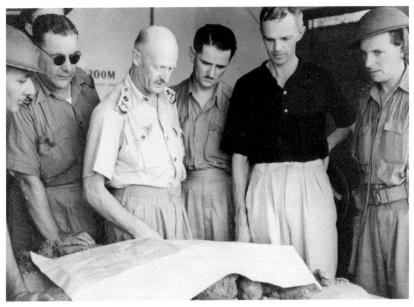

General Gordon Bennett briefing war correspondents
(Photograph courtesy Imperial War Museum, London)

A gathering of the major protagonists, September 1941, left to right: ACM Sir
Robert Brooke-Popham, Duff-Cooper, Sir Earle Page (Australia), Sir Archibald Clark-
Kerr (Ambassador to China) Sir Shenton Thomas and Vice-Admiral Geoffrey Layton
(Photograph courtesy Imperial War Museum, London)

General Percival with war correspondents
(Photograph courtesy Imperial War Museum, London)

The fraught relationship between generals Percival and
Gordon Bennett clearly illustrated
(Photograph courtesy Australian War Memorial)

General Percival and accompanying staff officers, Major Wild and brigadiers
Newbigging and Torrance, arrive at the Ford factory to surrender
(Photograph courtesy Imperial War Museum, London)

Women and children evacuate Penang
(Photograph courtesy Imperial War Museum, London)

The new Soviet ambassador to Washington, M. Litvinov, en route to take up his duties, calls on the Governor in Singapore
(Photograph courtesy Secker & Warburg)

A gathering of Malay sultans in Kuala Lumpur. Front row, left to right: Yang-di-Pertuan, Negri Sembilan; the Sultan of Perak; H.E. the Governor; Lady Thomas; the Sultan of Selangor; the Sultan of Pahang. Back row, left and centre: two ADCs; far right: Noel Ross, Private Secretary (Photograph courtesy Imperial War Museum, London)

Government House, Singapore, 1934
(Photograph courtesy Imperial War Museum, London)

5

CIVIL DEFENCE DISARRAY

In the post-war despatches written by each of the senior service commanders[1] and the many academic analyses of the disastrous Malayan Campaign, legitimate claims have been laid against the inadequate and ineffective arrangements made for civil defence and the poor coordination between the military and civil authorities. Civil defence was barely considered before the Japanese invasion. Perhaps more surprisingly, following the outbreak of war in Europe, there were still only vacuous verbal declarations of intent.[2] In the Extraordinary Meeting of the Legislative Council called on 26 September 1939, when the Governor addressed the gathering with a prepared statement about Britain's declaration of war against Nazi Germany, he added no warning or assessment of the possible knock-on effect this could have for Malaya. Expressions of loyalty and support for the King Emperor and the empire were announced and assurances given of raising further financial support for the imperial war effort but without a caveat. The Governor may have judged that a war many thousands of miles away to the west was of little immediate concern. But closer to home Japan was behaving outrageously. With information about Japanese behaviour generally available to the reading public, no attempt was made to give, at least, a cautious warning of possible future vulnerability. According to the minutes of this meeting, not even the GOC (Bond) who was there, made

---

[1] Supplements to *The London Gazette* 38183, 20 Jan. 1948.
[2] Proceedings of Legislative Council of the Straits Settlements, 1939.

any comment.[3] At succeeding council meetings during 1939 and early 1940, no plan for civil defence was ever introduced. It was after Thomas departed on leave that members of both councils start to show concern about the government's laissez-faire attitude. To be objective and make a balanced judgement of the criticism and initial apathy to civil defence levelled at the government, it is right to take account of the exceptional circumstances that existed in Malaya.

This campaign was unlike any other war that Britain had fought; Thomas pointed this out in his post-war notes.[4] Not only was the climate and terrain inhospitable, but it was a war of defence in a country that had never endured major conflict. Local people had no comprehension of what war meant. Malaya was a country governed by a foreign power which had assumed responsibility for its protection. The country was a mosaic of social and cultural values.[5] It would have been a mammoth task to equip and train several thousands of Malays, Indians and Chinese for the civil defence services. For a start, the majority spoke only their own language, a more basic issue than a lack of arms and equipment. Nothing of this kind had ever been undertaken in any British colony. Moreover, most of the British civil staff whose task it would have been to galvanize the population had no experience of war preparations or of military affairs in general. As noted, neither the Governor nor any of his senior officials had served in the forces during the First World War. Surprisingly, though, during post-war recriminations it was claimed that of the 224 officers in the MCS on January 1940, 61 of the more junior officials had, in fact, served in the Great War.[6] But at this time it was very apparent there was no grasp of the enormity of the civil defence task or the knowledge or skill to put the state on a war footing. Given this lack of conception among the civil authorities, senior military officers had undoubtedly a duty to exercise their knowledge, take responsibility for preparations, and insist that the administration listen to and follow their advice. It was an obvious military responsibility which they failed to acknowledge until it was too late.

---

[3] Ibid.
[4] Thomas Papers, Foreword "What Malaya Did". Mss. Ind. S. 341. RHL.
[5] Collection. Correspondence Dickinson/Bryson. Jan. 1969. RCS/BAM. 103/5/7. CU.
[6] Callahan, *The Worst Disaster*, p. 115.

Adding to the ordeal, without imposing martial law, there was the matter of different forms of governance. Officially, the Governor could only advise the UMS and had to accept the various UMS claims that they were addressing civil defence procedures. He was reluctant, through his advisers, to press matters further as he felt that insisting on civil defence measures could prejudice the economic directive imposed on him. After the war, in 1947, on his return to England Thomas wrote an early report about Malaya's war effort.[7] He wanted the authors of the official history to take account of what he believed was the very considerable contribution by civil administration during the conflict. He also included a comprehensive list of what he saw as the duties of the civil government about civil defence. It was indeed all-inclusive and covered just about every issue of civil defence. There is no known record, however, that the document was ever published either before or during the campaign. The existence of such a paper would have unquestionably helped all parties to know the scale of civil defence duties, and would have avoided later accusations of who was responsible for what. Conspicuously, even in this list there was no reference to passive defence measures such as the construction of air-raid shelters, ARP (Air Raid Precautions) wardens, warning systems, protective precautions, rescue teams and auxiliary fire services.

In 1957, following the publication of the official history,[8] and in spite of Thomas' attempted intervention, the civil authorities were heavily criticized for their inadequate and belated civil defence arrangements. In response, Thomas wrote a further personal report which he was unable to get published. It was to be one of many attempts to vindicate the colonial government's war preparations and was entitled "What Malaya Did".[9] He points out that as early as 1938, a defence committee existed and sub-committees of this organization "were responsible for planning the several aspects of civil defence".[10] Later that year, he adds, it became apparent this arrangement was unsuitable and the functions were taken over by departments of the ordinary type whose executive heads were

---

[7] Thomas Papers. Mss. Ind.s. 341. RHL.

[8] Kirby, *History of the Second World War*, passim.

[9] Thomas Papers. Mss. Ind.s.341. RHL.

[10] Ibid.

responsible to the government, not to the defence committee. It meant, in effect, that during this period there was no central authority coordinating the various elements of civil defence. For example, those government departments concerned with agriculture became responsible for rice production and the storage of reserves—at least in theory. Even this arrangement was unsatisfactory and, by October 1939, was replaced by a set of civil defence departments, each linked to the government through a new office of Secretary for Defence, with Vlieland in charge. Effectively, this office was the defence branch of the colonial and federal secretariats and the High Commissioner's office. The intention was to focus and coordinate civil defence policy and practice throughout Malaya, with the exception the Unfederated States. On the outbreak of the European war the defence committee, renamed the war committee, was still chaired by the Governor. The heads of the three services were members and, in due course, the committee was enlarged to include three unofficial members of the legislative and federal councils.[11] On the ground, these new arrangements made no difference to the existing lassitude, characterized by the fact that no written minutes of the meetings were compiled.

Thomas' *prima facie* assertion in his unpublished reports and his ceaseless *post facto exculpate* correspondence implies the inauguration, development and expansion of appropriate responsible authorities to meet the growing defence challenges. These assertions are entirely without substance. Most of the schemes did not start until late in 1940, when Thomas returned from leave, thus precious induction time was lost. There was no urgency or clarity in the written instructions to those in charge of these day-to-day matters. There was no coordination of effort, no written record of decisions agreed on.[12] Moreover, any such decisions would have applied technically only to the Straits Settlements, although the FMS would almost certainly have fallen into line. However, the UMS frequently balked at and occasionally refused to comply with civil defence directives, particularly if they involved expenditure or manpower. In reality, very few of the civil defence measures agreed at war committee level filtered down to subordinate authorities, particularly in

[11] Ibid.
[12] Vide Brooke-Popham Papers, 6/2/3 of 5 Dec. 1940. IWM.

the UMS. If they did they were either ignored, given only perfunctory attention or attempted in an amateurish manner. The war committee may have assumed their proposals were undertaken, but without a system of physical checks and written instructions, they were quite ignorant of the outcome. In many instances, instructions were passed by word of mouth to the parties concerned, and left at that. At the same time, the war committee itself was in turmoil with the army and air commanders disagreeing with each other,[13] and Vlieland adding to the dissension. The OAG, Jones, was confused and unable to assert his authority. All in all, civil defence matters were a low priority and given scant attention.[14] As noted, the issue of rice reserves (passive defence) did, however, receive venomous attention.

The commissioner of customs, in early 1939, was appointed Food Controller. To assist him a food stocks reserves committee was formed, consisting of experts with knowledge of the preservation of essential commodities. Its primary aim was to anticipate the possible restrictions on the import of these essentials in the event of war in the West. Rice was naturally the most important article of food; the annual consumption was about 900,000 tons, of which two-thirds were imported. The committee set about arranging to purchase enough supplies from external sources to last for at least six months and also prepare storage resources. One problem was that milled rice would not keep sweet for six months so un-milled *padi* (rice in the husk) had to be procured: it was bulkier, needing greater storage space and a nearby milling facility. (Later, it was found by experiment that if milled rice was stored after mixing with powdered lime it would remain sweet for much longer.)[15] It is clear from government memoranda that at no point did the civil authorities consult the military on the choice of storage sites.[16] Vlieland had already decided on his own account that the largest and most important storage depot would be near Alor Star in the very north of Malaya. Later, in his unpublished memoir, he stated:

---

[13] See Chapter 3.
[14] Ibid.
[15] Thomas Papers. Mss.Ind. Ocn. S.341. Oct. 1954.RHL.
[16] Ibid.

[T]he Alor Star granary scheme was a purely civil undertaking which was never mentioned still less debated in the War Committee .... The civil authorities that is to say the Governor, the Food Controller and I decided upon the storage of padi ... The Alor Star scheme was worked out largely by Sir Shenton himself without consulting the military who were in any case resolutely disinterested in anything we did in the Malay States. That particular stupidity was only forced on us by the military, by manoeuvre of dubious propriety, in November 1940.[17]

This statement contradicts General Bond's assertions in his diary entries throughout most of 1940. He writes of his exasperation with the OAG because the latter failed to curb the excesses of Vlieland whose independent decisions regarding storage, reserves and locations were taken without even consulting the government food controller, let alone the military.[18] Bond's key point was that the Alor Star granary was too far north for security and that the reserves should be either relocated or greatly reduced. In spite of these warnings, Vlieland went ahead with plans to increase the storage capacity at Alor Star. He later felt his decision was justified when Babington decided that the airfield at Alor Star was a vital forward air base, needing sizeable army protection. Moreover, with the arrival in theatre of two reinforcement Indian brigades, Vlieland persuaded the OAG to telegram the Secretary of State for the colonies in London, to confirm that with a sizeable military presence in the area of Alor Star, the granaries would be secure and reorganization of the rice stocks was unnecessary.

When Bond learnt of this exchange, taken without his knowledge, he enlisted the support of Admiral Layton. Jointly they informed the WO that Vlieland's comments had not been discussed with them and, in any case, they disagreed with his views. Bond noted in his diary: "Layton spoke to the AOC (Babington) who had reluctantly agreed to [the] undesirability of keeping food reserves in the front line. Vlieland was very upset at C-in-C's action which he regards as military interference."[19] At the same time, much to Vlieland's irritation, similar arguments arose about other food essentials with the military

---

[17] Vlieland Papers 3.3.1 LHCMA.
[18] Thomas Papers loc. cit.
[19] Ibid.

intervening when they learnt indirectly of a policy that would have a bearing on their own plans.

The matter of passive defence during 1940 was a topic that was of increasing concern to the population or, more correctly, that element of the population aware of the growing danger. With the deteriorating international situation, the predominantly European community became more restless about the government's laissez-faire approach and began to question its commitment to the matter. The subject was raised regularly both in Legislative Council meetings and in local newspapers. Many felt that few visible precautions were being put in place and urged the government not only to do something about it, but also to be seen doing something about it.[20] An unofficial member of the Straits Settlements Legislative Council, F.D. Bisseker, was a particular and conscientious campaigner about passive defence. In November 1940, he challenged the government's lack of energy or any dedication to what he considered essential preparations. In the council chamber, he made a lengthy and impassioned speech:

> We are not at concert pitch yet though, and much effort at organisation is necessary still in passive defence measures before they can grow into a state of efficiency which will permit of the units concerned rendering full service in the case of need. St John's Ambulance and the Auxiliary Fire Service are not equipped even yet. A.R.P. communications are inadequate and I doubt very much if there are stirrup pumps and self-organised rescue squads in even half a dozen houses and big blocks of buildings in the whole Colony. I know of no air-raid shelters and there is yet no evidence of that protection which effective sand-bagging can provide. I commend these deficiencies to the notice of the Secretary of Defence. The stressing of difficulties in providing these essential measures or the cry "it cannot be done" smack to me of defeatism. The sooner we realise they have got to be done the better will be our welfare.[21]

He went on to catalogue the deficiencies in equipment, the lack of practical support or indeed gratitude shown to the many volunteers. Furthermore, the absence of instruction, supervision and guidance had resulted in disillusioned advocates resigning. He then pointedly blamed

---

[20] *The Straits Times*, 25 Nov. 1940.
[21] Proceedings of Legislative Council of the Straits Settlements, 6 Nov. 1940.

the authorities for the inadequacies and, in particular, the Secretary for Defence. Bisseker believed Vlieland should personally be directing this task and making his presence visible throughout the nation, encouraging and inspecting the few schemes established. His address ranged over many related matters that he claimed were topics of great interest to the public. Why, he wanted to know, had the government not resolved the "question of taxation for the purpose of raising funds for the prosecution of the war – we are lamentably behind our time in our effort". And he noted that a joint (Straits Settlements and FMS) committee had been formed in September (1940) to examine civil defence matters and it was not until the end of October before they held their first meeting. When he enquired of a member why it had taken so long, he was told that there was not much enthusiasm for the task. The OAG replied that passive defence was now receiving his consideration and although he could not express himself positively, many of the matters mentioned were being "considered" and he was able to give this assurance. Moreover, regarding Bisseker's view of the functions of the Secretary for Defence, he felt that it was much more important that the Secretary for Defence should be in Singapore coordinating the defence measures.[22]

The next meeting of the Legislative Council took place in December 1940, by which time the Governor had returned from leave and was in the chair. Bisseker revisited the subject of passive defence and made another lengthy and heated address expressing profound disappointment that nothing appeared to have improved. There was, he said:

> No indication given that even an investigation would be made into some of my claims regarding lack of organisation and co-ordination, and much less was there any promise that if what I maintained to be the existing state of affairs was found to be correct, action taken to rectify would be taken.[23]

He was particularly incensed at the idea that "a case had to be made in each and every instance before further expenditure was embarked upon".

Bisseker drew attention to the poor comparison between Malaya's efforts and those in the UK, citing newspaper reports that London alone

---

[22] Ibid.

[23] Proceedings of the Legislative Council of the Straits Settlements, 9 Dec. 1940.

had provided public shelters for 1.4 million people and the government had ordered the provincial authorities throughout Great Britain to do likewise. Bisseker wanted to know why in these seriously worrying times the local government of Singapore could not also order the entire nation to begin vital and urgent preparations. The Governor's laconic reply encapsulates his apathy to the gathering storm. He believed that:

> [T]he public should themselves accept the responsibility of looking after themselves as we do at Home. It may be interesting to hon. Members to know in that part of East Kent in which I lived [on leave], save in one town, I do not think I saw a single public shelter within 10 miles of our village. Any shelters that we had were put up by ourselves and used by ourselves ... and in any case the matter is not easy, in fact, it is very complicated, and what we might do in Singapore would, I feel, not necessarily be suitable for Penang, Ipoh, Kuala Lumpur and so on.[24]

In the formal procedure of council meetings the Governor made his remark in the form of a closing address, so that it was impossible for members to refute his remarks. He was unkindly dismissive of Bisseker's obsession with passive defence. The following day's newspaper noted, however, "that comparisons with UK were dissimilar and entirely inappropriate".[25] No mention was made about his irritation with Bisseker and his almost dismissive contempt for the petty details of civil defence. It is also surprising to find, according to the minutes, that the GOC made no comment nor offered any advice. A forum like the formal council meeting would seem to have offered an unrivalled opportunity for a professional military comment about civil defence.

The reason for the lack of air-raid shelters in Singapore was actually known as early as 1937. The newly formed defence committee had, in fact, discussed the question. It concluded that owing to the high water table in Singapore shelters could not be sited underground, and the higher ground was mostly utilized as Chinese cemeteries and thus was inviolable. Earthed-up large concrete cylinders were proposed as a sensible and workable substitute. The government rejected this idea and decided to follow a plan similar to that employed by the Dutch authorities in the Netherlands East

---

[24] Ibid.
[25] *The Straits Times*, 10 Dec. 1940, leader.

Indies (NEI), which was to disperse the population on warning of an air raid to "Dispersal Camps". In Singapore, such camps with a capacity to house 350,000 people were later built, some miles out of the city, at a cost of over 1 million (local) dollars. Light, water, communal kitchens, stores of food, trained commandants and wardens were provided. Significantly, it was pointed out that shelters miles out of town were impractical in an emergency. Another proposal was to give protection for vital workers and others, with shelters above ground along some of the great wharves. The Singapore Harbour Board, an independent authority, decided against it[26]—a decision that would be deeply regretted.

Bisseker was general manager of a tin smelting works in Penang, where he also resided. He was elected to the Legislative Council as an unofficial member in February 1940. From the very beginning of his tenure, he pursued the authorities relentlessly over what he considered their apathetic approach to civil and passive defence. His persistence made him most unpopular with senior government figures. Governor Thomas later wrote: "Bisseker constituted himself the critic of everything that had been done. He himself had done nothing to help in defence preparations and was not even a member of any Passive Defence Unit."[27] This remark is not entirely true; Bisseker frequently volunteered to help but such was his unpopularity with the Governor, his offers were never taken up. He was, though, involved unofficially in several passive activities in Penang. Later, during the last days of Singapore, he played a major role in the civil defence arrangements as second-in-command to the Director General Civil Defence, Brigadier Ivan Simson. Even after a lengthy period in captivity, where he had time to reflect, Thomas still harboured a dislike of Bisseker. In correspondence to Sir John Shuckburg (Under-Secretary of State at the CO) on 14 November 1945, he said: "I hope you will sift most carefully any statement made by Bisseker of Penang. He is quite untrustworthy, and his war effort was confined to making opportunities for himself and others to escape."[28]

There was plainly a debilitating and acrimonious relationship between the Governor and this member of his Legislative Council who, from

---

[26] Maxwell, *The Civil Defence of Malaya*, p. 31.

[27] Letter. Thomas to S of S, 8 Feb. 1942. CO 967/78, NA.

[28] Letter. Thomas to Shuckburg, Colonial Office, 14 Nov. 1945. CO 967/75, NA.

other documentary evidence, was primarily concerned with spurring the authorities into constructive civil defence action. At a time when the authorities needed to project a united effort, such acrimony was disgraceful. As will be seen, Bisseker became an energetic and dominant figure in the final days of Singapore's descent. He continued to badger the government about civil defence throughout 1941, while at the same time giving credit when obvious advances in certain areas were achieved. But he was far from satisfied with the overall results. He was not the only member of the Legislative Council who expressed concern about civil defence matters. There were others, but he was undoubtedly the most voluble and persistent. The refrain of civil defence lethargy was also taken up by KL. The minutes of a Federal Council meeting held in October 1940 show that a council member, one W.G. Blunn, expressed similar dismay at the lack of tangible evidence of progress, or indeed the matter being taken seriously. He said that since a Secretary for Defence was appointed in January 1939:

> Very many minute papers must have been exchanged in the last twenty-two months between that officer in Singapore and the various officers concerned in the Federated Malay States. But as honourable members will agree, minute papers are rather like the music in the circular bass. In the words of the song, "they go round and around" until eventually something emerges. In the meantime however, people who may feel their lives are at stake, are inclined to become rather impatient, waiting for the outward and visible sign ... everybody should know exactly where to go, what to do and how to do it ... they should be instructed as to the signals which would be given in the event of an attack from the air and how to behave in such circumstances ... and enlightened as to the kind of shelter they should seek.[29]

A number of other members at this meeting, endorsing the same view as the colony, raised supplementary questions on passive defence matters. The president of the Federal Council was the High Commissioner but on this occasion, it was the OAG (Jones) who stood in, as Thomas was on leave. It must have been glaringly apparent to Jones that civil defence was now a countrywide concern and at the

---

[29] Minutes of Federal Council Meeting. Oct. 1940. Arkib Negara, Malaysia.

front of everyone's mind. It is difficult therefore to understand the Governor's argument, that allowing the military to be seen preparing defensive positions would harm the morale of the colony. People needed reassurance and it would certainly have been a comfort to see that at least the services were taking the possible dangers seriously and implementing appropriate action.

Two particular issues concerned Bisseker: the dissemination of information to the public to counter the propaganda being broadcast by foreign radios and the conflict for labour between the military and local businesses. The military was unable to offer a pay scale comparable with the civilian sector. As a result, it was unable to recruit badly needed labour. Bisseker believed the local government had a financial obligation to assist in the effort.[30]

On the matter of keeping the people informed, the Governor had strong feelings on being selective with official government information, particularly those statements he judged to be alarmist. He took a close interest in what particulars were released into the public domain. Within the government machinery there was already in place, before the war, a sponsored Department of Information. Until this point there was little for it to do and it met infrequently; in any case, its military-related content was heavily censored. After the outbreak of war, London appointed a Director of Propaganda, Sir George Sansom, and the department assumed a more prominent and important role. At the same time the military authorities set up a Services Public Relations Office but, as noted earlier, it was under the control of a long retired and disastrously incompetent naval officer. It caused more anguish among journalists than providing a service (see Chapter 6).

Among the list of civil defence duties of the civil government which Thomas catalogued, was the vital matter of the preparation and execution of various denial schemes. A list compiled after the war, there is no record of such a document existing before the campaign. It became abundantly clear during the invasion that little serious thought had been given to this crucial matter. In the middle of December 1941, when the Japanese were already well down Peninsula Malaya, London

---

[30] Proceedings of the Legislative Council of the Straits Settlements, 9 Dec. 1940.

became alarmed at the failure to deny them important resources, denial they hoped would impose a delay on the Japanese advance. In panic, they gave the quite impractical instruction of an unrestricted scorched-earth policy. From the colonial government's point of view, this would have been seriously damaging to the indigenous Asians who remained behind, however uncomfortable survival might be. Following a series of exchanges between Singapore and London, it was agreed that certain essentials such as public utilities, power plants, water supply and food produce would not be touched.[31] Businesses, estates and mines owned by Asians were also to be avoided unless they were obviously of particular value to the Japanese. Everything else of importance was to be destroyed. These urgent exchanges of communication at this point in the war exposes the astonishing inertia by both the military and civilians that no such plans had been prepared or even thought about. It is a particular denunciation of bad military planning. The speed of the retreat was so great that without preparation it was, in the end, almost impossible to apply a scorched-earth policy, except in a few cases. Eventually, decisions on these matters were delegated to the military commanders on the ground. In the case of large and important installations such as the coal mines in Selangor, the destruction of which would be complex and take some time, it was left to the mine-owners to comply. Not surprisingly, they turned to the army for assistance. Military sappers already under pressure were diverted from other essential tasks to attend to these demolitions.

As mentioned earlier, in addition to the regular forces, there was a small body of military volunteers in Malaya. In the event of an emergency they could be inducted to full-time service. The total number of volunteers was not large. In December 1939 there were 514 officers, 9,604 men in total; of this number 298 officers and 1,819 men were British.[32] By June

---

[31] The "scorched-earth" policy became a contentious subject. Thomas deemed that a sweeping application, as imposed by the Russians in their war with Germany, was impracticable and inappropriate to Malaya. He pointed out, in his comments on the draft history, that a comprehensive policy would have deprived the indigenous people of their means of survival. Besides, even in the worst case of defeat, it was expected that the British would soon return. See Thomas Papers and Kirby, *Singapore*, p. 159.

[32] "Local Forces Malaya, Strengths 1939". WO 193/914, NA.

1940, the numbers had dropped to 269 and 5,488 because a number had returned to the UK to enlist in Britain's armed forces. Of those remaining the Straits Settlements Volunteer Forces (SSVF) comprised the largest force, with four infantry battalions (two in Singapore, one in Malacca and one in Penang) in addition to some supporting units; a light artillery battery; an engineer unit; and some radio signallers, all in Singapore. There was also a small number of naval and air force volunteers. Also, each of the four FMS states had an infantry battalion and a small number of signallers and gunners. Three of the five states of the UMS (less Perlis and Terengganu) had between them one infantry battalion, and a very small number of others trained in miscellaneous military skills; in addition to the volunteers there was one regular Malay regiment, an infantry battalion—a second battalion was raised in April 1941. Regular British army officers commanded these forces while the NCOs were both British and Malay.

The number of militia volunteers should be set against the total number of British civilians of suitable age available for enlistment. In 1939 there were only 9,000 British males in Malaya. So worrying was the rush of young, able-bodied men to return to the UK to enlist, that the government had to impose a ban on further departures because these men held vital management jobs in crucial industries. From that time only a few with special circumstances were allowed to go. Of those who did not join the volunteers, a high proportion worked in one of the various civil defence organizations. It was calculated that after compulsory service was introduced in June 1940 and all the exemptions had been scrutinized, only 11 per cent of Malaya's European male population was exempt from war service for reasons other than health. Such decisions were invariably connected with the vital tin and rubber industries. In his 1947 report "Malaya's War Effort", Thomas gives examples of the detrimental consequences, pointing out how seriously affected some major industries were by the loss of senior management. Of the remainder not mobilized, the majority joined the revived civil defence organization. He also gives credit to the women, both European and Asian, who served the medical auxiliary service and other initiatives. He adds: "[T]he civil defence units represented an excellent cross-section of the population as a whole, operating in every district and made up of people of every race

... during the campaign most of them did their work well and stuck to their posts."[33]

The report dwells mostly on the island's efforts; the remainder of the Straits Settlements—Malacca, Penang and Province Wellesley—did follow closely the Singapore pattern. There is little mention, however, of civil defence efforts in the FMS and the UMS. The former did make similar, though less extensive, efforts as the Straits Settlements. The UMS, on the other hand, paid little attention to such preparations The counter argument put forward[34] was that a nationwide comprehensive civil defence scheme would have taken years and endless time to prepare and maintain. Not only was this impracticable, but it conflicted with Thomas' desire to present an image of confidence:

> 'It was the governor's wish that civil morale had to be maintained and confidence in the immediate future. Hence the Japanese threat was minimised and their ability to invade Malaya was belittled.'[35]

Governor Thomas caused confusion in the public mind by projecting an unconcern that flew in the face of evident Japanese bellicose behaviour. His casualness was at odds with the arrival of military reinforcements and contributed to a growing resentment among the European community at the upheaval new arrivals put upon their comfortable lives. In the many accounts of the fall of Singapore, there is a recurring refrain of early general mutual disdain. The soldiers arriving in Singapore from war-torn Britain had practically no understanding of the colonial environment. In particular, they had no knowledge of the delicate governmental relationship between the British administration and the Malay rulers. And they were taken aback by the detached, almost surreal view of the threat, and the affluent undisturbed lifestyle of the people.

One of those arriving from the UK at this time was Lieutenant Colonel Ashmore who recorded in his diary:

---

[33] Thomas Papers. MSS. Ind. Ocn. S 341.RHL. The figures Thomas quotes here are identical to those given in Maxwell's *The Civil Defence of Malaya*. Maxwell's book was published during Thomas' time in captivity. It is probably safe to assume he turned to this source for his facts.

[34] Maxwell, *The Civil Defence of Malaya*, p. 84 and passim.

[35] Sir W. Goode, Assistant Secretary for Civil Defence in Singapore, quoted in Callahan, *The Worst Disaster*, p. 243 and see Chapter 2, fn. 39.

The European population were possessed of a supreme confidence born of complete complacency. With a few notable exceptions, their attitude to the war in general and the chances of it coming to Malaya was one of complete indifference. I have heard it said by civilians that it would be better if the army were not in Malaya—they would attract the Japanese, whereas without them it would be possible to make satisfactory terms with the Japanese! That was in the summer of 1941.[36]

Even at the very senior levels, a civil servant in a position to know better was reported by Brooke-Popham to have said to him in relation to air-raid precautions, "My dear Air Marshal, I'm convinced that the possibilities of war against Japan are at least 500 to 1 against."[37]

To the military, intent upon preparing defences, what seemed to be obstructionism by civil servants was often no more than concern by the administration for the susceptibilities of the Asian population that they governed, and of the rights of the Malay States. A senior civil servant later wrote:

Co-operation was difficult. The Services and the civilians were working to conflicting directives, the first to get ready for war should it come; the second to maintain maximum production of tin and rubber and their swift despatch to Europe and America. This led to innumerable clashes of interest: priority for labour, for transport, for interference with normal business or damage to rubber estates or interruption of supplies and so on. Added to this was some irritation to the civilians to be ordered about somewhat peremptorily on occasions and to find their clubs and cinemas over-run by hordes of newcomers who seemed to have far more spare time and money than we did! Don't forget that the civilian population was generally working extremely hard; full blast at peacetime production and all that went with it plus mounting war work, usually at evenings and over weekends.[38]

A further irritant was that British service personnel in Singapore paid income tax at the very high wartime rates pertaining in Britain while the

---

[36] Lieutenant Colonel B.H. Ashmore, "Some Personal Observations on the Malayan Campaign", July 1942. Percival Papers. Box 5. IWM.

[37] Brooke-Popham Papers. 9/34. LHCMA.

[38] Sir W. Goode. Letter to Raymond Callahan quoted in his book *The Worst Disaster*, p. 114.

local civilians did not, a point the military resented and pointed out. The British expatriates and civil servants in Singapore were probably more resentful of the disruption to their well-regulated and comfortable lives caused by the influx of the military, than was the case in upcountry Malaya. In Singapore, the European civilians saw the military quite simply as brutal and licentious soldiery. A revealing incident is recounted in Russell Braddon's memoir *The Naked Island*. After enlisting in the Australian artillery he was posted to Singapore in August 1941, and had with him a letter of introduction to an elderly lady socialite who was a friend of his grandmother. He was told she could always be found in Raffles Hotel at Sunday lunch. He went to Raffles Hotel and was asked to leave almost immediately by one of the staff because a lady guest objected, and that the hotel was anyway "out of bounds" to soldiers. The lady who had objected to his presence, without knowing him at all, was none other than his grandmother's friend.[39]

In peninsular Malaya, many Europeans lived a different lifestyle, with a large number of them settled in remote areas. Of course, in major towns such as KL, Ipoh and Taiping there were significant numbers of such residents. For many of the upcountry groups, the arrival of the military brought a welcome variety to their often monotonous lives. There were, nonetheless, remarkable incidents in the northern, predominantly Malay States, where they were still oblivious of the danger. For instance, during vital deployment, British troops were asked to move further away because they were too near a Malay *kampong* (village). While it was difficult for the military to understand this prejudice because they presumed their presence in Malaya "to defend these people", it was equally hard for the administration to contend with the clash of cultures and persuade the Malays to accept these unusual circumstances. Many of the Malay kampongs were remote and lacked communication. Thus the arrival of military forces without warning or reason was bewildering for them.

In an interview with General Percival after the war, the writer James Leasor, in his study *Singapore: The Battle that Changed the World*, recorded Percival as saying:

> On the civil side, far too little attention had been paid to the people who did not regard themselves as British, but as Malays and Chinese. The civil

---

[39] Russell Braddon, *The Naked Island* (London: Pan Books, 1954), p. 42.

side did not seem to realise the complications of fighting in their own country. The civilian population were naturally saying to themselves, Who's coming out top dog here? And they were waiting to see who *was* going to be top dog, so there wasn't very much help from them.

"To start with, it took a very long time to get any overall decisions from the rulers out there, because in the end you had to go to about a dozen different people to get a decision. This occurred time and time again.

It caused great delays because a lot of these people were pretty dilatory in replying. It took weeks or months to get a decision on general policy regarding the building of fortifications and so on ....[40]

In Malaya, there was a political intelligence and security branch. Until the declaration of war in the West it was a small but efficient organization, concerned mainly with Malayan security, as reflected in its local title. After September 1939, it comprehensively extended its task beyond its parochial interests and increased its responsibilities. It consisted of a number of intelligence organizations, all of which were concerned with the local political scene. They also took an interest in the political affairs of neighbouring countries, especially those which affected them. The Inspector General of Police, SS (Straits Settlements) A.H. Dickinson was in overall charge, organizing its activities through a number of subsidiary bodies. Malayan Security coordinated the activities of all the Malayan police forces—the SS, FMS and UMS—in the collection and collation of all political matters affecting security. Malayan Security worked most closely with the FECB.

The FECB, in turn, maintained a close working liaison with intelligence officers and service attachés throughout all of East Asia.[41] Besides the naval, army and air intelligence sections, the FECB consisted of other specialized units: the Far Eastern Security Section; the Secret Intelligence Service (SIS) or MI6 Section; the shipping section; and the signals intelligence section. The Far Eastern Security Section was responsible for surveillance on persons or organizations working against British security in East Asia, particularly enemy agents engaged in subversion, espionage or sabotage. SIS had agents spread throughout

---

[40] Leasor, *Singapore*, p. 189.

[41] "Intelligence Organisation in the Far East", 4 Apr. 1940. WO 208/2049A. and WO193/920 Feb. 1941, NA.

the region, focusing mainly on Japanese activities and intentions. The shipping section traced and studied the movements of foreign shipping.[42]

The signal intelligence section concentrated on interception, deciphering, direction finding and traffic analysis of Japanese wireless messages. This work included the top-secret "Y" or "Ultra" deciphering of Japanese military and diplomatic codes. Thus, from its wide network and sources, the FECB was able to interpret the trends in East Asia and provide both Cs-in-C with up-to-date analysis of Japanese intentions. In addition, the land and air commanders had their own small intelligence gathering cells and provided them with situation reports. Furthermore, there were daily and bi-weekly intelligence summaries from London that covered the entire world and occasional parochial reports compiled by the Joint Intelligence Committee (JIC). In addition, the naval headquarters in Ottawa kept Singapore informed of changes in Japanese shipping patterns. There was also an exchange of information with Dutch and American service authorities in East Asia. A Defence Security Officer was responsible for military security and counter-intelligence within the forces, while the Malayan Security Service concentrated on internal security and Japanese infiltration in Malaya. Taken together, there was a comprehensive intelligence gathering and analysis system in place.

It is surprising, therefore, that in Malaya in early 1941 some intelligence specialists still believed that Japan was unlikely to risk hostilities with Britain and the USA simultaneously. There were a few who did not agree but, from the Governor downwards, among senior civil servants and the military, there was a conviction that, at best, there would be no war with Japan; at worst, Japan would not make a move until after February 1942.[43] When General Archibald Wavell, now C-in-C, American–Dutch–British–Australian Command (ABDACOM) visited the area in late 1941, he reported: "My impressions were that the whole atmosphere in Singapore was completely unwarlike, they did not expect a Japanese attack ... and were very far from being keyed up to war pitch."[44]

---

[42] Reports were based on direction finding and traffic analysis. See, for example, COIS Singapore to Admiralty, FEW 8. 12 Dec. 1940, NA.

[43] Wavell, "Operations in Malaya and Singapore", official report. CAB/66/26/44. July 1942, NA.

[44] Ibid.

One incident caused some uneasiness among the intelligence community and raised concern about the security of sensitive information passed to the Governor. During a dinner party in Government House at which several senior officers were present, a cipher telegram from London arrived for the Governor. Thomas summoned the Eurasian clerk in charge of his office to decode the cable. The next morning, one of the officers informed the Inspector General of Police (Dickinson) of the incident and commented that he was "horrified by the fact of entrusting a Eurasian subordinate, in wartime especially, [with] the decoding of secret cipher messages". The other military guests also complained separately to London. The result was a demand, from the highest levels, for an explanation from the Governor. His explanation was sufficient to placate the authorities. However, as Dickinson commented, "the feeling of suspicion and lack of confidence in the Governor to which the incident gave rise was never completely erased".[45]

The policing arrangements in Malaya reflected the different governmental administrations. The colony of the Straits Settlements had its own force, with an Inspector General at its head. The FMS also had its own Inspector General. The UMS had its own police force quite separate from each other and separate from the Straits Settlements and FMS. Neither of the inspector generals had any authority in the UMS and could only enter in an official capacity, by invitation of the ruler. In late 1940, after considerable debate, this agreement was changed: the introduction of a Malayan Security Intelligence Committee meant that the IGP of the Straits Settlements had the right of entry in respect of security matters. It then became possible to coordinate intelligence information across the whole of Malaya and, to some extent, across the region. The intelligence authorities declared that this move was "... the answer to the co-ordination of all police executive action and policy in the excessively complicated [from the police point of view] lay-out of the Peninsula".[46] By the time war came, it was still an immature organization.

---

[45] Peter Elphick, *Singapore: The Pregnable Fortress: A Study in Deception, Discord and Desertion* (London: Hodder & Stoughton, 1995), p. 152.

[46] Thomas Papers. Enclosure. Dickinson. "Memorandum on the organisation for the control of political intelligence in Malaya", Jan. 1946. Mss.Ind.Ocn.S. 341RHL.

In its embryonic period, there were incidents of poor coordination by inexperienced officials, particularly in the UMS.

The internal matters, which were of most concern to the security committee, ranged from determining the extent of Japanese penetration in Malaya and any attempts at subversion. The behaviour of the Chinese was scrutinized as well as their reaction to the growing danger. Similarly, the activities and conduct of the indigenous Malays and the other nationalities was closely monitored. Of these groups, the Japanese living and working in Malaya were the focus of close surveillance. At the time and after the war, opinion was divided about the impact and value their presence made on events.[47] Nearly every town throughout Malaya had a Japanese barber's shop and they controlled nearly all photographers, providing both a photographic service and development facilities. They also had a large fishing fleet, with bases in Singapore and Batavia, trawling the seas around Malaya and Netherlands East Indies.[48] In addition, there were a number of Japanese-owned tin mines and rubber estates. The traders had been in location long before international relations deteriorated, and most had, almost certainly, arrived in Malaya genuinely seeking work. Nevertheless, there is little doubt that their established presence and intimate knowledge of the country, and the peoples, was of value to the Japanese intelligence authorities. Out of loyalty, these traders would observe and report on matters they were asked to target. Doubtless there were "sleeper" agents among them and, indeed, they probably helped organize subversive activities. However, some British civil servants clung to the assumption that most were law-abiding citizens merely following their trade. Colonel Grimsdale, the senior Army Intelligence Officer in FECB, was of a different opinion. In his unpublished account he said:

> I remember being shown a police report on a certain Japanese [that] the Special Branch believed to be an important link in their intelligence organisation. Funds did not permit the thorough investigation which

---

[47] CO 273/671/9. 1943.

[48] Eric Robertson, *The Japanese File: Pre-war Penetration of Southeast Asia* (Hong Kong: Heinemann Asia, 1979, passim. Also see Margaret Shennan, *Out in the Midday Sun: The British in Malaya, 1880–1960* (London: John Murray, 2000), p. 213.

the case clearly merited, and the report concluded with a request for a comparatively small additional sum. The paper was annotated in the margin by the Governor himself. His comments included "this is pure alarmism". Further down I read "more alarmism"; at the end was the terrifying remark "there is no Japanese menace in Malaya." In the face of such official discouragement from the highest quarters, it is remarkable how much success the police had in tracking down some of the highly organised Japanese fifth column. But the lack of reasonable financial resources forced them to drop many promising lines of investigation and enabled the Japanese to develop their subversive activities largely unmolested.[49]

The Japanese Consul General in Singapore, Toyoda, was a known conduit for the transfer of intelligence information to Tokyo, and his encrypted signals, as noted, were monitored and decoded. Much of his intelligence material was of poor quality, often inaccurate and sometimes misleading.[50] By the law of averages, there were also times when he gained useful material.

In a lengthy note written by Dickinson after the war, in response to Thomas' ceaseless search for rebuttals of the charge of failure of his administration, he said:

> In the early days of the campaign there was a good deal of loose talk of a native Fifth Column. There is no evidence that any such thing existed as an organised entity ... The absence of an organised Fifth Column does not postulate the absence of a Japanese Intelligence-cum-Espionage organisation. The police for years had maintained as close a watch as circumstances permitted on the Japanese Community and its contacts. Intimate liaison was maintained with the Dutch Authorities in all Japanese affairs. But for the [UK Govt.] policy of 'appeasement' more action could have been taken on the evidence available than was in fact ever permitted. For thirty years, the Japanese community in Malaya had been permitted to pursue with complete immunity, the collection of intelligence and the mapping of the bye-ways of the countryside. Much of this 'intelligence' information was routine and available to anybody who wanted it, with common sense and a pair of eyes in his head ... The Japanese Community

[49] Grimsdale, unpublished manuscript. Con Shelf. 8521. IWM.
[50] Dickinson Papers. Mss. Ind. Ocn. S123. RHL.

of Malaya, some three thousand five hundred strong, was as a "security" [risk] but not a local political problem.[51]

In this document, Dickinson explains that, before the war, an assessment was drawn up of the likely behaviour of the indigenous people in the event of a Japanese invasion and that the loyalty and activities of the restless Chinese population were, in any case, continually the subject of close surveillance. As explained, the Chinese fell, broadly, into two main persuasions: those confessed communists, members of the Malayan Communist Party (MCP) who supported the communist regime in mainland China and those who sympathized with the government of Chiang Kai-shek, the Kuomintang. In addition, there was a more worrying, though small group, of pro-Wang Ching-wei: their sympathy lay with that group of Chinese in China, tolerant of Japanese occupation. (Wang Ching-wei was briefly leader of the Kuomintang after the death of Sun Yat-sen in 1924). The security committee claimed that the pro-Kuomintang group was probably the most powerful one, but the communists were the more active and vocal. The Wang Ching-wei party proved to be no great danger to the authorities and, in any case, on the outbreak of war, all known members were arrested and placed in detention. There was no evidence that they ever engaged in fifth column activity. The other important group of Chinese were, of course, those who were second- and third-generation citizens, and described themselves as "King's Chinese". They were genuine, loyal adherents of the British Empire but, as danger drew near, they became susceptible to pressure to declare an affiliation to either one of the other two main groups. The Kuomintang and the communists of Malaya later formed a United Front, following an uneasy truce between these two major parties in China. On the outbreak of the Malayan War all Chinese, with the exception of the Wang Ching-wei party, were absorbed into the United Front. According to Dickinson, in his report to the Governor, "the Chinese as a race were anti-Japanese and genuinely pro-British" but he qualified this remark by adding, "only providing the administration's sentiment coincided with their local interests, and did not clash directly with the dictates

---

[51] Ibid.

of Chungking".[52] The MCP, an almost entirely Chinese organization, similarly followed any lead given by the Communist Party of China.[53] In 1940, as mentioned in Chapter 2, the MCP planned and directed a number of violent strikes, seriously affecting the production of rubber and disrupting the allied war effort. It needed strong police action to restore the situation. It was noticeable that, following Germany's attack on Russia in June 1941, the MCP offered wholehearted cooperation to the authorities in Malaya against "our common enemy".[54] The fervent loyalty of Malayan-born Chinese was never in doubt and later criticism denounced the failure to enlist them as an irregular force to fight their most hated enemy. The government's reluctance to do so was because of the fear raised by Malays that they could not countenance an armed Chinese people in their midst.[55] The lack of national cohesion in this historically heterogeneous population was again a fundamental factor.

The indigenous Malays, as assessed by the security authorities, regarded themselves as the rightful ethnic natives of Malaya. Although there was no serious nationalist movement among the Malays in general, their local press had, for many years, expounded on Malay racial pride and general superiority.[56] The Malay intelligentsia showed signs of some movement towards nationalism, activated to some extent by influence from the Netherlands East Indies where nationalism was running strong, and by the local Malay press. Malay youth, cultivated by their more advanced and politically sensitive type of teacher, was beginning to stir. The Japanese administration, seeing possibilities in this youth movement (*Kesatuan Muda Melayu*), attempted to advance it by persuading a known Malay dissenter, Ibrahim Yaacob, to purchase a prominent Malay newspaper with Japanese capital. The scheme was brought to an abrupt end and Ibrahim arrested. It was generally acknowledged that the purely Malay

---

[52] Ibid.

[53] Purcell, *The Chinese in Malaya*, p. 218.

[54] Ibid.

[55] Peter Thompson, *The Battle for Singapore* (London: Portrait, 2005), p. 106. Thompson claims that when the proposal to arm the Chinese was put before the Governor he rejected it out of hand. See p. 617, n. 17.

[56] Testimony by Inspector General of Police (S.S.) A.H. Dickinson, in a report called for by Thomas after the war. "Memorandum on the Organisation for the Control of Political Intelligence in Malaya", Thomas Papers, 12 Jan. 1946.

political undercurrents were embryonic and of little cause for concern; most Malays then were dispassionate about politics. What was of more concern was their reliability under duress. It was thought that, in general, they would be loyal to the British interest but that no great reliance could be placed on them. It was expected that among the younger men would be a certain amount of cooperation with the Japanese army.[57]

The Indian element of the population consisted mainly of Hindus, although there was also a significant number of Sikhs and Muslims. Their normal behaviour was generally peaceful, and the labour classes were graded as "an ignorant section of the population, interested only in the quiet pursuit of their livelihood". They were nevertheless susceptible to the powerful persuasion of fervent Indian nationalists, embodied in the comparatively well-educated class of lawyers and teachers. This nationalist group, set up by well-organized local Indian associations answering to a Central Indian Association of Malaya, bid for complete control of the Indian population of the country on a strongly nationalist basis. While such associations were few in number, in 1940, their movement was seen as potentially powerful and dangerous.

The Sikh community came in for the most damning security assessment. Their group was strongly organized within itself through the influence of the gurudwaras (temples). Further, it was susceptible to the anti-British propaganda emanating from the many districts of the Punjab and, curiously, from America. According to Dickinson's report, it was a community that "contributed nothing to the welfare of Malaya, and could only be considered parasitic, stupid and likely to be openly anti-British in the event of disaster overtaking British arms".[58] In his post-war comments to Thomas, Dickinson remarked that, as it turned out,

> ... the Sikh community are reported to have behaved badly, co-operating fully with the Japanese in the more brutal aspects of their treatment of the civilian population. It must be added however that instances of great loyalty and devotion on the part of some individuals, have been recorded.[59]

---

[57] Ibid.
[58] Ibid.
[59] Ibid.

It is evident from the documentary evidence, both official and private, that the civil administration simply did not see a need for urgency in the introduction and preparation of civil defence measures.[60] The population, as represented by people like Bisseker on the Legislative Council, made their demands for action volubly and forcibly, but met with resistance and were regarded as alarmist. The government was at pains to project an image of calm and restraint. Even at this time little effort was made to alert the populace to the potential risks, or to inform them of the simple and basic protective precautions every household and business premise could organize, at no great expense. In spite of the mounting evidence from diverse but highly reliable sources of Japan's irrational behaviour, the Governor was still reluctant to acknowledge in public that there might be danger ahead. He even refused to authorize the building of shelters and his administration failed to demand concerted action from the Malay states. In summary, there was no unity of purpose. Astonishingly, the possible evacuation of civilians was never even confidentially discussed. Senior government officials in the Malay states were given no briefing whatsoever about their responsibilities in the event of an emergency. In this dismissive environment, the authorities disregarded the possibility of a scorched-earth policy and, bewilderingly, did not insist on the planned destruction of facilities that would be useful to an advancing enemy. This malaise also underlines the total absence of authority by senior military officers. At no point did they insist on a scorched-earth policy, nor did they demand that essential arrangements be prepared for civilians who may find themselves in a war zone—a serious negligence that was inexplicable.

---

[60] In particular, as noted, in the records of the proceedings of the Legislative Council S.S. and of the Federal Council, 1940 and 1941.

6

CONFRONTING THE ENEMY

By late 1941, the effects of the economic and trade freeze imposed on Japan by the USA, Britain and other Allies were having a crippling effect on the Japanese economy.[1] In an apparent attempt to get an agreement and break the deadlock Japan engaged in an endless round of diplomatic discussions with America; these talks took place in Washington. While these daily meetings were underway, however, USA intelligence intercepted the Japanese delegation's regular reports to Tokyo.[2] These disclosed that Japan had little intention of agreeing to the conditions for lifting the embargo. Covertly, Japan had already made up its mind that the only solution to its problems lay in acquiring its own independent supply of vital resources, by force if necessary, and not depend on western munificence. Singapore was aware, through British diplomatic channels, of the dangerous impasse in Washington, added to which there were now almost daily reports identifying the continuing build-up and deployment of Japanese forces in Southeast Asia.[3]

In the 12 months since the Governor returned from leave, both his administration and the military hierarchy had undergone considerable change. But even following the departure of Vlieland, the relationship between the two sides was still that of fractious turmoil. Allegations

---

[1] Nicholas Tarling, *A Sudden Rampage: The Japanese Occupation of Southeast Asia 1941–1945* (London: Hurst, 2001), p. 46.

[2] Decryption by "Magic", US decrypt of message from Tokyo to Berlin, 8 July 1941. Quoted in Feis, *The Road to Pearl Harbor*, p. 219.

[3] CAB 79/12 *Japanese Intentions*, 4 July 1941, NA.

continued to reach London of a lack of coordination and continuing disagreement between the civil and military authorities. To his chagrin, Thomas was now informed that a Minister Resident had been appointed and would join his administration. Alfred Duff Cooper, a minister of cabinet rank, arrived to investigate and report on these allegations. In addition, the replacement army and air commanders were now in post. Lieutenant General Arthur Percival commanded the army and Air Vice-Marshal Walter Pulford commanded the air force. On 5 November, Brooke-Popham learnt that he too was to be replaced. Churchill endorsed these changes and, in an attempt to soften the blow to Brooke-Popham's feelings, explained that the military emphasis had changed. The army, he reasoned, now bore the bigger responsibility: "the defence of Singapore should be entrusted to an army officer with up-to-date experience".[4] This was a smokescreen; there had been no change in the defensive plans, the central tenet of which still rested on the ability of the air force to destroy an approaching invasion fleet at sea. The officer chosen to replace Brooke-Popham was Lieutenant General Sir Henry Pownell.

From early 1941, the military authorities became progressively troubled by Japanese military behaviour and their increasingly brazen territorial expansion throughout southeast Asia. The flow of intelligence information grew and the analysts now believed that an invasion of Malaya was a serious possibility. Defence preparations—within the physical limits imposed upon them—were injected with new vigour. New military arrivals, including senior commanders, had to learn the detail of their areas of responsibility in a great hurry; busy people had to surrender valuable time to brief and instruct them. The civil administration, on the other hand, did not appear to be infected by the increasing sense of urgency among the ranks of the military. On 1 December, prompted by London, the colony was placed on a state of alert and a proclamation issued, calling up all the naval, army and air force volunteers. Thomas noted in his diary that he had received a telephone call from the CO: "7.00 am tel: [sic] from CO saying position getting worse" and "Meeting with Brooke-Popham, Percival and Jones [Colonial Secretary]. Called

<hr />

[4] Brooke-Popham papers. V/5/1. 5 Nov. 1941. LHCMA.

out the Volunteers."[5] The following day the Royal Navy's modest contribution to the defence of Singapore, in the form of Force Z, arrived at the naval base. Force Z consisted of two capital ships—*Prince of Wales* and *Repulse*—and four destroyers. It was planned that this Eastern Fleet would have the protection of an accompanying aircraft carrier, the *HMS Indomitable*, but the carrier grounded leaving its base in the West Indies. Admiral Sir Tom Phillips was the C-in-C of the fleet; his arrival heralded the departure of Admiral Layton.

The pace and tempo of government affairs did not change. Matters relating to war preparations continued at a ponderous rate and were beset by bureaucratic evasion of responsibility. The passing of memoranda seeking urgent decisions on defence matters still moved leisurely between departments. This state of affairs even continued after the outbreak of war until Thomas, belatedly, on 15 January 1942, declared that the time for passing interdepartmental memos was over. People had to take decisions.[6] This twilight period, just before the deluge, has been the described by several historians as surreal.

On 24 July 1941, the Vichy government announced that it had agreed to the "temporary occupation" by Japan of strategic bases and airfields in Indo-China as a "temporary measure undertaken to protect Indo–China". In the House of Commons the following day, the Foreign Secretary, Anthony Eden, pronounced that the Japanese government had presented demands to Vichy for the occupation of all naval and air bases in southern Indo-China. It was quite evident, he said, that the conclusion of a definite agreement was imminent, and it had been clear, for some time, that this aggression was premeditated. Perhaps in an attempt to alleviate concern, he added that certain defence measures had been enforced in Malaya "in view of the plain threat to our territories

---

[5] Thomas Diary. This diary is small, leather bound and pocket-sized. It contains condensed notes of the more substantial "My War Diary", 8 Dec. 1941–14 Feb. 1942; this was sent to the CO and stamped as received on 13 Apr. 1942. No satisfactory explanation has been forthcoming for this unusual practice of keeping two diaries. The small diary accompanied Thomas into captivity and he faithfully recorded his daily experiences, Mss. Ind. Ocn.341. RHL.

[6] Montgomery, *Shenton of Singapore*, p. 124.

which the Japanese action implies".[7] On 26 July, the *Straits Settlements Government Gazette* announced that Japanese assets in Malaya had been frozen. On 28 July, Hanoi officially announced that the Vichy government had permitted the Japanese to utilize eight aerodromes in southern Indo-China, including some on the Thai border, and that Japanese troops had begun disembarkation.[8]

Later in the year, on 26 November, the American consul in Hanoi learnt, through the French secret agency in Indo-China, that the Japanese (from Indo-China) would attack the Kra Isthmus on 1 December without previous warning, from the sea and by land. This message was repeated to Singapore the following day.[9] Thomas' reaction was to make a broadcast to the country stating that there was little to fear and if anything untoward should arise, arrangements were in place to deal with it.[10] On 5 December, London, recognizing that a serious situation was fast deteriorating, passed to Brooke-Popham the authority to launch Operation Matador. They added two riders; he had to be certain the Japanese were destined for the Kra Isthmus or they violated Thai territory.

As late as 6 December, when an invasion fleet was seen in the China Sea, the Governor, either as an act of bravado or plain disavowal, made some flippant remarks to Muriel Reilly, one of his cipher clerks. The conversation recorded in her unpublished diary seems to confirm his state of denial:[11]

> **6th December 1941.** He (Shenton Thomas) came into my room and sat down on the edge of my table and very solemnly said "well Mrs Reilly I have got bad news for you. We are at war!" I put down my pencil and said "well we've been expecting it for a long time now—let's be thankful it didn't happen a year ago when we had that scare" He looked at me over the top of his glasses and replied "oh! You didn't ask me with whom we are at war"—I answered "But of course you mean Japan" at which he laughed and said "Ha! I thought I would catch you—no, we are at

---

[7] Hansard Report, quoted in Maxwell, *The Civil Defence of Malaya*, p. 92.

[8] Ibid.

[9] Crosby, Bangkok to FO No. 861 repeated to Singapore, 27 Nov. 1941. FO 371/27767. Also WO 106/2514, NA.

[10] *The Straits Times* report, 1 Dec. 1941.

[11] Reilly, Mrs M. Diary. 91/14/1. IWM.

war with Finland." As he walked away laughing, I called after him "Oh! I thought you were going to prepare me to expect a Jap bomb on my head at any moment"—at that he returned and said "what did you say! Japanese bombs in Singapore! You can take it from me there will never be a Japanese bomb dropped in Singapore—there will never be a Japanese set foot in Malaya."

Singapore was now the focal point for international journalists, positioning themselves for the coming struggle; they also observed and reported the unreal normality of the population.[12]

In this same period, army manpower had been increased by reinforcements of young, recently trained recruits from India, and an Australian division, although in early 1941 this division was only one brigade strong. Another brigade later reinforced it. The division was commanded by a colourful but prickly Australian, Major General Gordon Bennett. However, vital military equipment had not been forthcoming; there were still no tanks or other armoured vehicles, and a serious shortage of artillery, heavy anti-aircraft guns and anti-tank weapons. The promised modern attack aircraft had not arrived—the Spitfires, Hurricanes and torpedo bombers that were to replace the dated and ancient Brewster Buffaloes, Hudsons and Vildebeeste. In December 1941, the British ground forces in Malaya stood at 88,600.[13] This number was still short of the figure that Percival and his predecessor had calculated was essential for the defence of Malaya: 100,000. In terms of combat troops, they were short of seventeen infantry battalions and two tank regiments. All the military forces suffered a woeful shortage of essential weaponry but above all else, the critical lack of modern aircraft. Above all other issues, this was the single most vital factor for the execution of the defensive plan.

The invasion of Malaya began in the early morning of 8 December 1941. It was timed to coincide with Japanese assaults on the Philippines, Guam, HK, Wake Island and Pearl Harbour. (In the case of Pearl Harbour, which lies east of the International Date Line, it was still 7 December.) The invasion began with seaborne landings at three places

[12] Barber, *Sinister Twilight*, p. 20.
[13] Ibid., p. 163.

in the northeast region of the Malay Peninsula. The main assault group landed unopposed at the long predicted coastal towns in Thailand, on the eastern seaboard of the Kra Isthmus, Singora and Patani. A third also identified at Kota Bharu in Kelantan, close to the Thai border. Two days previously, on 6 December 1941, at 1.40 pm, the approach of the Japanese invasion force was detected at sea, southeast of Cape Cambodia and 300 miles from north Malaya. A lone Hudson aircraft from Kota Bharu, which was then flying a reconnaissance mission in the area, reported its presence. It was seen to be a force of considerable size, at least 26 transports in two groups, with an accompanying armada of cruisers and destroyers for its protection.[14] The sighting was communicated immediately to GHQ Singapore and more than an hour later, at 3 pm, the information was passed to Percival who was in KL visiting III Corps headquarters. Percival and Heath, the Corps Commander, consulted a map and both concluded that on its present course the convoy was heading for Singora.[15] After the war, Percival wrote, in his "Despatches", that his "command was at the fullest degree of readiness, but there was no undue alarm, owing to the view that the Japanese expedition was directed towards Siam (Thailand)".[16] This is a surprising statement in the light of his prescient Appreciation of 1937. This was the very strategy he forecast that Japan would use to approach west Malaya. In apparent ambiguity, he added that they (he and Heath) believed that this sighting of an approaching invasion force would trigger an order [from the C-in-C] to proceed with Matador. If he believed the "expedition" caused "no undue alarm", why consider that Matador should be set in motion?[17]

The 11th Indian Division in the Alor Star area, chosen for Operation Matador, was on standby and at short notice to move. Heath now instructed the divisional commander, Major General D.M. Murray-Lyon, to reduce the warning time to "instant readiness" and to move trains and road transport to the start position. Percival caught the late afternoon civil flight back to Singapore and was in his headquarters at Fort Canning

---

[14] Kirby, *History of the Second World War*, p. 180.
[15] Percival, *The War in Malaya*, p. 106.
[16] Supplement to *The London Gazette* 38215, 26 Feb. 1948.
[17] Ibid.

by about 18.30. In his book, Percival comments that on arriving at his office, he "... was a little surprised to find out that Matador had not been ordered".[18] This is also a curious statement for two reasons. First, it reflects poorly on the relationship between himself and the C-in-C, in that he did not immediately telephone Brooke-Popham from KL to discuss the sighting, even if it was half-expected. It was, after all, a momentous event. Second, a large measure of his meagre forces was to be despatched into neutral Thailand. It would have been perfectly understandable, indeed expected, that the Army Commander seek clarification before despatching a major unit on a hazardous expedition. A further indication of this curious relationship is that Brooke-Popham turned to his naval colleague, Layton, to discuss the implications of the sighting. While it was perfectly reasonable to seek a nautical assessment of the navigational course of the flotilla, it was odd not to include both the ground and air commanders in these important deliberations. At that point, both Cs-in-C agreed that a decision on Matador be delayed to make quite certain that the convoy was, without doubt, heading for Thailand. There is no record of Percival, on his return, attempting to contact his C-in-C after learning that Matador had not been authorized. Indecisiveness about whether or not to authorize Matador was indicative of the irresolute command structure. The implications of authorizing Matador weighed heavy on Brooke-Popham's shoulders. His Chief of Staff, Major General I.S.O. Playfair, remarked that: "They have now made you responsible for declaring war" summed it up.[19]

It was not until late evening the following day (9 pm, 7 December), and after Brooke-Popham had confirmation of the direction and intention of the invasion force, that Percival went personally to see him to explain that it was now too late to undertake Matador.[20] Early on 8 December, Murray-Lyon, learning of the Singora landings and still without instructions, asked if he could now stand down his 11th Division. But it was not until the morning (10.15 am) of the following day, 9 December,

<hr>

[18] Percival, op. cit., p. 108.

[19] Ong, *Matador*, p. 205. Remarks recalled by Brooke-Popham after the war. Brooke-Popham papers. LHC.

[20] Gilchrist, *Malaya 1941* (London: Robert Hale, 1992), p. 116. Also Percival Despatch, etc., para. 124.

that Percival told Heath that he "could regard Matador operation as off and rolling stock held for that could be released".[21]

The Governor knew of the concerns being discussed regarding Matador. On 7 December, he received a copy of an urgent cable sent to London by Sir Josiah Crosby. On learning about the sighting, Crosby called on the Thai Foreign Minister:

> I have just seen Thai Minister and we send you the following message from us both. For God's sake do not allow British Forces to occupy one inch of Thai territory unless and until Japan has struck the first blow at Thailand.[22]

Undoubtedly, such a strong plea, compounded by the caveat already issued by London, did little to help Brooke-Popham make a dispassionate and purely military decision. This was not Crosby's first entreaty about not violating Thai territory. Some critics suggest that his 37 years of service in Bangkok and obvious affection for the Thais made him blind to their scheming dialogue with the Japanese.[23] Moreover, his diplomatic telegrams expounding Thai allegiance to the west and to Britain in particular were dangerously misleading. Sir Andrew Gilchrist, who at the time was a junior diplomat working for Crosby in Bangkok, notes that "rumours of a 'Matador' type operation by British forces were now [December 1941] in general circulation".[24] Moreover, a Magic[25] decrypt of a Japanese diplomatic telegram reported a suggestion by a pro-Japanese member of the Thai cabinet that the Japanese forces should provoke a British invasion of southern Thailand, enabling "Thailand to declare war on Britain as the aggressor".[26] It would seem that Crosby either ignored these objectionable indicators or simply did not want to believe them.

---

[21] Brian P. Farrell, *The Defence and Fall of Singapore 1940–1942* (Stroud, Gloucestershire: Tempus, 2005), p. 151.

[22] NA. FO 371/28163. 7 Dec. 1941.

[23] See, for example, Gilchrist, *Malaya 1941*, p. 28, which quotes a briefing note for the CIGS in Nov. 1941, describing the concern of military commanders about Crosby's relationship and charitable view of the Thai authorities' behaviour.

[24] Ibid., p. 115.

[25] The Americans called their decryption machine "Magic".

[26] Elphick, *Singapore*, p. 103.

According to his diary, Thomas learnt of the Japanese landings at Kota Bharu when Percival telephoned him at 1.15 am on 8 December. As prearranged with the police, he ordered the arrest of all Japanese in Singapore and the seizure of Japanese powerboats in harbour. Nearly every secondary source describing this event differs, both about the time that Thomas heard of the invasion, and his reaction. According to Noel Barber, he is alleged to have said, on hearing the news from Percival, "Well I suppose you will shove the little men off!"[27] This is a comment repeated in several books on the campaign. Thomas says that at the time of the call he was working on a cipher telegram and that later, at 4 am, he received a call from Pulford warning him of approaching hostile aircraft. He then phoned Rodgers of the Harbour Board and Jeans (head of ARP) to alert them. However, when the Japanese aircraft arrived over Singapore, the whole city was fully illuminated; there was no blackout. The official history states that the civil defence organization did not respond because the headquarters of the ARP was "not manned",[28] a version of events that obviously calls into question the veracity of Thomas' diary entries. The matter of the unpreparedness of civil defence of Singapore was investigated after the war; Thomas defended his position by claiming that he was not forewarned of the likelihood of an air raid. In addition, to support his case, he had a letter from the officer in charge of civil defence who wrote: "the point is that 'brown-out' [precautionary dimming of lights] was not ordered for the night of the 7/8 December, and my recollection is that it was not given on Service advice. Therefore, the A.R.P. was not manned, nor was the municipal services alerted in any way. They were in their beds as on any other night in peace-time."[29]

Brian Montgomery in *Shenton of Singapore: Governor and Prisoner of War* claims to have irrefutable evidence, both in a written account and in a verbal record by a naval officer, that Thomas was, in fact, at a vital conference at the naval base at 2.30 am on 8 December.[30] While he was there, an air raid warning red was declared, and the officers took shelter.

---

[27] Barber, *Sinister Twilight*, p. 28.

[28] Kirby, *History of the Second World War*, p. 183.

[29] Thomas Papers, "Comments on the Draft History of the War Against Japan", para. 95 (j). RHL.

[30] Montgomery, *Shenton of Singapore*, p. 5.

In addition to Thomas, the conference was attended by Brooke-Popham, Admiral Phillips (the new C-in-C, Far East Fleet), Pulford and senior army officers, with the exception of Percival. A number of staff officers also attended. It is claimed that this conference, called by Phillips, was the occasion for the decision to put to sea the two capital ships and their destroyer escort (*Force Z*) to meet the Japanese invasion in north Malaya, and, moreover, that Thomas' endorsement of the mission was pivotal. This decisive conference is also mentioned in Arthur Jacob Marder's book *Old Friends, New Enemies: The Royal Navy and the Imperial Japanese Army*.[31] However, no documentary evidence has been found that such a conference took place. According to Montgomery, no official minutes were kept for security reasons but he gives a very full account of the entire event, related to him by the naval officer, Lieutenant Commander J.W. McClelland. Montgomery explains that this officer was not part of the proceedings but deliberately slipped into the room at the request of Layton, who had not been invited to attend. McClelland wrote a full account of the meeting and, after the war, was interviewed by Montgomery to corroborate his record. It is very strange that Thomas makes no mention of this critical meeting, even in the privacy of his diary. The naval base was about 20 miles from Government House and, at that hour, it would have taken about 30 minutes to drive there. If the meeting did indeed take place, it is hard to imagine that Thomas was back at Government House by 4 am, in time to receive Pulford's warning of an air raid, which in any case would then have been superfluous.

This mysterious meeting is also given prominence by Sir Andrew Gilchrist in *Malaya 1941: The Fall of a Fighting Empire*. He insists that the gathering did take place and is credibly reported. Both Brooke-Popham and Thomas were people with whom Gilchrist was personally well acquainted, and he considers that the remarks attributed to both men during the meeting are entirely in character.[32] Gilchrist's endorsement only serves to make Thomas' failure to reveal this conference, in any of his records, quite extraordinary and raises further misgivings about the accuracy of his diary entries. What is not in contention is that Singapore

---

[31] Arthur Jacob Marder, *Old Friends, New Enemies: The Royal Navy and the Imperial Japanese Army* (Oxford: Clarendon Press and New Yo Oxford University Press 1981–90).

[32] Gilchrist, *Malaya 1941*, p. 126.

was bombed at 4.15 am on 8 December 1941. There was no air-raid warning, the city was fully illuminated and the civil defence organization was unprepared.

Later that day, Cs-in-C Brooke-Popham and Layton issued their infamous Order of the Day, stating confidently:

> We are ready. We have had plenty of warning and our preparations are made and tested .... We are confident. Our defences are strong and our weapons efficient .... Japan has made a grievous mistake .... We see before us a Japan drained for years by the exhausting claims of her wanton onslaught of China.[33]

Ten weeks later these public words were to ring hollow. When hardened members of the press corps received a copy of the order, they expressed their deep cynicism. George Hammond, editor of *The Tribune*, said: "I can't believe anybody could deliberately tell so many lies."[34]

The unit selected for Matador, the 11th Indian Division, consisted of two brigades only, under command of Major General Murray-Lyon. The division was deployed in north Malaya in the state of Kedah. As noted earlier, it was given dual and conflicting roles. First, it was to prepare for deployment to a defensive position near Jitra, 18 miles south of the Thai border, with the task of covering the important airfield at Alor Star. Alternatively, it was to remain on alert in anticipation of the Matador operation, an offensive advance. "The two possible roles, which were in no way compatible, increased immensely his [Murray-Lyon] difficulties."[35] In these circumstances, the Divisional Commander had little option but to have his command on continuous alert, ready to move at short notice. Indeed, he had already moved two of his battalions to the railway station at Anak Bukit, ready to entrain.[36] This high state of readiness meant that little time could be devoted to the construction of the defensive position. In any case, they needed to have ready loaded on transport, large quantities of stores for the rapid preparation of defensive positions at the chosen destination and for the possible repair of bridges en route.

---

[33] Brooke-Popham Papers, 6/5/33. 8 Dec. 1941. LHCMA.

[34] Barber, *Sinister Twilight*, p. 39.

[35] Ibid., p. 170.

[36] Percival, *The War in Malaya*, pp. 114–5.

These same materials were needed for the defensive site in Jitra. Murray-Lyon's plan envisaged the division departing from ten assembly points many miles apart: as time was going to be of the essence, he could make a quicker move from his deployment area if his forces were at instant readiness and not confined to trenches. During this waiting period, there was the additional handicap of appalling and incessant monsoon rain. The men were without protection or relief. "It was raining ... it hadn't stopped for days ... there was the devil's own deluge. I had never seen such a storm. You couldn't see more than twenty yards."[37] On 6 December 1941, the division first learnt of the sighting of the Japanese convoy in the Gulf of Thailand and ordered the highest state of readiness.[38] To add a further testing element to the divisional commander's mission, he was responsible for a small force (two battalions called Krohcol) tasked with advancing along the Kroh-Patani road to ambush any Japanese who might approach from that direction. Kroh, where the column was assembling, was 100 miles away from Murray-Lyon's headquarters, and communication was very unreliable.

Neither of these pre-emptive opening moves was successful. In the case of Matador, the lengthy period waiting for confirmation of the invasion fleet's destination left it too late to deploy the division. In the case of Krohcol, again, a late decision to order the move was followed by an advance of the column against some opposition, identified initially as Thai police but later suspected to be Japanese in Thai police uniforms.[39] These forces prevented Krochol from getting anywhere near its objective. With the cancellation of Matador, and at a very late point in the proceedings, the 11th Division turned to the alternative task deploying to defend the Jitra area. It was dismayed to find poorly and partially prepared defensive positions and trenches flooded with rain water. The division had to erect barbed-wire barriers, lay anti-tank mines and new telephone cables.[40] These wet and exhausted troops, some so raw they had never seen a tank, now confronted a rapidly advancing, battle-trained Japanese force

---

[37] Compton MacKenzie, *Eastern Epic* (London: Chatto & Windus, 1951), p. 247, quoted in the diary of Lieutenant Greer.

[38] Kirby, *History of the Second World War*, p. 180.

[39] Ibid., p. 186.

[40] Allen, *Singapore 1941–1942*, p. 124.

supported by tanks. The ensuing encounter was swift and brutal. The Jitra position was quickly overrun, with the Japanese employing a tactic that was to be a feature of their remorseless advance down the Malay Peninsula. They attacked the main defensive position frontally while at the same time sending supporting columns around the flanks to encircle the position. They cut the lines of communication and blocked any withdrawal routes, then fell upon the defenders from the rear.

This early engagement of the war in Malaya was disastrous and set a pattern and standard for subsequent actions in the campaign. The official history stated that the "action at Jitra was a major disaster for the British forces in Malaya ... and the deployment of 11th Division at Jitra led to defeat in detail".[41] Errors of command and control, lack of clarity of purpose, poor communication and inexperienced, demoralized troops facing a cohesive trained and resolute enemy were the main ingredients of failure.

A most serious flaw revealed during this action was the poor radio communication between all formations, upwards and downwards. Primarily, there were simply not enough radio sets available, but also the signal ranges between sets in close country was very poor.[42] In many instances, a despatch rider or the civil telegraph and telephone systems provided the only means of communication.[43] This was epitomized with the operator interrupting Brooke-Popham and Percival on a trunk call to say, "Your three minutes have expired, sir," and cut the connection in the middle of a discussion on a vital military matter.[44]

It could not have helped in communication that corps headquarters was located in KL, some 260 miles behind the forward units and the GOC in Singapore a further 230 miles away. Bizarrely, Percival even found time on 8 December, the morning of the invasion, to attend a meeting of the Straits Settlements Legislative Council. Thomas opened the council proceedings with what was either a show of British phlegm, or another example of his failure to grasp the significance of the outbreak of war with Japan.

---

41 Kirby, *History of the Second World War*, p. 210.

42 WO/172/176, NA.

43 Ibid.

44 Cecil Brown, *Suez to Singapore* (New York, NY: Random House, 1942), p. 364.

Before we proceed with the orders of the day I wish to make just a short statement. At 1 o'clock this morning a Japanese force attacked the beaches of Kota Bahru. The Force consisted of a cruiser, four destroyers, two armed merchantmen and some transports. They were engaged by our forces and the last news is that all the surface forces appear to be retiring and that the ships are sailing north. There were a certain number of Japanese left on the beaches. They have been roped in and those that are making off in boats are being machine-gunned. (Applause).

We are informed that the main landing is now taking place at Singora in Thailand, so that Thailand as well as the British Empire has been attacked without provocation and without cause ... The Council will now proceed with its business.[45]

There is no record, in the minutes, of Percival contributing to the proceedings.[46] However, after the war, Hugh Bryson, who was clerk to the Legislative Council, wrote that:

Percival came in about half way through the meeting and, the public having withdrawn, gave members a survey of the position in Kedah and the Kroh—Betong area; he appeared confident that he could hold, if not repel, the Japs [sic].[47]

The distance between commanders and the opening battle have been compared with fighting taking place on the borders of Scotland and corps HQ in Crewe with the GOC in the Isle of Wight. Senior commanders did not have the benefit of personal aircraft to cover these huge distances. When Percival needed to meet the Corps Commander in KL, he had to fly from Singapore by civil airline on an early morning flight. This facility was, understandably, suspended as the Japanese drew closer to the capital of the FMS and enemy aircraft dominated the skies over Malaya. Even the most senior commanders did not have their own air transport.[48]

The primary Japanese assault on Malayan soil took place on the east coast, at Kota Bharu. The first shot in the Malayan campaign was fired by the Indian 3rd Dogra Regiment's 18-pounder gun at enemy landing craft just after midnight on the 8 December 1941. By 12.25 am Japanese

[45] Proceedings of the Straits Settlements Legislative Council Meeting, 8 Dec. 1941.
[46] Ibid.
[47] Bryson Papers. BAM Collection. RCS/RCMS 103/5/7. CU.
[48] Callahan, *The Worst Disaster*, p. 219.

troops were ashore and by 1 am they had captured the pillboxes in the area of Badang. Savage fighting then took place for a number of hours, with several of the other pillboxes resisting to the last man but, by 4 am, the Japanese had a firm beachhead.[49]

Most of the RAF's strength was by now deployed in north Malaya. Of the 158 aircraft available to the air commander, 110 were in the north by dawn on 8 December. At 12.30 am, when Singapore heard the news of the landings, a few aircraft from Kota Bharu attacked the landing craft and succeeded in hitting all three Japanese transports, two of which sank. This notable success by a small number of Hudsons and old Vildebeest aircraft has been seized upon by adherents of air power as an example of what could have been achieved if the RAF had been reinforced by the 336 aircraft promised by the COS.[50]

At daylight, Japanese aircraft took to the air and demonstrated Japanese superiority in both flying ability and the quality of their aircraft. They attacked the major aerodromes on both coasts. British aircraft returning to the aerodromes on the west coast to refuel and rearm were attacked on the ground and their numbers fatally reduced. At Alor Star, a squadron of eight Blenheims caught on the ground were reduced to two aircraft. At Sungei Patani, south of Alor Star, two fighter squadrons similarly caught were reduced to four aircraft in each squadron. The remaining aircraft at Sungei Patani withdrew and repositioned at nearby Butterworth. Inexplicably, the ground staff hastily withdrew, leaving over 150,000 gallons of aviation fuel as well as the bomb stores and the runways intact. This is all the more extraordinary as there were no Japanese ground forces anywhere near Sungei Patani at the time. An early myth was already spreading through the jittery British forces that the Japanese were everywhere, could travel silently through "impenetrable" jungle and were unstoppable.

On the east coast, the three airfields had been under continual bombing and strafing throughout the day but the Japanese were careful to use only anti-personal and fragmentation bombs to avoid damaging the runways. Pulford ordered the remaining aircraft to withdraw to Kuantan. Again,

[49] Percival, *The War in Malaya*, pp. 118–20.
[50] Allen, *Singapore 1941–1942*, p. 118.

the RAF station staff, in panic, deserted the aerodromes. Although they had set fire to the buildings, they left the fuel, stores, runways and 550 tons of bombs intact. Fortunately, units of the 8th Indian Brigade managed at least to set fire to the abandoned fuel stores. Without instructions to the contrary, the brigade remained responsible for the defence of these abandoned facilities.[51] At the end of the day, only 50 operational aircraft remained in the north.

On 9 December, the second day of the war, the air situation deteriorated even more. Early that day, Pulford decided to reduce the concentration of aircraft at Kuantan. Lamentably, the Japanese got there first (they flew 120 sorties a day for the first three days of the war)[52] and destroyed seven aircraft on the ground. The remainder were ordered back to Singapore. Attempts to strike back at the Japanese led to further losses. Six Blenheims left Singapore that morning to attack the Singora area; they were to be joined by a fighter escort from north Malaya but the only two remaining fighters in the north were, at that time, heavily engaged in other tasks supporting the army. The Blenheims pressed on unescorted and were attacked by 30 enemy fighters. They lost half their number. A second strike was planned comprising the remnants from Singapore and the only remaining Blenheims in the north, but they were attacked on the ground at Butterworth before they could take off. All but one was destroyed. The Governor recorded in his diary:

> December 9.
> Enemy reinforcing in Kelantan and State Government move to Kuala Krai. Aerodromes in Kelantan, Alor Star, Sungei Patani and Kuantan badly bombed. More machines gone. Singapore quite composed and all first aid posts fully moved [sic]. All very reassuring.

In reality, there was no plan drawn up for the evacuation of either the state government or the civil population from the state of Kelantan, an Unfederated State. When firing was plainly heard on 8 December at about 1 am, the British adviser, A.C. Baker, rang around the British community warning them that women and children should be ready to leave the area as soon as possible. At 4.30 am, the Military Commander ordered them

---

[51] Farrell, *The Defence and Fall of Singapore*, p. 146.
[52] Richards and St George Saunders, *Royal Air Force 1939–1945*, p. 30.

to leave immediately. The women and children fled in their private cars to Kuala Krai, a railway town some distance in the interior. Some Europeans from the adjoining state of Terengganu (also an Unfederated State) heard of this instruction through friends and followed suit. They took only the minimum of belongings with them: they all believed that this was only a temporary arrangement, and when the "incursion" was suppressed they would return home.[53]

Key's 8th Brigade finally abandoned the two remaining airfields on the east coast on the night of the 10 December, destroying as much as they could. However, as the runways were grass there was little they could do to ruin the landing surfaces; in any case, the RAF had positioned dumps of material for repairing craters nearby. By the end of the day, British aircraft losses were crippling and the Japanese had secured total air supremacy across north Malaya. Only one Buffalo photo-reconnaissance aircraft remained in Butterworth. By the evening of 10 December and before the ground battle for the westcoast trunk road began in earnest, British airpower in Malaya had been virtually destroyed.[54]

10 December turned out to be an even blacker and more disastrous day for the British forces. Now without airpower, and adding to the unremitting despair, the two prestigious capital ships, the *Prince of Wales* and the *Repulse*, were sunk. After intense deliberations (mentioned above), Admiral Phillips, the Fleet Commander, decided to take the risk of attacking the Japanese naval forces still offshore and gathered opposite Singora. Phillips set sail from Singapore on the afternoon of 8 December at a time when the air situation in the north was critical but not hopeless. His Force Z consisted of the two capital ships and an escort of HM destroyers *Electra*, *Empress*, *Tenedos* and *HMAS Vampire*. Late in the afternoon of 9 December, enemy reconnaissance aircraft, whose presence was noted by the fleet, spotted Force Z. Critically, Phillips was unaware that a Japanese submarine had also sighted his squadron earlier that afternoon.[55] By then he knew that the RAF could not provide air cover over Singora, so he decided it would be sensible to return to

[53] Margaret Shennan, *Out in the Midday Sun: The British in Malaya, 1880–1960* (London: John Murray), p. 233 and passim.
[54] Richards and St George Saunders, *Royal Air Force 1939–1945*, p. 22.
[55] Kirby, *The War Against Japan*, p. 196.

Singapore. En route he picked up an Allied signal, suggesting there was an attempted enemy landing at Kuantan. As this was only a minor diversion from his return course, Phillips decided to investigate. His squadron was again spotted by Japanese air reconnaissance and both capital ships were attacked and sunk. The majority of the 3,000-strong crew from the two ships was rescued by the destroyers. Admiral Phillips and his flag captain, John Leach, both died. The reported landing at Kuantan, for which Z Force had diverted, was false. Admiral Layton, who was about to depart Singapore for his new command, was ordered to remain and reassume the appointment as C-in-C, Eastern Fleet.[56] His first decision was to order the remaining cruisers and destroyers away from Singapore to the safety of Java and Ceylon. The naval base was left empty. On 5 January 1942, Layton removed himself and the FECB to Java. Later, in mid-January, he was appointed C-in-C, Ceylon (Sri Lanka).[57]

After less than a week of war, the RAF had effectively been destroyed and the Royal Navy forced out of East Asia's seas. Only the army remained to defend the people of Malaya. The effect on the population's morale was immediate and devastating. A number of historians who have closely examined the loss of the capital ships consider that Pulford, in spite of radio silence imposed by Phillips on his task force, should at least have sent a reconnaissance aircraft to Kuantan to investigate the rumour of a landing. He would have been able to discredit the rumour, and most certainly would have found Force Z and sent assistance. Instead, he is reputed to have said to Palliser, the naval COS in Singapore, "My God, I hope you don't blame me for this. We didn't even know where you were."[58]

On this same day, 10 December, Duff Cooper took over as Chairman of the recently renamed War Council. On his appointment by Churchill as Resident Cabinet Minister in Singapore for Far Eastern affairs, he was given the authority to form a War Council. It was not an auspicious meeting. Both Brooke-Popham and Thomas told Duff Cooper that they intended to take their orders from their respective masters in London (the Chiefs of Staff and the CO) and saw little need for a War Council. The tone and mood of these meetings can be judged by the opening

[56] Kirby, *Official History*, p. 199.
[57] Ibid., p. 253.
[58] Leasor, *Singapore*, p. 197.

exchange. When Duff Cooper asked Brooke-Popham to let him have a list of his urgent military requirements, he was told that such a list had already been sent to the WO and turned down. Duff Cooper replied that he would immediately raise this issue directly with Churchill. An astonished Brooke-Popham told him that such a move would be seen as disloyal to the Chiefs of Staff. Dumbfounded, Duff Cooper recorded in his diary:

> I told him that if he thought loyalty to the Chiefs of Staff was of greater importance than winning the war I could not agree with him, and that if he really believed that the supply of certain weapons was essential there were no methods which he should not adopt to secure those weapons.[59]

The disastrous events during the first few days of the campaign, the crushing defeat at Jitra, the loss of the two capital ships and the destruction of most of the RAF were so momentous, that the outcome of the campaign was virtually determined at that point. The speed, momentum and pressure with which the Imperial Japanese Army launched and maintained its dogged drive south, stunned the defenders. Without air or sea power the ragged, beleaguered army reeled backwards, pausing once in a while for a half-hearted, but ineffective, stand against a relentless blitz.[60]

The Japanese forces, commanded by Lieutenant General Yamashita, advanced simultaneously on three axes, each a division strong, supported by light tanks, additional units and air support. Two divisions traversed the Kra Isthmus in parallel to the west coast of Malaya—from which they planned to make their main thrust—towards Alor Star, Kroh and Grik on the Perak River. The third division began its advance down the east coast, from Kota Bharu, following the line of the East Coast Railway towards Kuantan. The two advancing west coast columns converged or separated according to the terrain, roads and rivers along their routes. On both coasts, they additionally employed amphibious "leap-frogging" manoeuvres, inserting forces at points along the coast in the rear of the British positions.[61]

---

[59] Duff Cooper Papers. DUFC/3/7Churchill College Archives. CU.
[60] Kinvig, *Scapegoat*, passim.
[61] Kirby, *Official History*, passim.

From Jitra the army fell back on Gurun, about 30 miles further south, but its stand here was no more successful than the attempt at Jitra. As pressure mounted, Murray-Lyon ordered an immediate withdrawal some 7 miles further to put Muda River between his forces and the Japanese. By the morning of the 16 December his 11th Division, sorely depleted and exhausted, was behind the river, which he hoped would prove a formidable tank obstacle. In so doing, however, he irrationally left the island of Penang exposed.

The episode of the loss of Penang to the advancing Japanese was the first significant challenge to the administration's management of passive defence matters. It was, distressingly, to uncover evident inadequacies that caused international opprobrium and tainted the image of Thomas and his government. Penang was bombed on 11 December. It was a heavy raid which, in spite of the previous day's air raid on Butterworth's RAF airfield on the mainland opposite, came as a surprise to the people of the island. They rushed into the streets to watch the approaching formations and, too late, realized the danger. Hundreds were killed and thousands injured. It set in motion a saga which highlighted the inadequacy of civil defence and passive defence measures on the island, and brought into sharp focus the poor planning for such an eventuality.[62] The written records of the European civilians caught up in the early days of the fighting in Penang and north Malaya almost unanimously affirm the lack of information about the devastating events taking place around them.[63] In one particular memoir, Harvey Ryves, a British police officer working in north Kedah, deplored the complete absence of official communication about the military developments engulfing everyone, which was especially regrettable, he felt, in view of his appointment. In the end, he relied on people passing through his area, the beginning of the flood of refugees, to let him know what was going on so he in turn could warn others enabling them to take suitable action. He mentions an incident when a Mrs Scott, the wife of a rubber estate manager, went to find the British resident to get advice and help:

---

[62] Andrew Barber, *Penang at War: A History of Penang during and between the First and Second World Wars, 1914–1945* (Kuala Lumpur: AB &, 2010), p. 66 and passim.

[63] Shennan, *Out in the Midday Sun*, p. 233.

A couple of hours later she returned to say that the British Resident had issued orders that no women and children were to leave the state (Kedah) without permission. I was so amazed at hearing this report that I promptly phoned Jomaron, the District Officer, to ask if he had heard similar information. He hummed and hawed and made the extraordinary reply that women and children could leave, but the government could accept no responsibility if anything happened to them on the journey![64]

The raid on Penang was unopposed: by this time, there were no fighter aircraft in northern Malaya and no anti-aircraft defences on the island. The only regular battalion had been withdrawn to form part of Krohcol.[65] Air raids continued over three consecutive days, and the casualties were terrible from bombing and machine gunning in the crowded streets of Georgetown. All essential services broke down, the town was in flames, hundreds of corpses lay unburied and looting became endemic. Most of the native population fled to the relative safety of Penang Hill: disastrously, the labour force and the local police disappeared. The place was in utter confusion and panic, which in turn led to hasty and misguided decisions that were later the source of much recrimination and reflected badly on the entire administration. Subsequent enquiries, however, acknowledged the valuable part played by a number of Europeans, particularly women, who worked alongside Asian women, treating the injured and providing succour to the homeless. About half of the ARP Corps and the Medical Auxiliary Services remained at their posts.

Nevertheless, overall, in this first test of passive defence measures, there were glaring defects. Most of the important facilities, such as the fire service, ambulances and police, failed to function. It is a shocking fact that there were no air-raid shelters. On 15 December, the military garrison commander, Brigadier C.A. Lyon (not to be confused with Major General Murray-Lyon, the Divisional Commander) received instructions from General Heath that he was to make secret preparations for the evacuation of the garrison, including the Europeans. Moreover, he claimed afterwards that the evacuation orders were to be given verbally at 12 am on 16 December, and passed onto only those who had to coordinate them.

---

[64] Memoir of Harvey Ryves, policeman in north Malaya. 84/301 1941. IWM.
[65] Kirby, *History of the Second World War*, p. 218.

He informed the Resident Councillor, Leslie Forbes, of the plan. Forbes maintained that he had no hint of the intended secret evacuation. From the inquiry after the war, it is clear that the two did not get on. When asked about co-operation with the civil authorities at this time, Brigadier Lyon made a bizarre reply:

> Good co-operation was maintained with the naval staff, although the Commander felt obliged at the start to arrange for the removal of the pre-war SNO (senior naval officer). Airfields were demolished early and co-operation did not arise. Co-operation with the civil authorities was imperfect partly because senior civil officials did not get on with the Commander, nor had he a high estimation of the Chief Police Officer. In the crises, however, the Commander took charge and maintained close contact with the Resident Councillor.[66]

Fierce criticism, which followed this first ordered evacuation, was directed at the underhand way in which it was arranged and the discriminatory selection of those to be evacuated; the message was for the Europeans only. Without warning, the white women were told to prepare to leave that night and that it was a military order which they had to obey. It was established that it would, in any case, be impossible to evacuate Asian civilians since there was insufficient transport for their large numbers. In consequence, to avoid an unmanageable stampede, they would not be told. The evacuation that night, considering the haste imposed and the brevity of instructions, went relatively smoothly; the ferry taking them across to the mainland had to be manned by Royal Navy ratings, survivors from the recently sunk capital ships, because the Asian crew—Malay, Chinese and Indian—had deserted. A few Europeans, notably the medical superintendent, Dr Evans, refused to leave and insisted on remaining to look after the injured.

A manifestation of the poor scorched-earth planning together with the hasty withdrawal of the 11th Division led to a late and perfunctory attempt to destroy everything of use: defence stores, ammunition, quantities of petrol and oil, as well as equipment and machinery, the power station, the civil airport buildings and the Penlaga Cable station,

---

[66] WO 106/2552. "Report on sequence of events Penang Fortress 8th Dec. 1941", NA.

which was the terminal for the important telecommunications cable to India and the UK. Inevitably, some important omissions occurred which were to prove of inestimable advantage to the Japanese. The broadcasting station and a fleet of small boats and craft in the harbour were untouched as were 3,000 tons of tin in the form of ingots. The Japanese found 24 self-propelled craft and many large junks and barges in the harbour, all deserted by their crew and left in working order. The radio station was operated by the Japanese to broadcast propaganda throughout the remainder of the campaign. Indeed, almost right away, according to the written stories of survivors, Radio Penang started taunting: "Hello, Singapore, how do you like our bombing?"[67]

Previously, on 13 December, the Governor had sent a cipher cable to the Secretary of State for the Colonies in London:

> Penang has been raided several times by daylight and damage to Asiatic quarters has been extensive. So far as known, fatal casualties 200, wounded about 1000, all Asiatics. Owing to destruction of aerodromes in the North air defence has been impossible and the Asiatic morale in consequence bad. Military authorities in collaboration with the Resident Counsellor arranging to control the town. European women and children will be evacuated as soon as possible.[68]

It should be noted that, in this cable, he made specific mention of European women and children. In his diary entry that day, Thomas wrote that at the War Council, after some prevaricating remarks from Percival about the uncertainty of defending Penang, "it was decided that I should advise European women and children to leave and other Europeans who wanted to". He added:

> that was the Council minute, but my own note at the meeting was that European women and children should be allowed to go if they wish. Policy is to defend Penang. Difficulties great but that is the fixed decision. European men also should be allowed to go if they wish, but any who desire to stay and help—let them.[69]

---

[67] Shennan, *Out in the Midday Sun*, p. 236.
[68] CO 967/74. Cipher No. 627. Govt House, 1609. 13 Dec. 1941, NA.
[69] Thomas Papers.

In the light of later accusations, this addendum reads like an afterthought.

Percival had circulated a memo to the War Council before this meeting, outlining the pros and cons of withdrawal from Penang. However, as the members noted, it contained no firm conclusion or recommendation.[70] Presumably, Percival believed that after some discussion at the meeting he would have a consensus on a favoured solution, or that hearing other opinions would help him arrive at a decision; either way, presenting the options was the embodiment of the consummate staff officer. It was most certainly not the behaviour of a decisive leader. In the end, the decision was left to Heath. Duff Cooper, on the other hand, at what was described as a depressing meeting, considered that the situation was so serious that he proposed a radical change of strategy:

> We should now ask ourselves is it possible with barely four divisions (mainly Indian), with only three squadrons of fighter aircraft not all properly trained, without command of the sea, to defend a country the size of England? The Japanese can reinforce quicker, land anywhere. If not possible, then we should consider [a] change of plan. [The] real question is defence of the Naval Base by holding Johore .... There is a need to withdraw to Johore and hold the island to the last.[71]

At this stage both Thomas and Duff Cooper were not only directly concerned with the course of the battle, but also appeared to have become assertive enough to impose their opinions on the strategic direction of the campaign. Thomas did not agree with the major withdrawal proposed by Duff Cooper nor did he agree with Percival about withdrawing from Penang, but his logic suggests a concern more for his government's image than any military judgment. He believed the proposals would be very bad for public morale and did not want his administration to be associated with them. Thomas' diary and the War Council minutes reveal a growing gap between him and Percival and increasing animosity towards Duff Cooper. For example, in his diary he explains that his idea of "defend to the last man" differs from Percival's view, which had the additional qualification of "but only to the best of our ability". Equally, Percival

---

[70] Montgomery, *Shenton* of Singapore, p. 94.
[71] WO106/2568. "Minutes of War Council 13 Dec 1941", NA.

had little faith in Thomas holding fast to decisions they had reached between them. He went as far as having a stenographer accompany him to meetings with the Governor to record their discussions. Incredibly, Percival would not leave the building until he had Thomas' signature to them: this in the middle of a war.[72]

On 19 December, Penang was eventually abandoned and a week later Ipoh hastily evacuated. In the space of 16 days, the British forces were behind the Perak River with its left flank on the coast. North Malaya was effectively lost. With the capitulation of Penang and the planned withdrawal of his forces to a position further south, behind the Perak River, Heath (instructed by Percival), ordered all the European women and children to leave Perak State. Thomas learned of this instruction from Fraser, the Federal Secretary, in a telephone call from KL. Such a decision coming so soon after the Penang fiasco, immediately led Thomas to order this instruction to be cancelled as he considered it invalid and defeatist. Moreover, he said, it should not have been made without reference to him. He also sent telegrams to officials in Perak, one of which included the statement: "The evacuation of Perak is entirely unofficial and unnecessary, and liable to cause a panic amongst the Asiatics. Singapore is already overcrowded, and no one may go there."[73] His instructions to Fraser contained some draconian measures. Trains travelling south were forbidden to carry passengers who appeared to be evacuees, and first-class carriages were removed altogether to prevent Europeans from making off. Motor cars travelling south were turned back, petrol was no longer available to private individuals and they were not allowed to make long-distance telephone calls.[74] Thomas noted in his diary that, after his intervention, a "big row broke out" in the War Council. Duff Cooper told Thomas that he would make Heath's position untenable if he (Thomas) countermanded his orders. A most unpleasant and lengthy altercation followed with Thomas eventually, in a complete *volte-face*, conceding that, in future, "the civil government will not order the compulsory evacuation of civilians from any area, but if a military

[72] Kirby, *Singapore*, p. 195.
[73] Maxwell, *The Civil Defence of Malaya*, p. 111.
[74] CO 967/77 Duff Cooper, secret and personal letter to Churchill, 18 Dec. 1941, NA.

commander considers the military situation justifies it, he may order compulsory evacuation by the civilian population".[75] In Duff Cooper's letter to Churchill, describing this confrontation he wrote that Percival, who was also present at the meeting, said nothing "until I suggested that it was the first time in the history of the British Empire when it had been our policy to evacuate the troops first and leave the women and children to the tender mercies of a particularly cruel foe".[76]

Shortly after this episode, the Governor had to meet a delegation of Asians led by Bisseker, who asked him for an explanation of the racial discrimination at the heart of the Penang evacuation. He confesses in his diary that "it was one of the most difficult speeches he ever had to make", but he clearly attempted to divert the blame by adding that it was a decision taken without his knowledge. He added that he had given orders that, in future, European government officers would stay with the people to look after their needs regardless of the consequences.[77] This was quite untrue: none of the decisions regarding the withdrawal from Penang were taken without his knowledge.

The Penang evacuation was a further serious blow to everyone's morale, following as it did, and so soon after the loss of the *Prince of Wales* and the *Repulse*. Attempting to explain the calamity and play down the tactical impact of the loss, Duff Cooper broadcast to the population on 22 December. Unfortunately, instead of assuaging the people, his message compounded the problem by trying to reassure everyone that *all* civilians had been evacuated to safety. This was patently untrue; only the Europeans got out. The statement caused general uproar. From the minutes of the War Council meetings and Thomas' diary entries, debate on this absurd claim took up an unprecedented amount of valuable time. It led to the drafting and redrafting of a directive that was to be adhered to by all parties in the event of similar occurrences, a directive that, in any case, was now pointless.

After the war, in early 1948, Thomas was given a preview of the draft of the Penang episode that was to be included in the official history. In

---

[75] CO. 967/75. Thomas War Diary, NA.

[76] CO 967/77 Duff Cooper. Ibid., NA.

[77] Newspaper "Straits Budget", 25 Dec. 1941.

an attempt to salvage something from the harsh criticism it contained, he wrote a contrived version to its author, Major General Stanley Woodburn Kirby:

> The bad thing about Penang was its hasty evacuation by the whole of the European population with the exception of two or three who refused to move. The order was given by the military, and the civil government in Singapore knew nothing about it and would not have approved. This was made quite clear. We should have been able to point out the disastrous effect on morale of such a move. We stood for no racial discrimination (this should also be made clear) and my final telegram to the Resident Councillor dated the 16th read: 'In any evacuation, preference should be given to those who are essential to the war effort, without racial discrimination.' This order to the Resident Councillor came from me, and not Percival, as stated in the last paragraph of page 331. Duff Cooper was not in favour of the words underlined, but gave way. On December 23rd I received instructions from the Colonial Office supporting this policy: no other was of course possible if we were to retain any sort of respect.[78]

Woodburn Kirby ignored Thomas' version as quite inconsistent with the known facts.

On the east coast of Malaya, the Japanese made even more rapid progress because they met virtually no resistance. The British forces withdrew from Kuantan on 31 December, though they remained in position defending the airfield 9 miles from the town. At various points, on both coasts, the Japanese momentum was temporarily checked and heavy fighting took its toll in casualties on both sides. The Japanese, though, were able to replace their losses with fresh, trained units and this maintained pressure at every contact. They continued fighting day and night; they were able to rotate their front line troops with rested units from the rear. The Japanese army was determined and courageous, making its way through swamp and jungle using every means of transport available—trucks, buses, carts, horses and thousands of bicycles. These last enabled a silent approach and were also used to carry rations and reserves of small arms ammunition. This was a highly disciplined force

[78] Thomas Papers. Entry undated.

based on absolute despotism. It was inseparably linked with state religion and education.[79]

The British army, under General Percival, on the other hand, comprised an international medley coming from places as far apart as the UK, Australia, Malaya, Burma and British India. They fought under leaders divided by differences of nationality, outlook, background and political allegiance. Dietary differences alone added a huge administrative burden. They were armed and equipped as for a campaign in western Europe or the desert and relied on wheeled transport for administrative support, which in turn restricted them to roads and tracks and dependent on supplies of fuel and oil, a combination that created a logistical nightmare.[80] The main roads became vital supply routes. Inevitably, they became choked with endless columns of slow-moving trucks, obstructed by abandoned equipment and columns of refugees.

Military analysts almost unanimously agree that, at this point in the campaign, a strong Field Commander would have acknowledged the limited capability of his ill-trained forces, the grievous handicap of a shortage of appropriate equipment and, crucially, lack of air support. Such punishing circumstances called for a major strategic readjustment: a clean break from contact with the enemy, a lengthy withdrawal to well-prepared defensive positions much further to the rear. Heath proposed this very idea: that it was better to cut their losses and pull back over 300 miles to northern Johor into a properly sited, fortified and defendable location. This proposal was very much in line with that suggested earlier by Duff Cooper in the War Council meeting of 13 December. Percival refused to countenance such an idea. He maintained that it would mean giving up valuable territory without a fight, enabling the Japanese to use airfields closer to Singapore and facilitating attacks on Allied shipping, bringing desperately needed reinforcements, supplies and equipment. Moreover, it would leave the long east coast exposed and undefended. No

---

[79] David H. James, *The Rise and Fall of the Japanese Empire* (London: Allen & Unwin, 1951), p. 108. (Originally an ancient spiritual system rather than an organized religion, Shintoism became exceptionalist and militaristic at this period. After World War II, the emperor published a directive for the disestablishment of "state Shintoism" (1945) on the orders of the US Army.)

[80] Kirby, *Official History*, pp. 163–8.

one appears to have pointed out that Japanese aircraft had not attacked Singapore since the first night of the war and indeed did not again attack Singapore until their forces gathered in southern Johor.

On 18 December, what was to be the last formal Allied war conference was held in Singapore under the chairmanship of Duff Cooper. British, American, Dutch, Australian and New Zealand representatives had attended these infrequent gatherings. While they were intended to make recommendations for common Allied action, the conference did little more than discuss the situation throughout the Far East and keep abreast of developments and concerns in their respective regions. There was little more they could do; their pronouncements stated the obvious. The situation was bleak. More manpower and equipment was needed but, importantly, in this instance, they endorsed Percival's plan to hold the Japanese as far north in Malaya as possible to give time for reinforcements to arrive unmolested. Final *communiqués* went to each authority and, in the case of Duff Cooper, his went to the Chiefs of Staff in London and he added a passionate request for vital and urgent support.[81]

Feelings in the local War Council meetings ran high and became increasingly acrimonious. The senior civil members seemed less concerned with the direction of the war than with the trivia of bureaucracy and personal power. Duff Cooper, at this same point, took it upon himself to write confidentially, directly to Churchill. His letter was delivered by the hand of Captain Tennant, who was the captain of the *HMS Repulse* until it was destroyed. The letter conveyed his contempt of nearly every senior figure in both the government and the services. In his judgment, the Governor was a weak character whose opinions were a reflection of what the last person he talked to had said. In addition, he was served by:

> ... a sinister figure called Stanley Jones [Colonial Secretary] who is universally detested in the Colony, where he is accused of having been defeatist since the beginning of the war. His record in the way of preparations is certainly a black one—there are no air raid shelters, no trenches even, no tin hats or gas masks for the civilian population.

---

[81] CAB 66/22/22.

No preparations have been made for a system of food rationing, no registration of the inhabitants nor identity cards.

Duff Cooper added that he might later ask for empowerment to get rid of Jones and replace him with an "admirable man now in Kuala Lumpur called Hugh Fraser [Federal Secretary]". In a dismissive manner, he declared that Percival:

> ... is not a leader, he cannot take a large view; it is all a field day at Aldershot to him. He knows the rules so well and follows them so closely and is always waiting for the umpires whistle to signal the cease fire and hopes that when such a moment comes his military dispositions will be such as to receive approval.[82]

The letter[83] leaves the clear impression that, in his opinion, the senior figures in Singapore running the affairs of government and war were inferior people, supported by equally unimpressive subordinates, and that both the management of the country during the hostilities and the conduct of the campaign was incompetent. Conversely, although unspoken, this reflected the state of the relationships. Top officials seemed unable to discuss and resolve the most basic issues, were hypersensitive to perceived challenges to their dignity and were unable to put aside personal animosities and acrimony for the common good. By this stage of the war, the danger facing the country was ominous and getting worse by the day; still, petty bickering and inconsequential disputes dominated the agenda.

Air Chief Marshal Brooke-Popham handed over his portfolio of command to Lieutenant General Sir Henry Pownall on 23 December and, in a final gesture of authority before departing, he wrote an edict to senior air force commanders, expressing his dismay at the lack of determination and resolve shown by RAF personnel in the face of the enemy:

> During the last fortnight it has been necessary to order the evacuation of several aerodromes. It has come to my notice that in some cases the process has been carried out badly ... while there have been cases of

---

[82] CO 967/77 Duff Cooper, secret and personal letter to Churchill, 18 Dec. 1941, NA.
[83] Ibid.

gallantry ... there have also been instances where the air force appear to have abandoned aerodromes in a state approaching panic. Stores that will assist the enemy in his further advance have been left behind, material that is urgently required has been abandoned and a general state of chaos has been evident.[84]

In practically every instance involving the northern aerodromes the station staff withdrew without warning the army, who had the task of defending the airfields, and in the majority of cases the staff left so hurriedly that valuable stores, equipment and even prepared food lay unattended at their sudden departure.

On 26 December, the people of Singapore learnt that HK had surrendered the previous day, Christmas Day. On 27 December, Thomas called an extraordinary meeting of the Legislative Council.[85] The purpose was primarily to ratify the enactment of martial law which had, for some time, been the subject of impassioned discussion at the daily War Council meetings. Its introduction had been strenuously resisted by Percival on the grounds that he felt it unnecessary and that he could not, in any case, release a senior officer solely dedicated to fulfilling the role. Duff Cooper had supported the idea throughout because he felt the situation needed a supremo with absolute authority who would, through dictatorial powers, demand an instant reaction and response from everyone.

During this legislative meeting which, as it turned out, was the last one to be held, Bisseker grasped the opportunity to raise civil defence issues once again on the grounds that they had become matters of national survival. He demanded that the authorities start telling the people the truth, good or bad, about what was happening in the war. It was, he said, an endless series of shocks to learn—after the event—of Japanese progress down Malaya, while at the same time being reassured by the government that everything was all right and that the Japanese advance was checked. Moreover, he wanted to know, what were the lessons from Penang: "Had we learnt anything from the chaotic evacuation and if so, is it being promulgated to those who can prevent it happening again?" He catalogued civil defence measures which needed improving, including

---

[84] Brooke-Popham Papers 6/5/50. 24 Dec. 1941. LHCMA.
[85] Minutes of Legislative Council Proceedings, 27 Dec. 1941.

compilation of a list of qualified and skilled officials evacuated from upcountry, available in Singapore and in a position to help. Moreover, he believed that a central body was needed, with plenary powers solely concerned with coordinating passive and civil defence measures. His particular concern was that the country was not unified, not acting as a cohesive nation and, importantly, ignoring the energy and desire of the Chinese to play a major role in the current emergency. The Governor, without apparent conviction, tried to reassure Bisseker that these matters were in hand.[86]

On 29 December, Thomas left by car for KL, accompanied by his wife. He wanted to find out how the FMS administration was managing with the crisis. It was a brave and noble gesture at this time of danger, and recognized as such by most people. Shortly after his return, he chose to broadcast his impressions of conditions in upcountry Malaya, including how the people were coping. His account, however, seemed to reinforce the opinion of many that he had still not recognized the gravity of the situation. He avoided giving what everyone wanted to hear: an honest summary of the military situation. According to Cecil Brown, an American journalist with Columbia Broadcasting:

> He made an incredible broadcast. He spoke for about forty-five minutes about his tour up-country, but for almost the entire time he told about seeing a steam roller which got out of control, rolling backwards, and how the Indian driver finally saved it. The broadcast was also printed in the paper and took more than two columns .... He was not referring to any armed force, just talking about a steam roller.[87]

In his book, Brown describes the Governor:

> ... as an uninformed individual. A slave to service clichés, bromides and banalities. He lives in a dream world where reality seldom enters and where the main effort is to restrict the entrance of anything disturbing.[88]

Brown's acerbic and often prophetic comments in his own broadcasts to America about the state of affairs in Malaya were considered too

---

[86] Ibid.
[87] Brown, *From Suez to Singapore*, p. 388.
[88] Ibid.

dangerous for the morale of the Asian population. His accreditation papers were withdrawn in January 1942 and he had to leave the country.[89]

Earlier in the month, on 15 December, Duff Cooper, with the consent of the war committee, formed a separate civil defence advisory committee of which he was Chairman and which included, among others, the Inspector General of Police, Dickinson, and the Fortress Commander, Major General Keith Simmons. This committee met every day. While Thomas was visiting KL, Duff Cooper decided that civil defence was in urgent need of a dedicated, energetic professional to coordinate the whole range of civil defence issues. He identified Brigadier Ivan Simson—Percival's Chief Engineer—as the man for the job. Percival was not enthusiastic about the idea (nor indeed, initially, was Simson) but later accepted a compromise arrangement whereby Simson remained his Chief Engineer but had the additional role of Director General Civil Defence (DGCD). Simson had, for some time, been critical of the absence of almost any form of proper defensive fortifications and efficient civil defences measures and (reluctantly) believed the appointment might give him a late opportunity to correct this grave error. Duff Cooper then appointed Bisseker as Simson's deputy. When Thomas returned from upcountry and learned of these events, he was affronted that such a major governmental arrangement had been put in place without his consent. He recorded in his diary on 31 December:

> There is serious political trouble. Duff Cooper, being led by the nose by Bisseker and Seabridge [editor of Straits Times newspaper], demands a kind of Dictator for Civil Defence ... Duff Cooper has officially appointed Bisseker, and War Council has officially appointed Simson, all in my absence and without my knowledge, though neither has any authority to make any appointments under the civil government. I cannot agree to Bisseker; everyone would think I have gone mad, or had surrendered to DC [Duff Cooper].[90]

In the end, though most begrudgingly, he approved the appointments of Simson and Bisseker. Nevertheless, to demonstrate that he retained some power, he enforced strictures to Simson's authority. He limited his activities to Singapore Island only and, further, insisted that if anybody

---

[89] Ibid., p. 70.
[90] Thomas Diary.

challenged any of Simson's orders they had to refer the matter to the Malayan legal department and await its decision. Explicitly, Simson was prohibited from extending his area of responsibility into Johor because it was an Unfederated State and was not under the jurisdiction of the Governor:[91] to impose such a curb, on these grounds, when all around was remorseless military retreat fast approaching Johor, reveals a renunciation of reality. It was a decision which would prove fateful.[92]

The unpleasantness was further compounded when Simson and Bisseker approached Jones for help with finding a suitable office close to the civil authorities; they were rudely refused. Simson noted:"I was soon to discover that no civil servant would help Mr. Bisseker or anyone associated with him."[93] Simson and Bisseker eventually occupied the offices vacated by Duff Cooper after his departure.[94]

This trivia was acted out in Singapore while the British forces were engaged in a desperate struggle in central Malaya. The Governor was in bad humour, concerned more about the apparent usurping of his authority than the gravity of the danger. He broadcast a New Year's Day message to the people of Malaya; his remarks, in attempting to minimize the concern some people had about the introduction of martial law, caused more uncertainty than reassurance. He repeated his statement made at the Legislative Council meeting on 27 December:

> During the last few days Martial Law has been imposed in Singapore, but there is no need for anyone to worry about that. I signed the Proclamation because it was necessary to make certain that evil-doers against the State shall be punished quickly and it seemed to us that this could be best secured by the promulgation of Martial Law. I know you will agree that men who conspire against the State, which means their fellow countrymen in time of war, should be dealt with properly and quickly.[95]

---

[91] Ivan Simson, *Singapore: Too Little Too Late; Some Aspects of the Malayan Disaster in 1942* (London: Leo Cooper, 1970), p. 84.

[92] In a note in his papers Thomas has written: "The Sultan of Johore would not for a moment have agreed to a military officer exercising full powers in his State in respect of civil affairs" (Thomas Papers).

[93] Simson, *Singapore*, p. 84.

[94] Ibid.

[95] Legislative Council Proceedings, 27 Dec. 1941. Also Maxwell, *The Civil Defence of Malaya*, op. cit, p. 89.

Many people, within the country and outside it, interpreted his words as a claim that there were fifth columnists and conspirators at work. In reality—and as proved conclusively afterwards—there was no such organized element nor any fear of it. Thomas wanted to reassure the people that the new legislation was intended solely as a means of dealing expeditiously with the variety of circumstances that might arise during a state of emergency. Instead, he caused much alarm amongst the people, fuelled by journalists' conjectures about covert activities within the country.[96]

At this point, the authorities in London were beginning to sense that Thomas was in danger of losing touch with his responsibilities because of both the escalating pace of developments and his concern with administrative trivialities. The Secretary of State for the Colonies had to remind Thomas of the need to let Whitehall know what was happening. Thomas received a telegram:

> I regret to have to trouble you with enquiries at this time but I feel that I must ask to be kept informed of current developments affecting civil administration in the territories under your jurisdiction. For example where are the various Malaya Rulers? Is active cooperation of the Chinese community being organised in any particular forms either by government or spontaneously? [97]

There is no record in the Colonial Office files of a reply to this enquiry.

By 3 January 1942 the Allies had fallen back to the Slim River, about 50 miles north of KL. They had been forced to abandon Kampar which was acknowledged as the best and probably only defendable site in west Malaya. Recognizing the defence potential of the Kampar position, Simson—with the Corps Commander's agreement—proposed to Percival that he be allowed to construct heavy fortifications at Kampar as a fall-back position, and also additional defensive sites further in the rear. Percival adamantly refused to allow any such action on the grounds that "building of defences in rearward areas was bad for the morale of troops and civilians alike".[98] Even without such preparations, Kampar still

[96] *The Straits Times*, 28 Dec. 1941.
[97] CO 967/74. S of S to Governor, 2 Jan. 1942, NA.
[98] Kirby, *Singapore*, p. 168

managed to hold out for four days. The Japanese eventually outflanked the Kampar position by coming down Perak River in shallow draught boats, and made coastal landings using, among others, the flotilla of small craft abandoned in Penang.

The Slim River position was the next stage in the withdrawal, and was attacked in force on 7 January by tanks preceding infantry. Mines and obstructions impeded their progress for a while but eventually the Japanese breached the obstacles and a force of 20 tanks broke out and penetrated the British lines for 15 miles, inflicting heavy losses on the defenders. During the battle, seven British commanding officers were killed on one day alone and the 11th Division lost virtually all its artillery and transport. The position became untenable and Percival decided to give up central Malaya and make a substantial withdrawal to northern Johor. The Japanese entered an undefended and deserted KL on 11 January and found vast stores of food, maps and ordinance. Petrol and oil stocks had been set on fire. On Percival's instructions, the whole apparatus of civil government, European officials and residents were ordered to abandon KL, the last of them departing on 10 January.[99]

General Wavell had arrived in Singapore on 8 January on his way to Java to take up his appointment as Commander ABDA Command (American–British–Dutch–Australia Command). He selected Lembang in Java as the location of his headquarters. After calling on the Governor, he flew on to visit Heath in KL for a briefing and assessment of the military situation, and visit some units where possible. On his return to Singapore, he presented Percival with his own plan for the defence of north Johor. He had drawn this up without consulting Percival. As it turned out, the plan was quite different from what Percival had intended, and he was taken aback at the peremptory manner in which it was presented. It was clear that such imperious behaviour indicated that Wavell had lost confidence in Percival. Wavell had also been impressed by the energy and confidence radiated by the Australian General Bennett, and thought the Australians should play a greater role in the Johor defence plan.[100]

---

[99] Percival, official despatch.
[100] Ibid., p. 185.

Moreover, he put Bennett in charge of the forward areas on this briefest of acquaintance, upsetting the predetermined command arrangements and adding friction to the already strained relations between Bennett and Heath, the Corps Commander. Percival had no option but to redesign his plans in accordance with Wavell's wishes, including the withdrawal of the 9th Division from its defensive duties on the east coast. Ultimately, the defence of northern Johor followed a predictable pattern, except for one notable proactive action by the Australians, which seemed to justify Wavell's confidence in them. In their first engagement in the campaign, on 14 January, they laid a successful ambush near Gemas (Gemencheh), a position forward of the main defensive line. This allowed a vanguard of bicycle-borne Japanese infantry to pass over a bridge, before they demolished it. The trapped unit of nearly 600 were either killed or wounded.[101]

During the War Council meeting in Singapore that day, Duff Cooper announced the termination of his appointment as Minister Resident. He explained that, with the appointment of Wavell as Commander ABDA Command, the role he filled was absorbed into the new arrangement (see Chapter 2). In his diary, Thomas noted:

> In War Council Duff Cooper announced that Wavell's appointment had made his own unnecessary and he was leaving .... I said I thought his presence had been very useful ... Actually Duff Cooper's departure will be hailed with shouts of joy! He is suspect by most people; partly for his broadcast reference to evacuation of the "majority" of the population of Penang (well knowing it could only refer to the Europeans) and partly for the Simson-Bisseker-Seabridge racket. I shall see him out with a sigh of relief. A rotten judge of men, arrogant, obstinate, vain; how he could have crept into [Cabinet] Office is beyond me .... [102]

In the same entry, Thomas also mentions that Wavell had spoken with him about the military situation, and said that the "Japanese breakthrough at Slim River should not have happened if proper dispositions had been

---

[101] AWM 73 Series, Official History 1939–45. The Japanese Monograph Series 54 says simply: "our forces suffered many losses".

[102] Thomas Diary.

made. It was Paris's [he replaced Murray-Lyon] 11th Division. Poor wretched troops."[103]

What Thomas did not know was that, on 11 January, before his departure, Duff Cooper sent a final "Secret and Personal" cable to Churchill, which he copied to the Secretary of State for the Colonies and to Wavell:

> Before leaving Singapore I think it right to tell you that I believe certain changes in the local Administration are of first importance. A breakdown on civil side may well paralyse fighting services. There exists a widespread and profound lack of confidence in Administration.
>
> I believe simplest solution would be to declare a state of siege and appoint a military governor for the duration of the emergency. The obvious selection for appointment would be Fortress Commander, Major General Keith Simmons.
>
> I had already arranged appointment of Director General of Civil Defence, Brigadier Simson, who has done very well but whose hands are tied by Civil Authorities and who is not allowed by Governor to dismiss incompetent officials. He would continue to act under Military Governor.
>
> If these measures are considered too drastic, I would urge that Colonial Secretary should be replaced by Mr. Hugh Fraser who has done extremely well. I would also urge with equal candour that Mr. Jordan, Secretary for Chinese Affairs, should go. The Chinese who form the majority of the population of Singapore are behaving splendidly, have made up their internal quarrels and are united in their resolve to withstand the enemy. Mr. Jordan is unfortunately most unpopular with them he is tactless and rude and cannot assimilate the idea that some of those who gave the most trouble in the past and even the tougher communist element may prove most useful at present. The necessity for a Secretary for Chinese Affairs no longer exists ....[104]

Churchill's response to this damning cable was, first, one of dismay that conditions within the administration should have reached such a state without his knowledge; second, that Duff Cooper had not done something about it much earlier; and third, that the Governor must

---

[103] Brigadier ACM Paris had taken over from Major General Murray-Lyon, who had been relieved of his command.

[104] F.O. 371/31825. Secret and Personal cable to Churchill, 18 Jan. 1942, NA.

go.[105] His advisers consulted Wavell, who thought that such a change at that point would do more harm than good. He persuaded Churchill that replacing the Colonial Secretary with Fraser (Federal Secretary, ex-KL), could help resolve much of the trouble. Thomas was informed of this decision by cipher cable and, because of its confidential contents, he was advised to decipher it himself. His first reaction was to fear for his personal position. He thought he was dealing with an instruction for his own recall.[106] In his reply, he defended Jones vigorously and believed that Duff Cooper's time in Singapore was too brief for his judgement to be of value. The CO was adamant and Jones left Singapore shortly afterwards. Thomas' fearful reaction for his own position on reading the first few lines of the cable exposes a confused state of mind, certainly insecurity and arguably a loss of confidence. However, he had the honesty to disclose his insecurity to his diary.

The retreat of the British forces down the length of Malaya was relentless. At the daily War Council meetings the war's progress was discussed at length but little honest information was passed to the public. The majority of the population was ignorant of the real state of affairs. Most people relied on refugees, arriving in increasing numbers, for details of the fighting and the location of the Japanese army.

Simultaneous with the Gemas encounter, a serious threat was developing to the British left flank position at Muar. The Japanese had closed right up to the northern bank of the 600-yard-wide Muar River, posing a dangerous threat to one of the British main lines of communication south of the river along the Muar-Yong Peng road. On 16 January, they forced a crossing of the river and blocked the road. This part of the British front line was the responsibility of the newly arrived 45th Indian Brigade, made up of young, hastily trained recruits. The Japanese deployed their crack Imperial Guards Division against them. Adding to the brigade's ordeal, the battalions of this unit were given impossibly long frontages of river line to defend. Following their standard outflanking manoeuvre, the Japanese, in another amphibious hook, landed behind the 45th Brigade's position, with additional landings much further

[105] Prem. 3, 161/2. PM to Colonial Office, 12 Jan. 1942, NA.
[106] Thomas Diary.

behind, in the area of Batu Pahat. The 45th Brigade came under attack from the front, the west and the rear. The fighting was confused and intense but the predictable outcome was the almost total elimination of the 45th Brigade.

With the collapse of the Muar front, it was becoming obvious to Percival, as well as Wavell, that the strategy from this point on must be based on fighting delaying actions in Johor to give time for reinforcements to arrive. The final action would be the defence of Singapore. Wavell, on 19 January, instructed that plans for this eventuality be developed in full as soon as possible, but that they must be kept entirely secret and include the preparation of defences on the north side of the Island.

The trauma of battle and the confused, ferocious and devastating fighting was taking its toll on leaders at all levels through loss of commanding officers in battle and stress on the diminishing number of leaders remaining. Further, the almost non-existent communications between major formations resulted in senior commanders accusing each other of not resolutely sticking to their defensive tasks and making insidious accusations on the poor fighting quality of troops under their command. For the next eight days the fighting was almost unremitting, retreating periodically to turn and face the enemy. There were no longer any natural obstacles to help the defenders. The official British history was to record, most harshly: "During this period of eight days, from the 16 to 24 January, the Japanese out-generalled, out-manoeuvred and decisively defeated the British forces in Muar-Yong Peng-Batu Pahat triangle and won the battle for Johore."[107]

The Governor's entry for 21 January reads: "The behaviour of the military ever since the retreat began has been disgraceful ... if Singapore falls it will be the army's fault; they have been incredibly inefficient."[108] Percival issued orders, on 26 January, for the withdrawal of his forces onto Singapore Island; the move was to be complete by the night of 31 January. Thus, at the end of January 1942, Malaya was lost to the empire. It is not clear from Thomas' diary when he learnt officially that Malaya was to be abandoned.

Meg (Megan) Spooner, wife of Rear Admiral Jack Spooner, kept a

---

[107] Kirby, *History of the Second World War*, p. 467.
[108] CO 967/75. Quoted in Montgomery, *Shenton of Singapore*, p. 124.

diary. He was Commander of the naval base which, at this point, had no ships, but he was also in charge of the residue of British naval and civil personnel at the base. Meg Spooner's diary, quite unintentionally, sheds more light on the relationship between Percival and Thomas. While it is indiscreet and heavily flavoured with gossip, it shrewdly catches the atmosphere and urgency of events and the mounting tension at this time. In an entry on 27 January she wrote:

> Jack told War Council that soldiers were retiring onto the Island on the 30 January. H.E. [His Excellency] nearly passed out. Asked if it was true P[ercival] said "there is a possibility". J[ack] said "Possibility be damned your orders are out."[109]

This exchange reflects the nadir in affairs between the military and the administration. Peninsula Malaya was to be abandoned, and the Governor responsible for its governance and protection had not been informed. Percival either did not trust Thomas to keep this information secret or decided it was pointless to inform him.

Spooner himself was also guilty of arbitrary decisions. No doubt spurred by the imminent surrender of Malaya and mindful of the Admiralty instruction not to allow skilled personnel and vital equipment to fall into enemy hands, he evacuated the naval base without informing anyone. On 31 January, he ordered the entire European naval and civilian staff to leave the base and transferred most of them to Ceylon.[110] Thus, even before the last soldiers had crossed the causeway, the object of all the planning, striving and dying was deserted and left untouched for the victor. The following week, on 5 February, Thomas wrote in his diary:

> Brought up Naval Base evacuation at War Council with Percival and Spooner. Spooner said the military told him they wanted no navy personnel in operational area, so he took them all away. Percival said he had never been consulted in the matter at all. I said I could not understand how a great Base could be handed over by the Navy at the request of anyone but the G.O.C. Bretheron [personal friend of Thomas] says the whole place looks as if the staff left for lunch and never returned. Maps

---

[109] "Megan Spooner diary". LHCMA.
[110] Kirby, *Official History*, p. 365.

and plans left on office tables and so on. A dreadful thing.[111]

The Imperial Japanese Army assembled in Johor Bahru, waiting to launch its final assault with only a 1,000-yard stretch of water, the Straits of Johor, between it and Singapore. What remained of the British forces was in total disorder. The troops were exhausted, dispirited and, in many cases, without weapons and equipment, abandoned in the hurried and harried retreat. The army found no prepared fortifications on the much vaunted island fortress to offer it protection and behind which it could recover. There was no respite from the unforgiving foe. Its Commander had lost the confidence of his supreme commander. His strategy was regarded as suspect and, indeed, imperiously overridden by the visiting Wavell. In addition, Percival had a paranoia about preparing defensive positions along his withdrawal route. To compound the disorder, the leading British field commanders could not agree among themselves.[112] The Governor was barely consulted about the momentous events bearing down on his province and he had lost the confidence of his colonial masters in London. His government in Singapore was in confusion. The island was overwhelmed with refugees from upcountry. The public services, under increased demand and constant shelling, were struggling to provide minimum services. The fact that the Japanese were so close astonished nearly everyone because no warning had been given.[113] The government had not only lost the trust of the people but also paid the price for its less than honest propaganda. More astounding, however, internal bickering and individual hubris featured higher in importance than confronting its certain nemesis. The glaring answer to all this turmoil was identified months earlier and that was the establishment of a supreme head with total authority over all, a "supremo". The authorities in London, both civil and military, must stand accused of a serious failure of duty to grasp this problem early on and correct it. Their solution of two Cs-in-C was bewildering and unaccountable especially as neither had, in any case, complete, unfettered authority over the military forces in their area.

---

[111] Montgomery, *Shenton of Singapore*, p. 130.

[112] Allen, *Singapore*, pp. 188–201.

[113] Barber, *Sinister Twilight*, p. 158.

7

THE SIEGE OF SINGAPORE

When the last British battalion had crossed onto Singapore Island and the causeway connecting the island with the mainland was breached, an optimistic section of the civilian population of Singapore believed this final move would, in fact, be its saviour. The reasoning was that all British troops were now concentrated in a single garrison, which would present a formidable barrier against any attempt by the Japanese to invade the island. They were unaware, however, that there were no prepared defences anywhere on the island and, in particular, none along the northern shoreline. It was an area rarely visited by civilians because access was restricted to the military and, in any case, there was a coastal belt of mangrove swamp. With the arrival of the troops and the fleeing refugees from upcountry, the population of Singapore escalated from its pre-war 750,000 to about 1,400,000.[1] This placed not only the already stretched public services and food supplies under severe strain, but caused acute problems of accommodation. There are corroborated reports that the European population, even at this point, appeared to show little regard, or an illusory lack of concern, for the destruction around it, and the drama unfolding at its doorstep. The Europeans continued to carouse and socialize, visiting restaurants and hotels for dances, and even the Corps Commander, General Heath, is reported, in Meg Spooner's diary of 4 February, as attending a dinner party at the Spooners' house,

---

[1] The last decadal census was in Dec. 1941. There are no precise numbers for Jan. 1942, but government estimates arrived at the figure of 1.4 million. Thomas Papers.

together with "his young wife",[2] as if there were no threat to society at all. Meanwhile, the urgent question now facing the government was the matter of evacuating people, particularly European expatriates and, above all, wives and children, referred to in official correspondence as *bouches inutiles* (lit. useless mouths; in everyday jargon, members of the expatriate community was referred to as either "effectives" or "non-effectives"). In view of the Penang calamity, care was taken that equal account was given to any members of the ethnic community also wishing to leave. An immediate difficulty on the matter of evacuating the ethnic races was the strict and very modest pre-war quota of immigrants that countries such as Australia and the Netherlands East Indies continued to impose.

Within the administration, departments of government, with no instructions to the contrary, attempted to continue business as usual and some MCS officials evacuated from upcountry sought office space so that they could feel gainfully employed, even though in most cases there was nothing for them to do.[3] The War Council continued to meet daily but its deliberations were little more than listening to reports of Japanese progress. They were bereft of ideas and even in these critical times, arguments and disagreements continued to arise. The meetings also disclosed startling ignorance among senior government officers about the basic infrastructure and public utilities of their island.

The Japanese army meanwhile, between 1 and 7 February, gathered its amphibious landing craft, including tank-landing craft, assault teams and supporting units in various assembly areas around Johor Bahru, ready for the attack. The Japanese had complete air and naval supremacy and total freedom of action. Apart from occasional Allied shelling, their preparations were relatively undisturbed.[4]

There was confusion in the minds of most British expatriates about government regulations regarding evacuation. As early as September

---

[2] Spooner Diary. IWM.

[3] W.P. (42) 177, Apr. 1942. G. W. Seabridge, "Report to War Cabinet on the Fall of Singapore", NA.

[4] Clifford Kinvig, "General Percival and the Fall of Singapore", paper given at symposium "A Great Betrayal? The Fall of Singapore Revisited" (Singapore: National University of Singapore, 2002).

1939, on the outbreak of war in Europe, the government imposed a blanket ban on travel to ensure nobody could either leave or enter Malaya without an authorized permit. This control was introduced to prevent the departure of young European males anxious to enlist in the fight against Nazi Germany; many of these same young men held key appointments in the trade and industry of Malaya. At this critical time, it was essential not to lose them. The regulation was revised in March 1940 to allow free entry and departure to all women and children. Then, in June of the same year, to clarify any doubts, the government confirmed that exit would be refused to all males over the age of 18, that is, an age when they were liable for service with the volunteers or the local defence force. In October, all wives and children were allowed to come and go provided they were related to a resident European. Thus, the position at the end of 1940 was that no male European could leave Malaya, except in very special circumstances, but his wife and children could freely enter and leave the country.[5] There are no records to indicate that the authorities took the regulations to the next stage, that of discussing what organization, preparations and instructions needed to be in place for an emergency evacuation. At this point in 1940, the Governor was on home leave, and these regulations were introduced under the authority of the OAG, Stanley Jones.[6]

As noted in the previous chapter, in July 1941, Japan occupied Indo-China and the British government declared, in parliament, its concern that this action posed a threat to the region and, in particular, to Malaya. Historians analysing the events of the final days of Singapore identify the Japanese move into Indo-China in 1941 as the pivotal point at which the civil authorities should have acknowledged the gravity of the regional threat and begun their planning for the possible emergency evacuation of civilians. In Singapore, no such contingency plan was ever discussed and it is almost certainly because the Governor did not believe the Japanese would invade Malaya. In Thomas' opinion, if such plans became known it would not be considered sensible contingency planning but would instead be thought defeatist. It must also be said that the military

---

[5] Maxwell, *The Civil Defence of Malaya*, p. 91. See also CO 273/664/1 and CO 273/669/6.

[6] See Chapter 2.

authorities, with their misplaced optimism on Singapore's impregnability, did not stress the urgent necessity of any such action. However, shortly after Simson was appointed Director General Civil Defence, he did urge the Governor to evacuate the *bouches inutiles* as soon as possible. The Governor's approach was in stark contrast to that taken by the authorities in HK which, even before the outbreak of war in the west, had identified the evacuation of British women and children in an emergency as a major operation for which contingency plans were essential. There were, of course, notable differences: HK was highly vulnerable, with the Japanese already resting against its border with China. And it was never assessed as a defendable fortress. In August 1940, the situation was judged serious enough for the compulsory evacuation of non-service British women and children. It was certainly not a universally popular decision, was resisted by many and considered premature. Nevertheless, 3,474 evacuees were transferred without incident to a safe staging destination in the Philippines.[7] It did demonstrate, though, the considerable benefit of prudent contingency planning.

The Malayan exodus of evacuees, without sanction, had begun as early as 1 December. The announcement of compulsory enlistment for the volunteers alarmed the expatriate community and was followed, a few days later, by the enlistment of various local defence forces. This reaction gathered momentum down through the Peninsula, bringing many European expatriates from both the business community as well as government civil servants to Singapore. While the government continued to reassure people that this was no more than an elementary precaution, many realized it as a signal of great danger. Now the wives and children began to leave their homes in Malaya for Singapore to secure passage home to Europe. The influx increased weekly and began to overwhelm the reception arrangements hurriedly put in place to receive them.[8] The government set up a billeting committee to find accommodation for them in private houses, hostels, and any school or club building where it was possible to arrange bed and board. Similar assistance was given

---

[7] Fedorowich, "The Evacuation of Civilians from Hong Kong and Malaya/Singapore 1939–42".

[8] Shennan, *Out in the Midday Sun*, p. 248.

to the rest of the community, including the Eurasians, although, in most cases, each race was inclined to look after its own.[9]

The clamour for passage on ships leaving Singapore became a major administrative challenge. In response, the government created a committee headed by a high court judge, Justice J. Aitken, to decide the priority of requests. According to Duff Cooper, the Aitken committee never sat because the Governor "had been endeavouring to settle the whole matter without allowing the committee to meet, and behind their backs".[10] The selection criteria was to be absolutely impartial, with the provision that husbands who were required for national duty could not accompany their wives. When it eventually sat, the committee only resolved the question of whether a person and family were eligible to leave: it was then up to the individual to find a shipping line and book a passage. By failing to control the essential element of allocation of berths on available ships, the authorities caused great confusion and distress for many wives.[11] Not surprisingly, there were few requests from local nationals to leave; after all, Malaya was their only home.

By insisting on retaining peacetime bureaucratic regulations, the administration added untold complications and disorder. When women registered with the shipping lines for a passage they were asked for payment, or proof that payment was forthcoming. In the majority of cases these women had left their homes in a great hurry, without money, and could not contact their husbands for support, because their men were still upcountry either on essential work or conscripted for military duty. Adding to the turmoil was the demand that all passports must be in order and correct visas attached. This was an absurd request because many of the ships could not confirm, with any confidence, what their likely destination would be. Passengers were also told that UK regulations forbade them taking any currency greater than 10 pounds sterling in value out of the colony, and that all cash had to be reported to the exchange control. All personal jewellery had to be catalogued, and no one could

---

[9] Ibid.

[10] Fedorowich, "The Evacuation of Civilians from Hong Kong and Malaya/Singapore, 1939–42".

[11] Ibid.

take out a diamond larger than half a carat.[12] Dogmatically imposing these petty bureaucratic rules added untold distress and chaos to a procedure that was already failing to meet the urgency of the situation.

The ships that had brought supplies and reinforcements to Singapore were loaded with civilian evacuees and wounded service personnel for the return journey. On 21 January, Percival was able to cable London that 5,200 women and children were evacuated. There was, however, nearly the same number left behind still awaiting passage. So chaotic were the departure arrangements in the last week of December that several large transport vessels left the port either empty or only half-full.[13]

Air raids on Singapore, which had been heavy during January, continued unabated. Incessant artillery bombardment from the Japanese batteries in southern Johor added to the panic and misery. It was at about this time that the Governor's cipher clerk, Mrs Reilly, wrote in an undated diary entry that about 20 shells landed near Government House, with one hitting the grass bank outside, close to her office. Thomas was at the daily War Council meeting during the bombardment. When he returned, she told him what had happened. He retorted, "Shelled—rubbish—whoever said that!" He was taken to see the damage and was assured by the military officers present that it was indeed caused by 4-inch artillery shells.[14] It is difficult to understand that even with visible proof around him, the Governor still maintained this level of denial. The damage to the public utilities caused by these barrages was severe and continuous repairs to gas, electricity and water supplies were barely completed before they were shelled again. Control on consumption had to be imposed. Water gave the greatest concern. The two large reservoirs on the island, MacRitchie and Pierce, together could provide 14,500,000 gallons a day. However, the greatest volume of water, over 15,000,000 gallons a day, came from Johor Bahru. It was pumped from the station in Gunong Pulai via the causeway, thus the pipe carrying it was above ground. Indeed, the pipe was laid above ground for most of its journey across the island. When the causeway was breached on 31 January after

---

[12] Maxwell, op. cit.

[13] Fedorowich, "The Evacuation of Civilians from Hong Kong and Malaya/Singapore, 1939–42", op. cit.

[14] Diary of Mrs M. Reilly.

the final withdrawal, the pipe was also destroyed. This left the island dependent on its reservoirs. When this consequence was explained to the Governor he was rather surprised, as he noted in his diary on 30 January:

> Discovered in War Council that when the Johore causeway goes up, after our troops are across, the water mains supply to the Island will go too. I confess I did not realize the latter, and, as a number of taps have to be fitted to stand pipes which will have to come into use when house supplies are cut off, there is need for great haste. Curfew is being imposed from tonight from 9 pm to 5 am. More raids this morning and damage to godowns [warehouse] in the harbour area and in the coolie lines. Probably aimed at ships, such as the *Empress of Japan* which are taking away a lot of women ... Wavell for half-an-hour at 2.00 pm.[15]

It was a shocking admission that he did not know that the island's main water supply came from Johor. At the daily War Council meetings, discussions on the possibility of the island eventually being besieged would, almost surely, have included the important matter of the supply of reserves of food and water. The Governor's ignorance of the source of water begs the question: if he did not know where the island's most vital resource came from, why had he not asked?

On a more positive note, the food situation for the military garrison was satisfactory. There was meat for three months, flour and tinned vegetables for four months, and enough other items for five months. The stocks of food for the civil population would last for four months, with flour for six months and meat for nine months (a large proportion of meat comprised live animals under government control), which could also be used to supplement army stocks.[16]

When General Wavell visited the stricken army on 18 January, he instructed Percival to prepare a plan for the defence of Singapore. Percival's proposal for the defence of the island has been the subject of endless analysis by historians and military theorists, and the consensus

---

[15] Thomas Diary.

[16] Thomas Papers. In the Minutes of the War Council on 12 Dec. 1941 it was recorded that there was sufficient rice for 200 days. WO 106/2568. And Percival reported to Wavell in Jan. 1942 that there was a four-month supply of food for the population. See CAB 106/144, NA.

is that he got it completely wrong.[17] The most disputed and most glaring omission was his failure to allow properly constructed fortifications on the north shore of the island. His obsession, with which the Governor agreed, not to engender a rearward mentality by early defensive preparations, clouded his military judgement. Even though he must have recognized that his relentless retreat would lead, inexorably, to a final defence of Singapore, he still did not permit any construction work to that end. His senior engineer, Brigadier Simson, records a passionate appeal to Percival on 26 December, when the retreating army was still north of KL. He succeeded in meeting alone with Percival late at night to make his case for work to begin on defensive sites both in north Johor (a proposal supported by Heath), and on the north shore of Singapore. In his account of these events, Simson has described this crucial dialogue between two tired, exhausted men, one of whom—Percival—resented not so much the midnight intrusion of his Chief Engineer, but the inevitability of having to face the distasteful subject of rearward defensive sites yet again. With all the passion and conviction that Simson could muster, he told the general that there was still time, material and manpower for formidable obstacles to be erected. Defensive positions on the main Japanese thrust route and the likely assault beaches on the north of the island could still be prepared but he must begin right away because as the Japanese got closer, civilian labour would disappear. After hours of impassioned pleading from his senior engineer, Percival still refused and, when asked why, Simson got what he later described as the "frankly horrifying" answer: "I believe that defences of the sort you want to throw up are bad for morale of troops and civilians."[18]

In his new appointment, Wavell followed the progress of the battle in Malaya and Singapore with close attention in person. When, on 19 January, he instructed Percival by cable to prepare secret plans for a withdrawal onto the island he added:"Under cover of selecting positions for garrison of island ... you can work out [a] scheme for [a] large force and undertake some preparations such as obstacles or clearances ..." He was referring to the northern shore of Singapore and, as he had made

---

[17] See, for example, Kirby, *Singapore*, p. 222.
[18] Simson, *Singapore*, p. 69.

clear previously, with the Japanese approaching from Malaya it would be useless to hold troops in the wrong place on the southern beaches.[19]

In his post-war rebuttal, Governor Thomas claims to have been taken aback very late in the day when he was informed that there were no defensive positions or obstacles prepared on the north shore of the island. This statement is hard to believe, for it is safe to assume that it would most certainly have been one of the major topics, if not the main one, at the daily War Council meetings when all talk was then of the impending attack. He wrote to Wavell at the end of 1947, explaining that, soon after returning home in 1945, he contacted Bond (Percival's predecessor), to ask why no defences had been prepared either in south Johor or north of Singapore Island. He got an unsatisfactory answer and passed this onto Wavell, who replied:

> I do not know of course what secret reasons given to you for not constructing a defence line on the north of Singapore island were: but I do distinctly recollect that when I landed at Singapore on the morning of Jan 7th 1942 the first thing I asked to do was to inspect such defences. When I found that there were none I spoke with some asperity and I do remember Percival giving as a reason—I think the main one—for his neglect was that it would have a bad effect on civilian morale. My retort was that it would have a much worse effect on everyone's morale if its troops were driven into the island, as it seemed quite possible even then, and there were no defences. He also complained I remember of labour difficulties, which I said I found difficult to accept with such a large population in Singapore.[20]

On discovering the paucity of defence preparations on the northern shores, Wavell quickly warned London of this glaring omission. Later, when Churchill learnt of it, he wrote: "The possibility of Singapore having no landward defences no more entered my mind than that of a battleship being launched without a bottom."[21] To answer Thomas' question of no defences in south Johor, Bond was certainly in a position to do so. General Dobbie, Bond's predecessor, had ordered the building of a line of concrete machine-gun pillboxes across this area. He was

---

[19] Kirby, *History of the Second World War*, p. 316.

[20] Thomas Papers.

[21] Churchill, *History of the Second World War: Volume 4*, p. 43.

authorized a sum of £60,000 by London for their construction. With only £30,000 spent and the project half completed, Bond, on his arrival, and for no clear reason, cancelled the scheme. On defences "north of Singapore Island", it is uncertain if Thomas means northern Singapore or across the causeway in Johor which, as he pointed out to Simson, was an Unfederated State and he personally refused Simson permission to prepare any military defences in that location. Wavell certainly seemed to think that Thomas was referring to the northern shore of Singapore. In this same letter to Wavell, he (Thomas) says:

> I think I may say that from the day when the Japs [*sic*] entered Indo-China the average British civilian foresaw a land attack on Malaya but I am quite sure that none of us expected the route that took place and no one ever suggested it to me.

This is blatantly untrue. Every military Appreciation since 1937 pointed to a landing in the northeast, followed by a crossing of the Kra Isthmus to the west coast.[22] The main thrust south would be on this side of the country, parallel to the coast. This region of Peninsula Malaya offered not only the best terrain for the movement of large military formations but also a continuous road and rail network, and was a mixture of open and cultivated areas with a network of tracks and secondary roads which permitted the option of changes of axes. No discussion of the defence of Malaya after 1939 considered any other option a practical possibility. Furthermore, in the paper he submitted to the overseas defence committee in March 1940[23] in which he made a case for an increase in frontline aircraft, Thomas explained that all the storage facilities for reserves of food were per se on the west coast:

> In the present state of Malayan defence the Japanese can land in the Peninsula from the sea or enter it from Thailand ... [T]his means ... in most of the country on the western side of the central range of mountains, in Penang, and in Singapore. Supplies so stored would be at the mercy of the invader.[24]

---

[22] See, for example, ODC Paper No.15 of Mar. 1940, NA. Vlieland Appreciation. Personal papers 3.3.1. LHCMA.

[23] CO 967/75.Comments on O.D.C. Memo (40) 19 dated 20 Mar. 1940, NA.

[24] Ibid.

Most analysts agree with Percival's claim about the defence of the island, that, in general terms, with the forces at his disposal, there were only two options open to him. He could either disperse his resources around the island's coastal perimeter to prevent landings anywhere or, alternatively, have likely landing sites thinly covered, and concentrate his reserves ready for immediate counter attack at the point of landing. His final solution was an untidy compromise of the two. He dispersed valuable units to cover possible approaches from both the Malacca Straits on the west side and Mersing on the east side; additionally, he thinly deployed others along the southern coastline. He nevertheless considered that the main attack would be launched against the north coast, to the east of the causeway. Wavell agreed that the main assault would be directed at the north coast but strongly maintained that west of the causeway was the more likely objective.

The Governor continued to chair the daily meetings of the War Council and received increasingly depressing reports of destruction, damage and death. His diary also documents reports of drunken misconduct by British and Australian troops around Singapore to the point that he told Rear Admiral Spooner and the army's provost marshal to see that this behaviour stopped immediately: "We cannot allow our men to riot, and refuse it to Asiatics" [sic].[25] He also heard, first-hand, some depressing accounts of military actions in Malay from civil service colleagues arriving with the retreating army. In his diary of 2 February, where he catalogued the raids on the naval base oil tanks, godowns, railway station and oil barges, he added:

> Leslie Davies [previously his Private Secretary] turned up, having got through Johore with troops who were cut off, and then rescued by the navy. He said the Australian Air Force at Kuantan were dreadful. Panicked out at first bombing. I have heard the RAF panicked in exactly the same way at Alor Star.[26]

Until this point, Chinese labour had been reliable and essential for sustaining basic public services around the island and just as vital for providing the manual support at the docks. However, with mounting

---

[25] Thomas Diary.
[26] Ibid., passim.

aerial bombing in the dock area and loss of life increasing daily, the Chinese dockers were beginning to desert. Thomas visited the harbour area to see for himself the destruction and assess the problem. So concerned were both he and Percival because of the interruption caused to evacuating families and to the unloading vital military stores, that Thomas summoned the Chinese Mobilization Council and "told them plainly that unless they could prevent labour from running away they might find themselves doing coolie work for Japs [*sic*] at the point of a bayonet".[27] Two prominent Chinese businessmen, Lim Bo Seng and his brother, acted as liaison officers with the Mobilization Council and, even during the worst conditions, still managed to organize a daily workforce of 12,000 labourers. It was about this time that Thomas mentions meeting a deputation of Chinese communists, on the advice of the senior police officer, some of whom had been released from gaol, but all of whom had the common desire to fight the Japanese. They agreed to suppress their differences and join with Kuomintang supporters to do so. "They wished to form a united front with the sole purpose of resisting the invader."[28] Thomas gave his approval for the formation of a military unit under the command of Chinese-speaking John Dalley, a British special branch police officer. The unit was known as DALFORCE. In a broadcast on the following day, Thomas declared:

> You can realise the immense contribution which the Chinese can, and will, render to the war effort by mobilising themselves in this way, by helping to preserve the peace, by preventing panic, by assisting in the distribution of food, by producing labour, by joining the defence forces, and in a multitude of other ways. I have had similar assurances of unstinted co-operation from leaders of the Indian community, and I have, of course, accepted them with equal gratitude.[29]

Unfortunately, it was too late to take advantage of this initiative. Such a formidable grouping, with its passionate hatred of the Japanese, should have been conceived long before this point. However, as noted, the indigenous Malays were strongly against the training and arming of the

---

[27] Ibid.
[28] *The Straits Times*, 25 Dec. 1941.
[29] Ibid.

Chinese. There was now no time to train them, nor were there sufficient spare weapons to arm them all properly. In spite of these handicaps, they acquitted themselves bravely and ferociously and, after capitulation, took to the jungles of Malaya, where they later formed important resistance groups, ambushing convoys, destroying supplies and causing endless trouble to the Japanese occupation forces.[30]

A major complaint mentioned interminably in nearly every personal post-war account of this period was the lack of accurate information about the progress of the war. Indeed, there are intimations of disingenuous *communiqués* from the Government Information Office. People were endlessly bewildered by events overtaking them of which they had had no warning. In some cases, they alleged they had been led by the government into believing the situation was less serious than it was.[31] The newspapers complained the loudest and most frequently, demanding to know the truth. In their frustration with the authorities, journalists filed columns with reports of developments elsewhere in the international war scene. According to Cecil Brown, the Columbia Broadcasting System (CBS) war correspondent, they filed articles with headlines such as "Russians Pursue Nazis in Crimea", "Fresh Blows at Rommel's Forces" and "British Air and Sea Successes". They resorted to picking up any tidbit from outside the country or from international news agencies such as Reuters. In many cases, the information was out of date by the time it was printed. A notable example of withholding bad news was the report of the loss of the airfield at Kelantan. The Japanese captured this important aerodrome not long after they landed at Kota Bharu at the outbreak of hostilities (on 8 December) but no news of this event was disclosed until 22 December, when the military authorities issued the following *communiqué*:

> Owing the loss of aerodrome facilities in Northern Kelantan, and the vulnerability of the communications, it was decided some days ago to withdraw from the area north of Kuala Krai. This operation, involving a series of carefully co-ordinated movements by night, has been successfully carried out by the military commander concerned. During the last few days, the enemy's land and air forces have attempted to interfere with the

[30] Kevin Blackburn and Daniel Ju Ern Chew, "Dalforce at the Fall of Singapore in 1942", *Journal of Chinese Overseas* 1, 2 (2005): et seq.

[31] Brown, *Suez to Singapore*, p. 415 et seq.

operation. In spite of this, the greater part of the force and the majority of the stores and equipment have been brought out.[32]

The Kota Bharu aerodrome was one of the air bases hastily evacuated by the air force on the night of 10–11 December. By then they had lost most of their aircraft and were now vulnerable to continuous attack from Japanese planes flying from southern Thailand. The runways were grass and the RAF had left dumps of repair material close at hand (see Chapter 5). Moreover, by 22 December, when the *communiqué* was released, the Japanese were unquestionably winning the war, Kedah and Perlis had been lost, Penang had been evacuated and the Japanese army on the west coast had reached the Perak River. On the east coast, they were approaching Kuala Terengganu.

By this time, the government had appointed, as Director General Propaganda, Sir George Sansom. In the minutes of the War Council meeting on 18 December, he drew attention to the fact that:

> Foreign Correspondents [are] profoundly disturbed at the situation reports, which hide the true picture, and are not believed by white or Asiatic communities in the war areas. [The] situation is known to be bad up country; news seeping through to Singapore is causing loss of civilian morale.[33]

Duff Cooper, who was chairman at that time, replied that the first rule was to say nothing to help the enemy. Sansom agreed that security was paramount but pointed out, quite properly, that it was the military who decided which fighting details to disclose. Through its propaganda department, it was the final authority and vetted the journalists' copy before dispatch. However, it was with his department that the press had fierce and daily disputes. He emphasized that it was therefore vital that the current situation be honestly disclosed. It is not clear from the records whether the incorrect or inaccurate information that was given to the journalists was by design or blunder.

Military headquarters in Singapore suffered equally from scant information since communications with the forward formations were appalling. Their image was not helped, however, by the choice of retired

---

[32] Maxwell, *The Civil Defence of Malaya*, p. 78.
[33] WO 106/2568. War Council Minutes 18 Dec. 1941, NA.

naval officer Commander Burroughs (Chapter 2) as head of public relations, a man who readily admitted he had no experience for the job. The clash between press and censor began from the outset of the campaign. One of the earliest communiqués was misleading; it was also the source used for the Governor's incorrect statement to the Legislative Council on 8 December (Chapter 5). It implied that the first landing at Kota Bharu was successfully repelled and the few enemy troops which had managed to get ashore were rounded up, while their surface craft withdrew at high speed. This statement was quite inaccurate but never corrected. The Japanese, as described, successfully landed a sizeable force, then after a fierce but brief fight secured the beachhead and later took possession of the airfield. The departing craft were only returning to their base after effectively completing their part of the operation.

The *Straits Times*, like other newspapers, resorted to using outside sources for pithy and scant information, and made clear that its copy was reliant on external informants. For example, on 15 January, it printed:

> A British United Press correspondent, quoted by the B.B.C., says that the slaughter of the Japanese in some areas of the Malayan front is unbelievable. Our concentrated fire has mown down wave after wave of them and whole detachments have been blown to bits.

On 21 January it printed: "It is learned in London, said the B.B.C. last night that in spite of the enemy's claims, there are no Japanese troops within 76 miles of Singapore." And on 29 January it printed: "A B.B.C. broadcast this morning says that Ipoh is suffering incessant bombardment from the air."[34]

Each of these reports was wrong. There was at no time anything that could be described as wholesale slaughter of the Japanese forces; indeed, on 15 January, the British were desperately struggling in central Malaya around the town of Gemas. On 21 January, the Japanese were within 76 miles of Singapore. In addition, on 29 January, they were now within a few miles of Singapore, and Ipoh had been in Japanese hands for nearly six weeks. The Japanese, meanwhile, broadcast daily from the captured station at Penang with reports of their progress, often exaggerated, but as it was the only available source of current campaign news, the populace

---

[34] *The Straits Times*, 29 Jan. 1942.

listened and was confused. Government *communiqués* were composed of bland and vague adjectives such as "heavy and confused fighting", "enemy attacks in strength" and "local penetrations". The press correspondents continued their own daily battle with the censors. At that time there were 20 war correspondents in Singapore, all demanding they be told the truth about the conflict and, more importantly, allowed to print it. Brown, described by his colleagues as something of a maverick, endlessly challenged the censor about the content of his reports for CBS. He mentions in his book a number of occasions when his broadcast notes were rejected. On 29 December he wanted to say, within the context of his address, that "the British administration seems to have disappeared in these towns in the threatened areas". However, he was told all he could say was that "people have to shift for themselves as there is no European authority to turn to".

In a later broadcast, he wanted to explain the effect on the USA, of losing important tin-producing areas in central Malaya to the Japanese.

Fifty per cent of the tin-ore production of Malaya is now in Japanese hands ... The United States has been taking seventy per cent of this country's output. This means that the Japanese, by occupying the territory they have, are denying the United States thirty thousand tons of tin ore a year ...[35]

The censor cut most of this material and would not let Brown say that 50 per cent of the tin-ore production was now in Japanese hands; instead, he could say that "a large area, from which tin ore comes, is divided with the Japanese".[36] Brown's loss of accreditation and dismissal from Singapore on 23 January was because, the British authorities claimed, his broadcasts to America could be picked up in Malaya and had a depressing effect on local morale. On 5 January the editor of the *Straits Times*, G.W. Seabridge, summed up the situation in a passionate and reasoned leader article:

Malaya has now been in the front line for a month. The Northern Settlement [Penang] is in enemy hands, and fighting is taking place within 200 miles of Singapore. This island has been bombed on several

---

[35] Brown, *Suez to Singapore*, p. 382 and passim.
[36] Ibid.

occasions with 'slight damage to civilian property' and 'a few civilian casualties.' That is a reasonably accurate summary of all the people of this country have been told of the fighting that is going around them. Vague 'lines' have been mentioned and there have been sundry 'strategic withdrawals.' Such generalities provide a very flimsy basis indeed for detailed comment—so flimsy that we do not propose to attempt a task which is very nearly impossible of achievement ... The view we propose to put forward here is the view of the middle-class Asiatic who has been asked to help in maintaining morale but finds himself quite unable to do so ... If the newspapers and the newspaper reading public are to be any help in combating rumour, they must be supplied with the only things which are of the slightest value in carrying out the task. And those things are facts.[37]

The Governor took offence at many of the reports and remarks in the national newspapers but, specifically, those in the *Straits Times*, which persistently and pointedly accused the administration, and in particular the Governor, of failing to prepare and galvanize the country for war and now failed to tell them what was happening. This same newspaper and editor had, in pre-war years, warmly applauded Thomas: "He did well from the start. The business community found him approachable, friendly and sound."[38] Thomas now made it perfectly clear that he did not like Seabridge. The antagonism between them had rumbled on since well before the invasion and reached its nadir when Seabridge strongly endorsed Duff Cooper's appointment of Simson as Director General Civil Defence. The Governor claimed that this action made his position untenable.

No convincing reason can be found for the reluctance by the authorities, both the administration and the military, to keep the public truthfully informed of the real state of the war. Indeed there is the argument put forward by Elphick that if the real picture had been disclosed, a more measured and orderly evacuation could have been organized earlier, avoiding the late chaotic and perilous rush.[39]

---

[37] *The Straits Times*, 5 Jan. 1942. As reported in Maxwell, *The Civil Defence of Malaya*, p. 80.

[38] Quoted in Heussler, *British Rule in Malaya*, p. 252.

[39] Elphick, *Singapore*, p. 275.

Duff Cooper's early decree that no announcements were to be made that might be helpful to the enemy, seems to have assumed the authority of a rigid canon. With people having to rely on second-hand information, enemy propaganda and Japanese leaflets dropped by plane, all confidence was lost. The press pointed out that bad news was better than no news. When the truth was eventually known—an inevitability—the authorities would lose all credibility and had little chance of restoring loyalty. The ethnic Malay, Chinese and Indians, who spoke only their own language and lived in remote areas, were solely reliant on rumours that inevitably eroded all respect for their departing European bosses. Public confidence was further shaken when the Governor issued his fallacious memorandum in mid-January with the intention of infusing a sense of urgency in his civil servants. In allowing his directive to be made public, he hoped to reassure everyone that he was galvanizing his staff; instead it shocked them to learn that even at that late date such bureaucracy still existed:

> The day of minute papers has gone. There must be no more passing of files from one department to the other, and from one office in a department to another. It is the duty of every officer to act, and if he feels the decision is beyond him he must go and get it. Similarly, the day of letters and reports is over ... Every officer must accept his responsibility to the full in the taking of decisions ... The essential thing is speed in action. Nothing matters which is not directly concerned with defence, and no one should be troubled with it.[40]

Thomas had this instruction published in full in the newspapers on 17 January, and broadcast it himself later. By this date not only were Penang and Malacca in Japanese hands, but eight Malay States were also conquered and, in the final state, Johor, a desperate fight was underway. The public reaction was one of incredulity, with the *Straits Times* declaring that it was an appalling revelation two and quarter years late.[41] While causing dismay and despondency, this statement only confirmed what many had suspected for some time.

The Japanese assault on the island began on the night of 8 February 1942, and the Governor learned of it in a phone call form Percival. In

[40] *The Straits Times*, 17 Jan. 1942.
[41] Ibid.

turn, he passed a warning to Simson (DGCD) and the police, noting in his diary that shelling was disturbingly close to Government House and now, with an experienced ear, he was able to add "that it was the same 4-inch gun". At the War Council meeting in the morning (9 February), he learnt about the poor performance of the Australian contingent and later recorded in his diary: "[T]he Australians are not fighting well. They have been heavily shelled and many found wandering about the roads." Privately, he unburdened his frustration with the military hierarchy:

> Not easy to proceed with denial schemes when we are given no progress reports. Absence of personality in High Command most unfortunate. Percival doubtless good on paper but not a leader and his staff are small men. Simmons [Fortress Commander] is excellent and Bennett and Key are staunch fighters, but there is no one to whom the troops can look to. RAF much worse—Pulford nice but no more.

He also claims to have suggested to Percival that Simmons or Bennett become GOC Fortress with himself as GOC in C[hief] but as Percival explained, the fortress was now the only area they had. It made no sense and, in any case, they were both junior in seniority to Heath who would have to be first choice. Thomas added that Heath was a tired man who had retreated over 400 miles in a few weeks, and no one had any confidence in him. He then confessed in his diary: "we need someone really big here".[42] In spite of claiming difficulty over introducing denial schemes he nevertheless ordered the implementation of the civil denial scheme on 9 February, and controversially, without informing either Percival or Simson, ordered the withdrawal of all European technical staff from the Singapore Harbour Board installations on the following day. This latter order caused untold problems and virtually brought the one organization still working efficiently, to a halt. The hard-pressed army had to find manpower from its dwindling resources to keep the docks working. Defending this decision after the war, Thomas said that he was ordered by telegram, on 27 January, that all such men (and others) were needed in India. "I see no reason why the military should have been consulted."[43]

Not long after Simson had assumed his appointment as DGCD, he

---

[42] Thomas Diaries, op. cit.
[43] Thomas Papers.

recommended to the Governor that a phased scorched-earth policy be prepared. Thomas prevaricated and it was not until late January, by which time Simson had been appointed onto the War Council, that he got a decision. The plan was that the public utilities would remain untouched, and the civil administration would organize the demolition of rubber and tin stocks, radio stations, currency and, importantly, alcohol. Simson had also requested the destruction of 40 Chinese-owned engineering works but Thomas refused; such an action would crush Chinese morale. He agreed, however, to the destruction of 47 British-owned engineering plants. The demolition was eventually carried out by the military but in the face of strong and active opposition from owners and/or agents. By this point, there was little effective government authority and the military had to assist with the destruction of the other facilities which the administration had previously agreed were their responsibility.[44]

After only two days of fighting, the battle situation was quite desperate. Percival informed the Governor that "the Japanese had progressed more quickly than expected. 300 RAF ground staff ran away from Tengah aerodrome last night."[45] As Wavell had predicted, the Japanese had landed on the northwest coast of the island, an area held by the Australian 22nd Brigade (Brigadier H.B. Taylor). The reports from this formation were sparse and confused but it was clear that the Australians had offered little resistance. Their Commander, General Bennett, recorded in his diary:

> Word came through from a few men who escaped that 2/18th and the 2/20th battalions had been overrun. No word had been received from the 2/19th. All battalions were out of touch with [22nd] brigade. The enemy bombardment had destroyed all beach lights and beach guns and machine-guns and caused heavy casualties among gunners .... during the afternoon General Percival called and seemed very worried. [46]

The island consisted largely of plantations, jungle and mangrove but was flat, with very little high ground. Good roads radiated out from the city in every direction. In addition to the four airbases and the naval

---

[44] Simson, *Singapore*, pp. 97–9.
[45] Thomas Diary, 10 Feb. 1942.
[46] Compton MacKenzie, *Eastern Epic* (London: Chatto & Windus, 1951), p. 384.

base in the north, the only urban zone was the city, sprawled along the central area of the south coast.[47] In the important northwest region of Singapore Island there was a coastal belt of mangrove swamp which, with a minimum of preparation, could have become a formidable obstacle, but it was not constructed. In these conditions the confused, fluid battle and control of units and sub-units on the front line was chaotic, and in some cases non-existent, with subordinate commanders taking decisions without consulting their formation headquarters. The result was the abandonment of critical blocking positions for no clear reason and, in some cases, without firing a shot. The Australian 27th Brigade made the most inexplicable retreat. It was deployed to cover the causeway, alongside and to the east, of their compatriot 22nd Brigade. After learning of the plight of the 22nd Brigade and without waiting for instructions, the brigade commander (D.S. Maxwell) decided that the battle was already lost and ordered his men to pull back, leaving an alarming 4,000-yard gap in the forward defensive line.[48] When Wavell and Percival visited General Bennett early on 10 February, they found he had little information about the units under his command in the western area, and did not even know that his 27th Australian Brigade had also withdrawn in the night. Counter-attacks were ordered but in such confusion that they never materialized.

Later, on 11 February, Wavell flew out of Singapore after what turned out to be his final visit. Afterwards, he recorded in his despatches:

> I ordered Percival to stage a counter-attack with all troops possible, but I left Singapore on the morning of February 11th without much confidence in any prolonged resistance.[49]

Before departing, he called on Thomas for their final talks. In a rare display of emotion, Wavell repeated, "It shouldn't have happened." He believed the rot started with the poor deployment and defence, first at Slim River and later in Muar. He confessed that on his previous visit (30

---

[47] Farrell, *The Defence and Fall of Singapore 1940–1942* (Stroud, Gloucestershire: Tempus, 2005), p. 314.

[48] Kirby, *The War against Japan*, p. 383.

[49] General Sir A. Wavell, "Despatch by Supreme Commander ABDA on Operations in South-East Pacific.15 Jan 42 to 25 Feb 42" (London: HMSO, 1948), para. 27.

January) he had considered relieving Percival of his command "but, it's not easy to get leaders nowadays".[50]

Thomas now decided that the all-important ciphers, less one, be removed right away to the safety of the British Consul General in Batavia. His cipher clerk, Mrs Reilly, was ordered to leave Singapore because, if captured, the nature of her work would have made her the object of interrogation. She noted in her diary that when she informed the Governor of this order, he did not believe that events were so serious for such an early, hurried departure. When she explained that the Japanese had reached the area of the golf course (about 5 miles from Government House), he thought this was incorrect and that they were still many miles away (the Japanese arrived outside her house that afternoon). Mrs Reilly recorded that he acknowledged that:

> the Japanese had broken through the Australians, but that a small party of A&SH [Argyll & Sutherland Highlanders] had been rushed to the breach and they together with the Indians on the left and right flanks, had pushed the Japs [sic] back two miles.[51]

Thomas then added: "The Australians certainly have let us down— right from the beginning when they panicked from Kuantan Aerodrome and left all their planes on the ground intact for the Japs to seize."[52] In a later entry in the diary, Reilly wrote:

> [T]he Air Vice Marshal [Pulford] came into the room. I was shocked at his appearance. He was obviously in a state of nervous tension—almost mental it appeared to me—and he kept walking up and down the room muttering to himself and thumping tables and chairs as he passed and every now and then stopping in front of me and saying "this is a dreadful state of affairs—the whole show is damnable. An Air Force with no planes and no aerodrome—what the hell can we do. What can we do!"[53]

On 30 January, Pulford had been ordered to reposition the few fighter aircraft, less one squadron, to the relative safety of the Netherlands East Indies. On 11 February, Wavell ordered the transfer of the remaining

---

[50] Montgomery, *Shenton of Singapore*, p. 131.
[51] Reilly Diary.
[52] Ibid.
[53] Ibid.

aircraft; by the time of Reilly's diary entry there were no RAF aircraft remaining on the island and only limited sorties were being flown from airfields in Palembang, Sumatra.

The night of 10–11 February was disastrous. The Japanese, with tank support, broke through the weak and poorly defended positions guarding the main north-south arterial road and onto Bukit Timah Heights (177 metres). Then, oddly, they halted. It is generally agreed that had they continued, the way was open to them to enter the city area on the morning of 11 February. After the war, it was learnt that, at this point, the Japanese were in danger of out-running their administrative support; they were particularly short of artillery shells and small arms ammunition and had to pause for resupply.[54] Within the Allied camp, confusion and recrimination reigned. In attempts to move units and sub-units from one sector to another, either in support of hard-pressed troops, to fill gaps or endeavour a counter-attack, coordination and communication was almost non-existent. Many subordinate commanders, at any one time, were not sure under whose command they belonged. Orders were now reliant upon despatch riders and liaison officers.[55]

The British tactics during the island fight were little different from the pattern followed during the retreat down Malaya. There were no innovative responses to the relentless Japanese thrusts: when a position was breached, units fell back to a mythical line drawn on a map and from there to another until they arrived a few miles beyond the city limits. With the garrison holding this shrinking perimeter, the administrative situation was becoming desperate. About a million Asians were confined in a semi-circle with a radius of roughly 4½ miles from the waterfront (approximately an area of 30 square miles) and, because of their proximity to the military, were clearly regarded by the Japanese as a legitimate target for aircraft and artillery fire. The area was a dense mass of military transport, mostly abandoned, and confused troops wandering without direction. The streets were littered with putrefying corpses, the numbers overwhelming the auxiliary removal services. Bomb-damaged and collapsed buildings, entombing more dead bodies, and cratered roads

---

[54] Tsuji, *Singapore*, p. 260.
[55] CAB/66/26/44. "Report on Operations in Malay and Singapore. 27 Jul 1942", NA.

completed the grim picture. Both the main water reservoirs were now in Japanese hands, although they had not cut the supply: it was thought that they allowed a continued supply for fear of inheriting a typhoid epidemic. The garrison's food reserves were down to seven days, due to the loss of the Bukit Timah depots. Petrol was scarce, but reserves of ammunition were adequate.[56] A failure of pre-war civil defence planning for food reserves now manifested itself. In the dock area, 64 godowns had been used to store thousands of tons of flour, rice and other commodities. This was a serious planning error because the docks were an obvious and legitimate military target. In January, too late, Simson tried to rescue the situation, but a lack of labour, transport and alternative storage facilities prevented any substantial recovery of essential stocks. Forty-six godowns were destroyed including their contents; the remainder were seriously damaged and much of the contents ruined.[57]

The government no longer functioned as a governing body. I have not found any record or reference to the possibility of establishing a government in exile, as was the case in Burma where the Governor, Dorman-Smith, withdrew with a number of his staff to Simla, India.[58] However, in fairness and with hindsight, finding a suitable island or other location in the region outside Japanese reach would have been almost impossible, added to which Thomas and his wife had made clear they were not going to leave Singapore.[59] They refused an offer from Wavell, during their farewell meeting, to go with him to Java. Even so, it is odd that such a possibility does not appear to have been even discussed.

Civil servants who handled the evacuation and those trying to maintain public utilities continued to work and provide as much help as conditions permitted. The major offices of state and the municipal departments no longer existed. The Governor alone, with his immediate staff, worked from Government House because it was nigh impossible to travel with certainty around Singapore. Government House also provided refuge for a number of evacuees and itself became the target of incessant

[56] Kirby, *Singapore*, p. 245.

[57] Ibid.

[58] Jon Latimer, *Burma: The Forgotten War* (London: John Murray, 2004), p. 321 and passim.

[59] Montgomery, *Shenton of Singapore*, p. 138.

bombing and shelling. It was hit several times, resulting in the death of loyal servants and members of the military guard. Governor Thomas had refused several requests to move to a safer area of town; however, his wife Daisy had now fallen ill with dysentery. By 13 February, even Thomas agreed that the building was uninhabitable; he moved that day into two rooms in the Singapore Club, which was located in the Fullerton Building on the waterfront. The War Council had ceased to exist, having held its final meeting on the 10 February. Percival kept Thomas informed of the military activity, making personal visits as the public telephone system no longer worked. On 14 February (the day before final surrender), he told Thomas that the position was no worse and therefore they would carry on.[60] On the vital matter of the water supply, Percival warned Thomas that such was the damage that the supply had to be severely restricted and might last no more than 48 hours. Thomas, in turn, informed the CO:

General Officer Commanding informs me that Singapore City now closely invested .... Water supplies very badly damaged and unlikely to last more than twenty-four hours. Many dead lying in the streets and burial impossible. We are faced with total deprivation of water, which must result in pestilence. I felt it my duty to bring this to the notice of the General Officer Commanding.[61]

On 13 February, the frenzied evacuation of civilians continued. It was to be the last day of officially controlled evacuation and thus labelled Black Friday.[62] Japanese aircraft unremittingly blocked the departure of ships by bombing, machine-gunning and then pursuing them at sea. Some harrowing attacks sank a number of vessels that had cleared Singapore and made it to the open sea, with a huge loss of life.

In the bureaucratic bedlam throughout this time, an unpleasant accusation was levelled against Simson. He was allocated 300 places out of the final 1,200 evacuees and agreed they should be reserved primarily for young technical staff from the MCS, especially the public works department (PWD) whose experiences and expertise, it was judged, would be invaluable elsewhere. Out of the odd assortment of 40 vessels

[60] Thomas Diary.
[61] Quoted in Barber, *Sinister Twilight*, p. 229.
[62] Ibid.

remaining for the final departure, Simson was assigned 13 of them. His major problem, however, was to get the message to the selected names. With no communication and people being forced to move frequently to avoid bombing and due to the ever-changing military front, many of those selected could not be contacted. Rather than waste these valuable places, Simson, together with Bisseker, decided to issue their own permits to those most desperate, even if they did not meet the PWD criteria. Without consulting the Governor or the Aitken committee they issued permits to the old, and to women and children. Some 320 passes in all, signed by Simson, were given to others to distribute, but with first call to as many DGCD staff as possible. Simson refuted the allegation made later by the Governor that Bisseker took care to make sure he was one of the fortunate. Simson states categorically, in his book, that he expressly ordered Bisseker to leave and, what is more, did so with Thomas' agreement.[63] Among those with permits to evacuate were both Rear Admiral Spooner and Air Vice Marshal Pulford.

This episode and similar badly managed arrangements, all caused by shocking indifference to contingency planning, left the way open to all sorts of acrimony and accusations of favouritism. All of Simson's 13 vessels which departed Singapore on 13 February were sunk with a heavy loss of life; both Spooner and Pulford later perished, after being forced to make for an uninhabited island. Bisseker survived and eventually returned to England.[64]

Until the very end, there were astonishing incidents of staggering incompetence and intransigent bureaucracy: the Chief Officer of the SS *Empire Star* ordered off his ship a number of wives (about 40) together with their children, when it was discovered they did not have the correct permits.[65] By 15 February, when Singapore surrendered, over 10,000 women and children had been evacuated: 7,174 Europeans, 2,305 Indian and 1,250 Chinese. About 200 European women and children were left behind, most of whom ended up in captivity.[66]

---

[63] Simson, *Singapore*, p. 85.

[64] Simson Papers. Correspondence Simson/Bisseker 1957. LHCMA.

[65] K. Fedorowich. "The Evacuation of Civilians from Hong Kong and Malaya", conference paper (Singapore: National University of Singapore, 2012).

[66] Ibid.

Throughout the fighting on the Island, Wavell continuously implored Percival to fight to the last and asserted that there should be no thought of surrender while there were soldiers to fight and ammunition to fight with. Wavell, in turn, had been subjected to pressure by Churchill to ensure that Percival not be allowed to consider capitulation, that he should only finally succumb at the end of a tenacious siege, which embodied all the doggedness and resourcefulness of British arms. Churchill claims that it was mid-January 1942 when he first became aware of the lack of prepared defence in north Singapore. He cabled Wavell on 14 January and enquired "[W]hat are defences and obstructions on landward side?"[67] Wavell replied:

> Until recently all plans based on repulsing seaborne attack on island, and holding land attack in Johore or further north, and little or nothing was done to construct defences on [the] north side of island to prevent crossing of Johore Strait ...[68]

Churchill sent a minute to General Ismay to be brought up at the COS committee:

> I confess to being staggered by Wavell's telegram ... merely to have seaward defences and no forts or fixed defences to protect their rear is not to be excused on any grounds .... I warn you this will be one of the biggest scandals that could possibly be exposed ...[69]

He then listed ten measures needed for defending the northern shore. Seven of the ten points quite clearly came from an earlier report by Simson that had been sent to London, recommending these same preparations.[70] In a cable on 20 January to Wavell to ensure there was no ambiguity. He said:

> I want to make it absolutely clear that I expect every inch of ground to be defended, every scrap of material or defences to be blown to pieces

---

[67] PREM. 3. 169/2. 15 Jan. 1942, NA.

[68] Ibid.

[69] Sir Winston Churchill, *The Second World War, Volume 4: The Hinge of Fate* (London: Cassell, 1951), p. 44.

[70] CO967/77. The Simson list was compiled for Duff Cooper who sent it to Churchill, NA. Also quoted in Barber, *Sinister Twilight*, p. 105.

to prevent capture by the enemy and no question of surrender to be entertained until after protracted fighting in the ruins of Singapore City.[71]

With these imperatives ringing in his ears, Percival must have been confused by the contradiction between the scorched-earth policy demanded by his authorities, with all this implied regarding the destruction of all military materiel, and on the other hand the demand that he continue fighting to the end.[72]

On Wavell's return to Java after his final visit on 11 February, when he recognized that the end in Singapore could not be far off, he cabled the prime minister:

> Battle for Singapore is not going well. Japanese with their usual infiltration tactics are getting on much more rapidly than they should in the west of the island. I ordered Percival to stage counter-attack with all troops possible on that front ... everything possible is being done to produce more offensive spirit and optimistic outlook. But I cannot pretend that these efforts have been entirely successful up to date. I have given the most categorical orders that there is to be no thought of surrender, and that all troops are to continue fighting to the end.[73]

From the many eyewitness accounts made known later, there was a serious and noticeable deterioration in the morale of the troops engaged in the final struggle. Barely trained soldiers of the reinforcing 18th Indian Division and other units, which had been arriving during January, were committed to battle against a seasoned enemy without, in some cases, essential equipment, and no chance to adjust to a tropical environment. Many of these reinforcements had been at sea destined for other theatres, primarily the Middle East or Burma; they arrived in Singapore very bewildered and disoriented and were immediately deployed onto the front line. Reports of the shameful behaviour of Australian troops in particular caused serious concern. They had run away from the fighting and were seen wandering half-dressed, unarmed and drunk around the city precincts.[74] They commandeered private cars to get to the quayside

---

[71] Ibid.

[72] See, for example, Kinvig, *Scapegoat*, Chapter 18, loc. cit.

[73] Kirby, *The War against Japan*, p. 388.

[74] Report given by Percival at War Council and recorded in Thomas Diary, 9 Feb. 1942.

to board ships, pushing aside women and children in the process. J. Brash, a government servant who escaped to Bangalore, wrote a letter to a relative in Australia:

> [T]he one man who could tell the truth but instead has told a pack of lies is Gordon Bennett. The one and only reason for the sudden collapse of the Singapore defences was the Australian troops. That Singapore might have fallen in any event after a long struggle may be true, but if on Monday night, Tuesday morning [9/10 Feb] the Australian troops who were allotted the task of holding the Bukit Timah Road had not just thrown down their arms and run into Singapore it may have been a very different story ... It really was disgusting performance. Why they were given the Bukit Timah god knows after the pitiful performance at Batu Pahat where they just collapsed. Anyway they broke into all the houses on the way into Singapore and those that came into ours, we asked if they would like tea or breakfast and they said no! no! we don't want to wait all we want is ships to take us away. I have never seen men such cowards and so thoroughly frightened.[75]

Mrs Reilly gave examples of the complete breakdown of leadership, poor communication and misinformation. She wrote later of her last journey with her husband, who drove her from home to Government House, where she was to decipher an urgent telegram from London. On the way she saw "hundreds and hundreds of Aussies straggling along the Johore – Singapore main road – others sitting on the sidewalks, most of them clad only in shorts – no arms – no equipment". Her car stopped and gave a lift to two soldiers who asked Reilly's husband if it was true that the British forces were going to surrender when the Japanese reached the Botanic Gardens. If this was true, they felt there was little point in continuing to fight and lose more lives. After strongly rebuffing such nonsense, Mr Reilly asked them to speak to their officers to put an end to such rumours—only to be told that most of the officers had already left.[76]

On 13 February, with the garrison now within the final crowded perimeter and Bukit Timah and the main reservoirs in Japanese hands, Percival called a meeting of his senior commanders and principal staff

---

[75] W.O.106/2550B. Letter, Brash to Brash, 3 Mar. 1942, NA.
[76] Reilly Diary. 91/14/1. Op. cit.

officers to discuss the situation.[77] The Governor was not included in these talks. Percival first debated the possibility of a last, all-out counter attack to attempt to retake Bukit Timah. No one was in favour; it was felt there was little chance of success, the troops were exhausted and their morale was rock-bottom. Heath and Bennett advocated capitulation. Both argued that if the Japanese troops entered the city area they would run amok and the population would be subjected to the same havoc suffered by Nanking. Nevertheless, with Wavell's strictures in the forefront of his mind and despite the gravity of the situation, Percival decided to continue the struggle. He had, in fact, warned Wavell the day before of the dire situation and asked for discretionary powers to decide whether to surrender. Wavell, clearly not wanting to be the architect of such an important decision, urged him to continue to inflict maximum damage on the enemy, if necessary in house-to-house fighting: "Where water supply exists for troops they must repeat must go on fighting. Your gallant stand is serving its purpose and must be continued to the limit of endurance."[78]

Percival visited the Governor at the Singapore Club at about 10.30 am the following day to brief him on the latest state of affairs. It is safe to assume that the grave military situation was discussed and even the question of possible surrender, but in his diary Thomas alludes only to his great concern about the danger of an epidemic if the water was suddenly cut off.[79] Certainly, the dwindling volume of available drinking water was a serious concern, but this was the result of damage to the pipes carrying the water rather than the supply being disconnected. Percival spent much valuable time in these final hours dealing with the potential water crises, including calling a meeting at the offices of the Chairman of the municipality. While not wishing to minimize the gravity of this issue, it begs the question whether this was not a matter best left to the Chief Engineer and his team, leaving Percival free to deal with vital battle matters.

At 9.30 am on 15 February, Percival again held a conference of the senior commanders and principal staff officers at his headquarters at Fort Canning. The only member of the civil government present was

---

[77] CAB/66/26/44. Report titled "Operations in Malaya and Singapore" drawn up by Major Thomas, on instructions of Wavell.

[78] Kirby, *The War against Japan*, p. 411.

[79] Thomas Diary, op. cit.

the Inspector General of Police, Dickinson. Percival began by listening to a battle situation report, which described how little enemy activity there had been during the night. On the administrative side, he learned that while there were enough reserves of food to last for several days and ammunition, though short, was not by any means exhausted, the greatest danger was the failing water supply. He returned to the options: either go onto the offensive in a last effort or surrender. The formation commanders unanimously agreed that a counter-attack was impracticable. Percival then agreed that he would capitulate. A vignette, described by a staff officer, Major Cyril Wilde, who was note-taker at this final meeting, was his description of Bennett. After the surrender decision had been agreed on and the discussion had moved onto the practicalities, Bennett said, without convincing anyone, and quite out of context, "Maybe we should try one last counter-attack." The idea was received in silence; most believed he said it purely for the historical record.[80] By 11.45 am, Percival was at the Singapore Club where he informed Thomas of the decision. Afterwards he sent a final signal to Wavell, following which all communication with Singapore ceased:"Owing to losses from enemy action, water, petrol, food and ammunition practically finished. Unable therefore to continue the fight any longer. All ranks have done their best and grateful for your help."[81]

In the last hectic hours before the agreed time of ceasefire (to be at 8.30 pm that evening, 15 February), Thomas and his few staff spent the time trying to put in place arrangements for their incarceration, making final administrative decisions and cabling London before communication ended. He also drafted a statement with the agreement of the Japanese. It was to be published in the following day's newspapers and broadcast by him, explaining the implications of the surrender to the public and what the Japanese now expected of them. On the question of political protocol, he was determined—unlike Sir Mark Young, the Governor of HK who surrendered the Crown colony unconditionally—that it should be understood by the Japanese that it was a surrender by the British military forces; it was not the Crown Colony of the Straits Settlements, and that he

---

[80] C. Wilde, "Note on the Capitulation of Singapore", quoted in Allen, "The Surrender of Singapore", p. 178.

[81] Kirby, *The War against Japan*, p. 415.

as Governor would not sign any instrument of surrender. However, he sent a representative to the meeting: Hugh Fraser, the Colonial Secretary.[82]

Not everyone seems to have been aware of imminent surrender. John Forrester, a volunteer who previously worked for the trading firm Harrison & Crosfield, recorded:

> We were sitting in a compound owned by a Chinese millionaire with our Bren carriers all around us and thinking what a peaceful time it was when somebody said "Oh, we've surrendered." We just couldn't believe it, because there was plenty of water, and our Bren carriers were full of petrol. We thought the man who'd brought the news about the surrender was some fifth columnist and somebody even suggested shooting him. We were particularly amazed and dumbfounded because, although we had been to various corners of Singapore Island, we had never actually seen a Japanese or fired a shot in anger. We had done nothing worthwhile to stop the capture of Singapore. We had done nothing.[83]

As this chapter has shown, relations between the civil and military authorities reached their nadir. Neither side trusted the other: the civil authorities raged against the incompetence of the military and the military, in turn, had no respect for a government that had lost control of the most basic functions of civil administration as well as the confidence of the people. Exactly 70 days after landing in northeast Malaya, one of Britain's most important overseas possessions had fallen into the hands of the Japanese enemy. A pitiful, badly managed campaign came to an end. In their pre-war planning, the Japanese had calculated that the operation would take 100 days; they had achieved their objective, even to their own great surprise, in considerably less than that. Their staggering success was achieved partly by maintaining a ceaseless momentum with unremitting pressure. The Japanese soldiers were highly motivated and faced poorly trained and inadequately prepared troops. In addition, to a significant degree, the riven British administration was unable to prioritize its responses to Japanese aggression and unable to coordinate both the civil tasks of protecting a country, the people and its resources, with the military aim of defending a naval base.

---

[82] Montgomery, *Shenton of Singapore*, p. 143.

[83] Charles Allen, *Tales from the South China Seas: Images of the British in South-east Asia in the Twentieth Century* (Preston, Lancashire: Abacus, 1990), p. 263.

8

AFTERMATH

The loss of the "Impregnable Fortress" so swiftly, and as seen from Britain, so easily, was unprecedented in the annals of British history. In spite of the increasingly ominous portent throughout the campaign, the end stunned the British nation and the watching world. Conversely, Japan's swift success brought with it the considerable challenge of both protecting what it had gained and rebuilding the damaged countrywide infrastructure to provide the resources it so badly needed to sustain their war effort. It also needed to restore urgently the agriculture and manufacturing base of the country to provide both work and food for the people that were now its responsibility. It was a challenge for which the Japanese were ill-suited, with their inherent arrogance, disdain for the other Asian nations, hatred of the Chinese and lack of previous experience. The expansion of Japan's Far Eastern empire had been achieved sometimes under the pretext of a Greater East Asia Co-Prosperity Sphere, but mostly by force. The Japanese had no experience, or indeed any understanding, of benevolent rule. What the sword had gained was to be administered by oppression. Masanobu Tsuji, General Yamashita's operations officer, admits, "[N]o plans had been discussed for the administration of the occupied territories. This question should have been settled in advance."[1] Following an acrimonious navy/army debate about administrative responsibility, it was decided that it was to be an army responsibility, with the Minister for War in overall charge.

---

[1] Tsuji, *Singapore*, p. 23.

Immediately following the ceasefire, surviving British senior officials, in both the military and civil organizations, took it upon themselves to re-establish a semblance of authority in the war-torn island. The most serious worries were the outbreak of disease, burial of the dead and widespread looting, not just by the civilian residents, but also service personnel. These self-appointed leaders also set about trying to restore the more vital public services and utilities and impose some order on a suddenly leaderless people.[2]

In nearly every post-war account of the day of surrender, the return of silence, following the cessation of bombing and shelling, is the first and most common recorded impression. The bomb-damaged city and its precincts were eerily quiet and empty.[3] Slowly and cautiously, people emerged from their refuges to examine their devastated surroundings and experience the first taste of Japanese authority. At first, there was little evidence of the victor's presence. Under a strict injunction from their commander, Yamashita, the Japanese combat troops were restrained from entering the city for fear of causing mayhem and indulging in a drunken rampage.[4] Yamashita also insisted that his forces would make only a modest triumphal entry into the city because "[T]his battle is no more than a prelude ... and immediately after a commemoration service we will begin operations in Sumatra."[5] The first few Japanese figures who appeared publicly were equally concerned to get the infrastructure functioning and to restore the essential facilities for basic living.

The Governor and his wife, Daisy, remained in Fullerton Building during the day of surrender, learning the details of the day's events from visitors, including Fraser, the Colonial Secretary, and Percival. Next day he was taken to Fort Canning to meet the Japanese and agreed to the setting up of various committees to deal with critical matters concerning the restoration of basic public utilities and other levels of administration. Afterwards, he was allowed the use of an official car to collect some of his

---

[2] Montgomery, *Shenton of Singapore*, p. 143.

[3] Every personal account of the surrender records this impression. See also Henry P. Frei, "The Island Battle", paper given at conference (Singapore: National University of Singapore, 2002).

[4] Tsuji, *Singapore*, p. 274.

[5] Ibid.

belongings from Government House. In this early period, a large number of military personnel and civilian specialists were ordered to repair or rebuild vital elements of the infrastructure such as bridges and roads, restore power and light supplies and repair communication lines. An incongruous aspect of these activities was that Thomas had to discuss most of them with the Japanese ex-Consul General to Singapore, Toyoda Kaoru, whom he had arrested and imprisoned with another 40 Japanese nationals, on the outbreak of war.[6] Toyoda proved to be very helpful and accommodating, including getting passes and transport for Thomas and others so that they could attend to the business of restoration.

The total number of Allied prisoners of war (POWs) taken at the fall of Singapore is estimated at 100,000. A more precise calculation was impossible because of the uncounted wounded, injured and those who had attempted to escape. Later official figures give the total British, Australian, Indian and volunteer forces lost in battle and in the surrender as 138,708.[7] Japanese records show that captured British, Australian, New Zealand and Dutch troops in Singapore amounted to more than 40,000, with the number of civilians at 3,000.[8] It is often overlooked that in the fighting down through Peninsula Malaya and before the battle reached Singapore, the Japanese had already taken more than 11,000 POWs, including over 10,000 Indian officers and men and approximately 1,200 of other nationalities.[9]

At the time the decision to surrender was agreed, Percival debated with the others the possibility of the military attempting to escape from Singapore to avoid becoming prisoners of war.[10] Curiously, General Heath, whose wife was pregnant, asked Percival at the end of January, and before the Japanese had even attacked the island, if he could leave Malaya, but Percival refused.[11] It was implicit that, until the official hour of surrender, the armed forces would remain under arms and thereby under

---

[6] Montgomery, *Shenton of Singapore*, p. 143.

[7] Kirby, *Singapore*, p. 250.

[8] Farrell, *The Defence and Fall of Singapore 1940–1942*, p. 385.

[9] J. Flower, "Allied Prisoners of War: The Malayan Campaign", paper given at conference (Singapore: National University of Singapore, 2002).

[10] Kirby, *The War against Japan*, p. 410. And see Percival, *The War in Malaya*, p. 286.

[11] Kinvig, *Scapegoat*, p. 227.

the jurisdiction of the military authorities. An exception was granted for those whose military skills would be valuable for the continuance of the war and those whose recent employment would leave them vulnerable to severe interrogation: they were permitted to attempt escape immediately. After the surrender hour, any others who wished could follow suit. What was not specifically brought up (but by the terms of military doctrine generally assumed) was that normal military responsibilities would exist; senior commanders would remain with their men as long as possible to supervise arrangements for their imprisonment and see that some form of command structure remained in place.

General Bennett, the commander of the Australian Imperial Forces, apparently ignoring this implicit responsibility, hastily left his command in what was later revealed as questionable circumstances. He escaped together with two of his junior staff officers. The events surrounding his departure and his subsequent explanation were considered most unusual and the Australian military authorities decided to call for an official enquiry. Investigations uncovered the fact that Bennett had been considering escape for some time and certainly before the end of the fighting.[12] In itself, this revelation throws into doubt the strength of Bennett's conviction to fight the Japanese tenaciously and to the end. Moreover, the account of his escape, his boorish behaviour and totally selfish disregard for others during the flight caused many, particularly within the Australian high command, to question the quality of his leadership and to reassess his performance as Chief of the Australian military in Malaya.[13] The official military court of inquiry and a later royal commission into the whole event highlighted three controversial issues that were never satisfactorily resolved: whether Bennett departed before the official deadline; whether he should rightfully have left his men at this crucial time; and whether he properly appointed a successor. It was irrefutable that he failed to tell his Commander, Percival, of his intentions or even give a hint. Bennett's improbable and outrageous defence was that he had acquired valuable experience and knowledge fighting the Japanese and it was important that this information be brought home to meet the continuing Japanese threat

---

[12] A.B. Lodge, *The Fall of General Gordon Bennett* (Sydney and Boston: Allen & Unwin, 1986), p. 197.

[13] Ibid.

in the region, particularly the threat to Australia. He was also publicly scathing about the fighting ability of the Indian and British troops and the calibre of their commanders.[14] His later career never fully recovered from the stigma attached to his contentious and premature escape. Never again was he allowed to command combat troops.[15]

Changi Prison was quite inadequate for the large number of military POWs and, in any case, was scheduled to hold civilians. The Changi military garrison complex was selected instead. Several large barracks, including Selarang Barracks at the eastern end of the island, were designated as the site for the POWs. When Percival heard this news, he asked to speak with the Japanese Commander. Eventually a Lieutenant Colonel Sugita arrived, and Governor Thomas joined the meeting. Thomas and Percival made it clear that the chosen area could hold no more than a few thousand soldiers, and certainly not the 50,000 proposed. Their appeal was to no avail. Sugita informed them that Yamashita himself had selected the Changi area and the prisoners were to march off right away.[16] As it turned out, the British military commanders were left to themselves to allocate accommodation and arrange administration, including catering and medical facilities for the injured. Senior officers were initially put into military houses within the barrack compounds together with their immediate staff. The soldiers were given all the available barrack rooms as well as tents erected within the compounds. During this interregnum, before the Japanese themselves got organized, they were content to leave the POWs to run their own affairs. Cramped though these conditions were, these first weeks proved to be a time of relative ease in comparison with the hardships the prisoners were to endure later.

Regardless of rank, prisoners were subject to abuse, ill-treatment and periods of solitary confinement for what the guards considered disrespect or non-compliance. Percival was no exception; he was placed in solitary confinement for refusing to enforce excessive and gratuitous punishment that the Japanese wanted imposed on the POWs. Conditions in the hot and humid climate deteriorated, the enclosures became

---

[14] Ibid., p. 212.

[15] Lodge, passim.

[16] James, *The Rise and Fall of the Japanese Empire*, p. 239.

increasingly overcrowded, there was no electricity or sanitation, and limited food and water.[17] In mid-1942, the most senior officers were moved to Formosa, cramped in the holds of cargo ships and, two years later, transferred to Manchuria. The conditions in both these places were little better than in Singapore. Constantly deprived of all the necessities of life, it was a harrowing time for all the men. Other suffering took place in mid-1942 when many of those held in Singapore, including civilians, were transferred to build the infamous Thai-Burma Railway. In addition, a great number went to camps in Saigon, Taiwan, Korea and Japan to perform forced labour under brutal conditions.[18]

Civilian prisoners fared little better. Governor Thomas made frequent complaints about the behaviour of the guards and the living conditions in Changi Prison, and refused to cooperate in propaganda films which were intended to depict how well he and the other civilian prisoners were being cared for. He was also sentenced to 14 days' solitary confinement in a tiny concrete cell, the first three days without food.[19] On another occasion, he was locked alone in a separate lavatory for 24 hours when some offensive remark he made was overheard.[20] The Governor, like the other senior figures, was transferred first to Formosa and later to Manchuria. His wife was imprisoned in Changi Prison in a separate female area, as was the heavily pregnant wife of General Heath. Initially there were 430 women and children detained, but by 1943 this number had risen to 700.[21] Between three and five women and children were confined in prison cells designed for one person. When Heath's wife came to give birth, she was taken to a hospital in Singapore city. Afterwards she was sent back to her cell with her child. Both survived the war, as did Lady Thomas.

An early political casualty of the fall of Singapore was the impact on relations between Australian and the UK. Most Australians looked

---

[17] Kinvig, *Scapegoat*, p. 231.

[18] Nakahara Michiko, "The Civilian Women's Internment Camp in Singapore: The World of *POW WOW*", in *New Perspectives on the Japanese Occupation in Malaya and Singapore 1941–1945*, ed. Akashi Yoji and Mako Yoshimura (Singapore: NUS Press, 2008), p. 186.

[19] Thomas Papers.

[20] Ibid.

[21] Michiko, "The Civilian Women's Internment Camp in Singapore", p. 186.

upon the affair as a British disaster in which the Australian armed forces, as victims caught up in the debacle, had paid a heavy penalty. Prime Minister Curtin of Australia believed that Churchill had betrayed his country. When cables from his representative in London, Sir Earle Page, indicated that the British government, at a very late stage, was beginning to recognize the possibility that Singapore might be lost, Curtin appealed to London.[22] Churchill was, of course, concerned at the implications of such a likelihood, and of the equally ominous success the Japanese were making in Corregidor in the Philippines. More than any other issue he feared for the safety of India: this could only be ensured by a successful defence in Burma. The defence committee therefore considered the evacuation of Malaya and Singapore. When Curtin was made aware of this speculation, he sent an urgent cable to Churchill:

> After all the assurances we have been given the evacuation of Singapore would be regarded here and elsewhere as an inexcusable betrayal. Singapore is a central fortress in the system of the Empire and local defence. As stated in my telegram, we understood that it was to be made impregnable, and in any event it was to be capable of holding out for a prolonged period until the arrival of the main fleet.[23]

In response, Churchill dismissed Australia's anguished appeal. It would not advance the overall strategic plan for Southeast Asia because, he believed, this parochial view failed to take account of the wider strategic threat. He nevertheless agreed that a reinforcing British 18th Division would proceed to Singapore rather than to Persia, as originally intended. The division arrived too late. It was, in any case, quite unprepared for jungle warfare and lost a large proportion of its equipment when Japanese aircraft sank the ship *Empress of Asia* carrying its stores, as it approached Singapore on 5 February. The loss of Singapore was pivotal in Anglo-Australian relations. Australia became more assertive and displayed greater self-interest. Curtin's scepticism about future British intentions in Southeast Asia was soon reflected in his adamant refusal to agree to the planned redeployment of the Australian division from north Africa to Burma. Instead, he insisted they should return to Australia to fight in

---

[22] Churchill, *The Second World War, Volume 4: The Hinge of Fate*, p. 51.
[23] Ibid.

New Guinea.[24] He claimed that the loss of Singapore had left his country vulnerable and that its protection now lay in the hands of General MacArthur of the USA, who was then doggedly fighting his way through the Philippines. Curtin offered MacArthur the use of the Australian forces. In the event, the Japanese threat to Australia did not amount to much. Although MacArthur acknowledged the additional Australian force deployed in New Guinea, he did not call upon them for direct employment in his battle plan. Effectively, from that point, the Australian contribution to continuing war in the Far East was circumscribed.[25]

The extent of dissatisfaction with British imperial rule that surfaced among the India contingent was also an important issue at this time, even though it had little direct influence on the course of the campaign. As noted above, during the retreat, as many as 10,000 Indian officers and soldiers were captured or deserted. A further 45,000 men joined them after capitulation. Of this total, an estimated 20,000 were persuaded to switch sides and join the recently formed Indian National Army (INA). Another 20,000 joined between June and August 1942. [26]

The INA, an unofficial armed force, was formed by a group of Indian political dissidents who belonged to the Indian Independence League (IIL), a militant offshoot of the Indian Congress Party. Their objective was to rid India of British rule. As a fighting force, they proved of little use to the Japanese because of the caveats their leaders imposed on their employment. For example, they were not to be used to fight against Indian troops on the Allied side. They were, however, successfully engaged in anti-British propaganda, intelligence and sabotage work, not only in the region but also in India and Ceylon.

The future administration of Malaya and Singapore was in the hands of a military garrison, supported by Japanese government officials in key administrative roles and qualified civilians in major posts in the private and commercial sector. Known as the Military Administrative Department (*Gunseibu*), it functioned for three years and eight months. From the few

[24] Ibid., pp. 136–46.

[25] Max Hastings, *Nemesis: The Battle for Japan, 1944–45* (London: Harper Press, 2007), pp. 363–72.

[26] Alan Warren, *Singapore: Britain's Greatest Defeat* (London and New York: Hambledon and London, 2002), p. 235.

surviving Japanese documents released in the 1960s[27] and since translated into English by Japanese scholars, it is clear that Japanese planning for the administration of conquered territories was at best sketchy, and in many instances entirely ad hoc.[28] It certainly did not match the thoroughness of the planning and execution of its military strategy. For example, it was not until February 1941, on the initiative of the military general staff, that a study group formed to consider the administration of occupied areas. Its sketchy draft conclusions, incorporated into the "Principles for the Administration of the Occupied Southern Regions" gave only general objectives such as:

1. Acquisition of vital materials as rapidly as possible for national defence.
2. Restoration of law and order.
3. Self sufficiency for troops in the occupied territories.

And in the specific case of Malaya:

1. Because the Straits Settlements of Singapore, Malacca, and Penang were important military administrative centres, they were to be controlled by the Japanese Army.
2. The four Federated states (Perak, Selangor, Negri Sembilan and Pahang) were to be supervised and recognised under their respective Sultans.
3. The four 'Unfederated states' former Thai territories—Terengganu. Kelantan, Kedah and Perlis—were 'expected' to revert to Thailand in the future.[29]

It is noticeable that military requirements dominated the planning. There was no visionary policy for economic restoration and security. Directly after the surrender and before an established administration was in place, Yamashita addressed the people:

---

[27] In 1945, with the prospect of the Allies returning and invading Malaya, the Japanese burnt most of their official documents. Akashi Yoji, "Japanese Research Activities in Occupied Malaya/Syonan, 1943–45", in *New Perspectives on the Japanese Occupation in Malaya and Singapore 1941–1945*, ed. Akashi Yoji and Mako Yoshimura (Singapore: NUS Press, 2008), p. 158.

[28] Akashi Yoji and Mako Yoshimura, *New Perspectives on the Japanese Occupation in Malaya and Singapore, 1941–1945*, passim.

[29] Ibid., p. 4.

We hope that we sweep away the arrogant and unrighteous British elements and share pain and rejoicing with all concerned people in a spirit of "give and take", and also hope to promote the social development by establishing the East Asia Co-prosperity Sphere on which the New Order of justice has to be attained under the "Great Spirit of Cosmocracy" giving all content to the respective race and individual according to their talents and faculties.

Nippon armies wish Malayan people to understand the real intention of Nippon and to co-operate with Nippon Army toward the prompt establishment of the New Order and the Co-prosperity sphere.

The pronouncement was baseless, judged by the behaviour of the military authorities at the time of the statement and their subsequent pre-planned ruthlessness. Early arrangements for control and administration called for certain national reorganization. The FMS and UMS were dissolved and Peninsula Malaya was divided into ten provinces, or *shu*. Eight were made up of the nine Malay States (Perlis, the smallest state, was absorbed into Kedah. The other two were Penang and Malacca. Singapore was renamed *Syonan-to* (Shining South) and was a separate municipality under a Japanese mayor. Malaya was later renamed Malai. In June 1943 Imperial Headquarters, Tokyo, decided to transfer Kedah/Perlis, Kelantan and Terengganu back to Thai control. As mentioned earlier, these states had been acquired by treaty by the British from Thailand in 1909 (see Chapter 2).

The officer given the responsibility for the military administration (*Gunsei*) of Singapore and Malaya was the 25th army's Deputy Chief-of-Staff, Major General Manaki Takanobu. His assistant and the more dominant figure was Colonel Watanabe Wataru.

Very shortly after capitulation the Japanese authorities in Singapore entered upon what is now termed as ethnic cleansing. Before the final surrender, they had in place a secret plan to exterminate dissident Chinese. The Japanese believed they would be a source of trouble and, in any case, they were perceived as the traditional enemy, particularly the mainland Chinese.[30] The programme, called *sook chin* (purification by elimination)

---

[30] H. Hirofumi, "Massacre of Chinese in Singapore and its Coverage in Post-war Japan", paper given at conference "Malaya and Singapore during the Japanese Occupation" (Singapore: National University of Singapore).

was indiscriminately and ruthlessly imposed. In the scale of horror and
atrocities perpetrated by the Japanese, it has been ranked third after
Nanking and Manila.[31] Calculations made after the war by the Singapore
authorities estimate that 50,000 dissidents were massacred.[32] Japanese
scholar Akashi Yoji considers this particular incident and a later demand
that the Chinese should make a "gift" of ¥50,000,000 to the Japanese
government as leaving an indelible stain on the Japanese administration
in Malaya. He argues that these measures had an irreversible effect on
Japanese efforts to gain the cooperation of the Chinese community.[33]
They also provided the Malayan Peoples Anti-Japanese Party (MPAJA)
with a propaganda windfall, contributing to their anti-Japanese solidarity
and legitimizing their resistance.[34]

Predictably, the Japanese were compelled to restore former municipal
departments, reinstate local staff and retain about a hundred experienced
British civilian internees, to assist until replacements arrived from Japan.
Those released from gaol to assist in re-establishing and restoring the
utilities and infrastructure of Singapore remained out of prison for days,
sometimes weeks. When their replacements arrived from Japan, it was
evident that they were of poor quality and ill-educated, because the
abler men were in the armed forces, or seconded to appointments that
were more important. The result was inefficiency and corruption.[35] The
Director of Fisheries, William Birtwistle, with his unrivalled knowledge
of the fishermen who provided so much food for the city's population,
was ordered by the Governor to remain at his post and kept out of gaol.
In addition, many prisoners who were seen as convenient and available
labour were quite illegally and in contravention of the Geneva Convention

[31] Henry P. Frei, *Guns of February: Ordinary Japanese Soldiers' Views of the Malayan Campaign and the Fall of Singapore, 1941–1942* (Singapore: Singapore University Press, 2004), p. xxvii.

[32] Ibid., p. 153.

[33] Akashi Yoji, "Colonel Watanabe Wataru: The Architect of the Malayan Military Administration, December 1941–March 1943", in *New Perspectives on the Japanese Occupation in Malaya and Singapore 1941–1945*, ed. Akashi Yoji and Mako Yoshimura (Singapore: NUS Press, 2008), pp. 40–1.

[34] Ibid., p. 42.

[35] Corner, *The Marquis, a Tale of Syonan-to*, p. 132.

(to which Japan was a signatory) used as labourers in a massive clean-up and rehabilitation operation.

Engaging the help of these members of the MCS gave rise to some curious incidents, one of which occurred directly after the surrender. On 17 February, the Assistant Director of the Gardens Department of the Straits Settlements, John Corner, approached Thomas, whom he knew well. A dedicated but friendless botanist, Corner appeared to have a myopic academic concern for the preservation of the many botanical records that he and others had accumulated during their work in Malaya. Thus he asked Thomas to write a note to the Japanese authorities on his behalf. He pleaded that he should not be imprisoned but allowed to continue his research, the compilation of extensive records, and to oversee the preservation of the "scientific treasure houses of knowledge". Corner notes that in the confusion and rush of the moment, Thomas scribbled a pencilled note in line with this appeal. The actual note did not survive the war but at the time eventually ended up with a Professor Tanakadate, the official assigned to be in charge of scientific affairs.[36] The Japanese agreed to the arrangement and Corner subsequently spent the entire period of occupation in comfort, gainfully employed. At times, he even had use of an official car to move freely around both Malaya and Singapore. His behaviour was branded by most of his compatriots as collaboration. Consumed by his myopic interests he failed to recognize the implications of his fraternization and the insignificance of these botanical records, precious though they were, compared with the scale of death and destruction in Southeast Asia. Certainly, his comfortable lifestyle was in stark contrast to those incarcerated in Changi Prison. In his book *The Marquis, a Tale of Syonan-to* (1981),[37] he describes this period and mainly justifies his cooperation with the Japanese, unashamedly recording his "good fortune" and admiration for the Japanese with whom he worked. At one point, at the end of 1942, Tanakadate decided to give

---

[36] The note was crucial as evidence to support Corner's claim that the Governor agreed to his proposal. However, in his book he said the note was either lost or destroyed. In June 2001, *The Straits Times*, in an article, claimed that, in fact, its existence was confirmed because Tanakadate had published the Governor's note in a Japanese newspaper in June 1942.

[37] Corner, *The Marquis, a Tale of Syonan-to*.

a public lecture in English about Japanese culture, and asked Corner to draft a speech for him. It contained these words:

> The present war started with self-sacrifice on the part of some young *Nippon-zin*. And I refer to the gallant attack by our submarines on Pearl Harbour where those young men courageously sacrificed their lives at the altar of national necessity.[38]

If Corner believed this, he was either unaware of the unprovoked attack of noted "infamy" or was less troubled with exactitude and more concerned with gratifying his captors. In another act of what might be generously described as misguided loyalty, Corner heard of the imminent trial of Yamashita in Manila at the end of the war and wrote to the military court, pleading for Yamashita's life on the grounds that he had only done his duty: "... in all fairness he only carried out the instructions of General Tojo and had conserved scientific and historical institutes in Singapore and Malaya".[39]

The core of the Malayan economy—rubber and tin—was now isolated from its overseas markets. The major source of national income disappeared almost overnight. In any case, Japan had already decided that the production of rubber and tin in Malaya exceeded the demands of the domestic industries in Japan and the production of these commodities was to be reduced. Nonetheless, anticipating a great demand for these materials in the post-war world (see Chapter 2, fn. 31) the production systems were preserved in readiness to meet the need of not only the Greater East Asia Co-Prosperity Sphere but also global demand.[40] In the meantime, estates and mines were either reduced or stopped altogether. In turn, not only were labourers put out of work but also all the associated industries that serviced the production of these raw materials suffered a decline. It was not long before the unemployed workforce was reduced to poverty and living on the bread line. The Japanese Labour Inspector for Kelantan was compelled to write to the authorities in Singapore:

---

[38] Ibid., p. 174.

[39] Ibid., p. 72.

[40] Yoshimura Mako, "Japan's Economic Policy for Occupied Malaya", in *New Perspectives on the Japanese Occupation in Malaya and Singapore, 1941–1945*, ed. Akashi Yoji and Mako Yoshimura (Singapore: NUS Press, 2008), p. 115.

A major portion of the unemployed labourers, Indians and Chinese, are almost starving ... and some of these people have slowly drifted into towns and are maintaining themselves by begging on the streets and diseases are taking a heavy toll on them due to the absence of medical aid.[41]

Malaya then suffered food shortages. As a country it had never been self-sufficient in rice production, importing almost 60 per cent annually. Now, the neighbouring countries who had previously provided this staple product were themselves caught up in war and unable to grow or export it. Moreover, merchant shipping carrying such cargos were now the target of attacks by Allied submarines.

With the declining food situation, the general health of the people deteriorated. Many basic foods were unavailable or prohibitively expensive on the black market. Children, particularly, suffered through a lack of vitamins. Previously contained diseases such as beriberi reappeared and took a heavy toll. Medical stocks soon ran down and as there was little chance of replenishment, even common diseases and mild illnesses became difficult to treat. As breeding grounds of the *Aedes* mosquito were left untreated, malaria reappeared because the oil-based liquid remedy (crude oil and kerosene) could no longer be produced.

The demand for labour rose again in 1943, as the effect of increasingly successful Allied attacks on merchant shipping began to take its toll. The transport of essential goods, especially military necessities, had to be switched to rail. Several major projects were initiated—a Trans-Sumatran railway, a line across the Kra Isthmus and the notorious Thai-Burma Railway. Labour was also needed for the construction of an airfield as well as a number of local projects. Wages were poor and working conditions appalling. At many sites, the labourers themselves had to build their own accommodation and dig fresh water wells outside official working hours. "On one project that employed 2,500 labourers in 1942 and 1943 to build a landing ground at Port Swettenham [Malaya] the state Medical Department reported that three to four workers died of

---

[41] Paul H. Kratoska, *Asian Labour in the Wartime Japanese Empire* (Singapore: Singapore University Press 2006 [2005]), p. 239.

malaria or malnutrition each day."[42] The conditions of many of the 62,000 European POWs sent to work on the Thai-Burma Railway (where 12,399 died) is well-documented but rarely mentioned is the tale of suffering and death of the 182,496 Malayan and Burmese and other Asians sent to work on this same railway. Of this number, the Japanese officially acknowledge the death of 42,214 but 92,220 labourers are unaccounted for and the explanation offered is that they deserted to escape the endemic cholera epidemic. As they were never again seen and the chances of survival in the jungle in their emaciated condition were negligible, it is safe to assume they also perished. Other estimates put the Asian workforce as high as 269,948 and the number of deaths as 72,996 but it is acknowledged that the figures are unreliable, particularly for Burma.[43]

Percival and Thomas survived their imprisonment and both, in time, returned safely home. While he was held in various internment camps, Percival began writing an account of his part in the catastrophe. He knew that if he returned to England, an official dispatch would be required from him and these notes written on a variety of scraps of paper were his *aide-memoire*. However, on his final and hurried move from a camp in Moksak, Formosa (Taiwan) to Manchuria, he had to destroy the notes to avoid them being discovered in the inevitable pre-move search. As he recalled, "The work of eight months was burned in eight seconds."[44] The war ended while he was in the Manchurian camp. In a generous gesture that smacked of *schadenfreude*, General MacArthur arranged for Percival to be flown first to Tokyo to attend the Japanese surrender ceremony on the battleship *Missouri* and then to Manila to witness his nemesis Yamashita sign the surrender there. He recalled:

> As Yamashita entered the room, I saw one eyebrow lifted and a look of surprise cross his face—but only for a moment. His face quickly resumed that sphinx-like mask common to all Japanese, and he showed no further interest.[45]

Yamashita later confided that he saw Percival's presence as an act

---

[42] Ibid., p. 241.
[43] Ibid
[44] Kinvig, *Scapegoat*, p. 234.
[45] Percival, *The War in Malaya*, p. 326.

of humiliation and revenge. So unbearable was the humiliation that he considered suicide.[46]

He was hailed a national hero in Japan following his successful capture of Malaya and Singapore. However, not long afterwards, he caused the displeasure of the Prime Minister, General Tojo. While addressing the community leaders in Singapore on the emperor's birthday, Yamashita carelessly informed them that they had become citizens of imperial Japan. It brought a swift rebuke from Tokyo: he could not make political statements of this nature and only the imperial authorities in Tokyo could take such decisions. On 12 July, he left Singapore for Manchukuo. He suffered the indignity of being ordered to leave Singapore directly for Manchukuo and was refused the customary honour of an audience with the emperor in Tokyo, a traditional custom reserved for successful commanders to present their "memorials".[47] He remained in Manchukuo until October 1944.He was then sent to the Philippines to take command of the Fourteenth Army in the last stages of the hopeless defensive war against MacArthur. After Japan surrendered, Yamashita was indicted as a war criminal on charges of serious negligence of the rules of war and allowing his troops to commit atrocities. He was found guilty and hanged.

Thomas also started compiling notes and, at one stage while in the same camp as Brigadier Ivan Simson in Formosa, showed Simson his written version of the final civilian evacuation arrangements. It was an event which clearly troubled Thomas, and he was sure it would be the source of heated recrimination. His recollection and description of the last hurried mass departures of 13 February from Singapore were quite different from those of Simson. In particular, he strongly denied the Brigadier's claim that he (Thomas) had agreed that Bisseker be allowed to leave along with Nunn, head of the PWD. In his book *Singapore* (1970), Simson returned to this issue and stuck firmly to his conviction that while it was he who authorized the evacuation of Bisseker and Nunn, he did so only after clearing it with Thomas.

The imperial Japanese authorities' intentions for the future of Malaya

---

[46] Akashi Yoji, "General Yamashita Tomoyuki: Commander of the Twenty Fifth Army", in *A Great Betrayal: The Fall of Singapore Revisited*, ed. Brian P. Farrell and Sandy Hunter (Singapore: Marshall Cavendish, 2009), p. 146.

[47] Akashi, Yoji, "General Yamashita Tomoyuki".

did not include independence: in their view the country should become a permanent colony of Japan, a decision reaffirmed by the Ministry of Foreign Affairs in February 1945.[48] This decision was a purely pragmatic one, lacking any vision for the future. The Japanese needed the natural resources available in Malaya and were determined that their enemies, and the West in general, should not have access to them. While they controlled the country they controlled its resources. This policy ignored their assertion of seeking a Greater East Asia Co-Prosperity Sphere. Thus the military administration, devoid of an incentive, showed little sense of purpose apart from supporting the war effort. During the period of Japanese rule, even this limited objective was not met; there was little the people of Malaya could do to assist the war effort, and the Japanese were unable to overcome the shortages of food, clothing and other necessities for the defeated population.

> Japan did not manage to make its colonies serve its economic needs. A brief phase of constructive imperialism in 1942 soon gave way to the politics of scarcity and plunder. Japan's military ascendancy was short lived, and the resurgence of Allied naval power after the battle of Midway in mid 1942 meant that strategic goods from South East Asia could not be shipped back to Japan in any meaningful quantity. The great rubber estates of Malaya became virtual wastelands in which the remaining labourers scraped a subsistence by growing food on roughly cleared ground.[49]

With the departure of the Europeans, the economy of *Syonan-to* became virtually a Chinese one.[50] The Japanese faced the quandary of relying economically on the Chinese but not trusting them. Their solution was to allow the Chinese to retain their economic position but have all business activity under Japanese domination. Chinese businessmen were forced to cooperate with the Gunsei or politically identify with the Wang Ching Wei faction.[51]

---

[48] Yoshimura Mako, "Japan's Economic Policy for Occupied Malaya", p. 115.

[49] Christopher Bayly and Timothy Harper, *Forgotten Armies: The Fall of British Asia, 1941–1945* (London: Penguin, 2005), p. 11.

[50] Lee Ting Hui, "Singapore under the Japanese 1941–1945", *Journal of the South Seas Society* 17 (1961): 55–6.

[51] Lee Ting Hui, "Japanese Racial Policies in Singapore", *Journal of South Seas Society* 17 (1961): 55–65.

The majority of Chinese were inherently anti-Japanese, an aversion which surfaced in 1931 with the infamous Manchurian incident: this was a staged pretext for Japan's invasion of Manchuria. Their hostility was aggravated by the outbreak of the Sino-Japanese war of 1937. As recounted by Lee Ting Hui:

> [the] crude Japanese policy [towards the Chinese] was a failure. Collaborators there were; but on the whole "outwardly there was compliance ... inwardly there was an ever growing hatred." The anti-Japanese movement at the end of the occupation was stronger than ever.[52]

No Japanese figure of stature emerged to promote fair rule firmly and efficiently or to take advantage of the country's talent and natural resources. There was no Japanese guidance of how to govern successfully the people of Malaya and Singapore or of how to gain their respect let alone their loyalty. Throughout their history, the Japanese have never had the experience of ruling a foreign country benevolently. Their brutal repression and ceaseless demands aggravated a highly precarious situation. All the descriptions of their period of occupation leaves the distinct impression of an insecure ascendency and a temporary supremacy.

From the British government's point of view the Japanese invasion and occupation, though of relatively short duration, produced great changes throughout Southeast Asia.[53] While it is undoubtedly true that the people of Malaya were genuinely glad to see the Japanese depart and the British return, conditions and relations between the colonial power and the Malayan people were never to be the same.[54] Many were determined that the return of the British should be of short duration only. A genuine Malayan nationalism gave rise to an independence movement. In 1946 the Straits Settlements ceased to exist, Singapore became a separate colony and, by 1959, it was a separate state with a large measure of self-government. Penang and Malacca merged with the nine Malay States.

---

[52] Ibid.

[53] Nicholas Tarling, *The Fall of Imperial Britain in South-East Asia* (Singapore and New York: Oxford University Press,1993), p. 144.

[54] Wang Gungwu, "Malayan Nationalism", *Royal Central Asian Society Journal* 49, 3–4 (1962): 317–28.

Briefly during this process, the British attempted to restore their pre-war constitutional powers in the Peninsula through a short-lived Malayan Union,in 1947. This was seen as a clumsy attempt to break away from the long tradition of indirect rule and bring the UMS under more direct governance. The Malays, however, saw this as a threat to their survival as the dominant community and reacted in an uncharacteristically aggressive manner. This indirectly boosted Malay nationalism. The Federation of Malaya, an agreement that included special guarantees of the rights for Malays, including the position of sultans, and the establishment of a colonial government, soon replaced the Malayan Union, in 1948.[55] These developments marginalized the MCP, which reacted by embarking upon guerrilla insurgency, later described as an "emergency". The emergency lasted 12 years. Malayan nationalism reached its culmination on *Merdeka* (Freedom) Day, 31 August 1957.

In an interesting footnote to history, HM High Commissioner to Singapore, 28 years after the event, wrote in his valedictory despatch the acerbic comment:

> [N]o Singaporean has ever mentioned February 1942 to me in criticism or reproach. [However] I am reminded of the shame ... not only an appalling military disaster but the most shameful disgrace in Britain's imperial history. ... One may not regret the passing of empire but no loyal British subject living in Singapore can forget that it was here that the hollowness of the imperial ethos was so cruelly and so shamefully exposed. And it does not relieve me to recall that the military pomp and ostentation—not to say arrogance—with which we reoccupied Singapore was a sham and a fraud, for we reoccupied it not by our own efforts, but by an American atom bomb dropped on Hiroshima .... [56]

---

[55] Winstedt, *Malaya and its History,* pp. 140–2.

[56] Valedictory Despatch, Sir Arthur De La Mare, HM High Commissioner to Singapore, Oct. 1972. Quoted in Matthew Parris and A. Bryson, *Parting Shots,* London: Penguin Books, 2011.

9

CONCLUSION

The loss of Malaya and Singapore to the Japanese, in February 1942, was not solely because the British establishment, military and civilian, was in disarray and disagreement, though that certainly propagated the seeds of failure. It was because the British imperial forces were crushingly defeated in battle by a resolute, fearless, disciplined and dedicated army. The campaign was a humiliating military disaster, arguably the worst in the history of the British army. The disaster arose from a combination of numerous occurrences, avoidable and unavoidable, which merged to infect and destroy the cohesion and determination of the defender. International precedence, a clash of priorities, ill-equipped and ill-trained forces, poor leadership and a divided, indecisive Singapore War Committee all contributed to the tragedy.

A large measure of responsibility for this tragedy must rest with the authorities in London, both the CO and the WO. They failed to agree early enough that Japanese behaviour in the Far East posed a serious threat to British interests and then, later, when danger was imminent, failed to combine and jointly direct the civil/military authorities. Worse still, the CO independently told the Governor to focus his attention on the production of important war resources while the WO ordered the military to protect the naval base on Singapore Island: two tasks that competed for the limited labour force and inexorably led each side to adopt different and parochial perspectives. The glaring solution, acknowledged far too late, was to appoint an overall supremo, a person with total authority to impose directives on all parties. It was an important lesson, used later to valuable effect in other places such as Ceylon (Sri Lanka). Nonetheless, poor civil-military relations alone did not cause the defeat of British arms. Even before the war began there were other overarching factors that determined the loss of the island.

Most important, the impoverished and debilitated British imperial power was no longer in a position to meet the widespread demands, particularly military demands, of its far-flung empire. Indeed, the signs of overstretch were obvious well before these events but the huge burden of the Great War accentuated the failing. A dispassionate audit of responsibilities, at that point, taking into account the vast resources needed to manage and protect the empire's assets, would have exposed the near impossibility of coping with worldwide conflict. Humanity had changed as never before: war itself was transformed. The British Empire, the largest in the history of the world, had far outstripped its ability to safeguard its territories. One glaring manifestation of this weakness was Britain's inability to provide the resources—armed forces, armaments and equipment—for Singapore to have any effective defence. The very decision to build a naval base in Singapore was an admission that Britain simply could not sustain a two ocean navy. The base built in the Far East was big enough to harbour a British fleet should it need to rush there to meet a threat to its possessions and dominions. Britain simply did not have the means to keep permanently a fleet both in home waters and in the Far East.

The administration in charge of this important and exposed possession had changed very little in substance and procedure from Victorian days. The untidy, unwieldy colonial administration was the result of governmental evolution over a period of 150 years. In that time, it successfully oversaw the development and growth of the country's natural resources, its economy, infrastructure and the well-being of the people. It evolved piecemeal—organically, and thus perhaps effectively for a while—as British authority extended throughout the Peninsula. Its success was evident to the extent that Malaya became a leading world producer of rubber and tin and the people enjoyed the benefits of a thriving economy, which in turn enhanced their quality of life. Competent, dedicated and loyal staff, mainly officers from the prestigious MCS, ran the show. It was a service, however, that had never faced international hostilities or threats in any form. There was no comprehension whatsoever of the consequences of such a calamity.

A thorough post-war CO inquiry concluded that the civil-military relationship went through three phases before the fall of Singapore in 1942.[1] The first period, before war broke out in Europe, was marked by widespread resentment at the growing military presence in the area and the attendant material demands and inconveniences. The second was caused by the outbreak of the Nazi war in 1939, for the two arms of the administration had different objectives. The situation led to a serious clash between the civil and military authorities: an issue of such import should have been resolved in London.

The third phase came in 1941 when a number of very senior personnel changes took place. The Secretary for Defence was removed, a Minister Resident was added to the hierarchy and the C-in-C, Far East was under notice to be replaced. Moreover, at the last minute, even this decision was amended when the selected replacement, Lieutenant General Bernard Paget, was withdrawn on Churchill's orders and Lieutenant General Sir Henry Pownall appointed in his place. These striking changes amid the gathering storm soured relations across the senior echelons of both civil and military services, and led to apathetic cooperation, resentment and disagreement. There was a complete lack of any harmonious, constructive, united effort throughout this period. Added to the command disunity was the plethora of independent branches of the home government that came into being. The authors of the report did, however, add the perceptive rider "that however thorough planning and administration may be, everything must in the last resort depend very largely on the personalities of the men at the top".[2] The authority to install an overall supremo came too late.[3]

---

[1] CO 967/80 "Lessons from the disasters in HK and Malaya", NA.

[2] Ibid.

[3] As mentioned earlier this authority was established, though much too late, in the person of Wavell and ABDA Command. See Kirby, *War Against Japan,* pp. 263–8. In Ceylon Admiral Layton, lately of Singapore, was superimposed over the civil government as well as over the three Fighting Services. See also "Lessons to be learnt from the experiences of Hong Kong and Malaya from the point of view of the Colonial Administration in war time" and correspondence. CO 967/80, NA.

The *raison d'être* for the entire military-civil endeavour was the defence of the naval base in Singapore—the focus of ever-changing tactical plans. The safety of this vital base was considered paramount to the protection of Britain's Far East assets. The early assumption was that an attack on the base could only come from the sea thus fortifications were designed to meet such a threat. At the same time, with the development of the torpedo bomber, it was apparent that the RAF also had an important contribution to make and thus the air force became an integral part of the defence equation. As weaponry evolved technologically and the Malayan hinterland opened up, the plan for defence had to change. The changes all pointed to a need for more aircraft, warships and soldiers, none of which were immediately available. Singapore was warned that the likelihood of them becoming available later was slim indeed. In the event, no additional aircraft came: a token and vulnerable naval force arrived to be destroyed in the opening moves of the campaign. Meagre army units were deployed late and were inadequate in number, adolescent and untrained. The finger of accusation has been pointed at Churchill, not for ignoring the pleas for help from Singapore but for giving others he considered more deserving, the limited tools at his disposal. To be rational, however, the dilemma facing Churchill and his advisers' needs to be placed in context. The year 1941 was the nadir of Britain's war; the army was in retreat in the western desert, the battle of the Atlantic was close to destroying the nation's vital supply line, Russia had been invaded and was calling for help. Churchill did not want, and the nation could not sustain, a war on two fronts. He wanted no behaviour in the East that Japan could claim was provocative and use as an excuse for war. Added to this, he believed that America's mighty sixth fleet harbouring in Hawaii would be a deterrent to Japan misbehaving. Within these parameters, he saw other worldwide demands as more urgent.

The loss of Singapore, preceded by the surrender of HK and the hasty retreat from Burma, cast a harsh, unflattering light on British power. These calamitous failures were the catalyst for the decline of the British Empire. The fragility of British authority had been exposed. "What it led to was the demise of Britain as a world power, and her reduction to an American satellite."[4] In India, it gave new impetus to nationalist

---

[4] Callahan, *The Worst Disaster*, p. 271.

rumblings that existed before the war. An Indian officer of the Baluch Regiment recorded his reaction to the news from Singapore:

> Firstly, it had a tremendous effect on our people—we felt the shame that they had surrendered. Secondly, the fact of the tremendous defeat inflicted on the—till then omnipotent—British had an underlay of feeling that the white races weren't all that superior ... The news had tremendous effect on those Indian soldiers who had always felt that the British were supermen.[5]

Nearly every historian and scholar has portrayed Governor Thomas as, at best, incompetent and, less kindly, as obstructionist. In his book, *Shenton of Singapore: Governor and Prisoner of War* (1984), Brian Montgomery, while treating his subject with perhaps undue sensitivity, got closest to the truth:

> [Shenton was]not a great man ... but he was an admirable man, determined to do his best for the people under his charge, completely dedicated to the public service, not a prig in anyway, but a strong and upright character with a deep sense of duty .... not devious in any way.[6]

From his colonial education and subsequent experience, limited to Africa only, Thomas knew very little about the regular armed forces or military matters in general. As a member of the colonial service, not the MCS, he was seen in Malaya as "something of an interloper by what was, quite literally, the freemasonry of the Malayan Civil Service stablishment".[7] His failure to learn the Malay language was a further irritant to those who worked closely with him:

> [H]ow could a Governor who knew not a word of the local language impress his views on people? You can't really be impressive if you have to pause at the end of every sentence while your words are translated by a very bored interpreter (who probably hasn't your faith in any case) [to] paraphrase your appeal.[8]

Thomas appears not to have noticed his deficiencies. Certainly, none

---

[5] Trevor Royle, *The Last Days of the Raj* (London: Michael Joseph, 1989), p. 77.

[6] Montgomery, *Shenton of Singapore*, p. 203.

[7] Bayly and Harper, *Forgotten Armies,* p. 109.

[8] Correspondence Dickinson/Bryson. Jan 1970. BAM Collection. RCS/RCMS 103/4/2/15. CU.

of his diary entries or later writings mention them. The result was that in times of tension he appeared to lack the confidence to state his own unequivocal views. He inclined to the views of the person making the more forceful case, believing they had the experience and background. Later he would confess in his diary to important but publicly undeclared opinions, as was the case with the Penang civilian evacuation calamity (see Chapter 4). If he had had the courage to declare these suppressed judgments in an open forum, it is possible that his standing and image, if nothing else, would have risen significantly.

The momentous world events preceding and portending the fall of Singapore needed a leader of vision and Herculean demeanour—Thomas was none of these. He was a competent colonial civil servant; nowhere was he even described as a "good" one, thus was quite the wrong person to face the mammoth task of rousing and preparing a nation for war. Even if the blunder of his appointment could have been foreseen, the London authorities were in no position to replace him. His character, personality and myopic view of his administrative responsibilities made him the wrong person in the wrong place at the wrong time. In early 1942, after the fall of Singapore, Lord Cranborne, Thomas' chief at the CO, wrote:

> From the Governor downwards they seem to have been incapable of dealing with an abnormal situation. This, more than any inherent rigidity in the system, seems to be the real cause for criticism. Clearly the Governor should have been replaced earlier.[9]

Furthermore, Thomas lacked any staff of conspicuous ability, with perhaps the exception of Hugh Fraser, the Federal Secretary, who was called to Singapore to replace Stanley Jones (sacked at the behest of Duff Cooper).

A senior member of his staff who played a controversial role in the unhappy relations between the civil and the military administrations, C.A. Vlieland, was a man described by many as clever but abrasive, arrogant and delusionary. Vlieland was dismissive of the military and its tactical planning, believing he knew better. Indeed, without consulting anyone, he wrote the astute forecast of likely Japanese tactics in the fight for Singapore

[9] John Charmley, *Duff Cooper, the Authorized Biography* (London: Weidenfeld & Nicolson, 1986), p. 160.

though, as pointed out, there is a strong suspicion that he plagiarized the Dobbie Appreciation.[10] Thomas clearly had high regard for him, high enough to authorize Vlieland not to accept any interference from the Acting Governor and others on the defence committee while Thomas was on leave in 1940. It was a directive that Vlieland saw as licence to feed his authoritarianism, evident in his arbitrary selection of sites in north Malaya for the storage of rice reserves.[11] Not only was this instruction illustrative of Thomas' limited grasp of the importance of defence affairs, but also a reflection of his poor judgement of the professional contribution other members had to offer. According to one of his principal subordinates, Thomas' decision to leave Vlieland in charge during his extended period of leave, and at a time of menacing developments, made the former appear more complacent about the situation than he in fact was.[12] On Thomas' return he had to ask for Vlieland's resignation, so strong was the antagonism the latter had provoked among his colleagues.

Thomas was perhaps not so much complacent as sceptic. In spite of all mounting evidence, he simply did not believe—or, more accurately, did not want to believe—that the Japanese would invade Malaya. When it was reported that they had indeed landed he seemed unconcerned, as demonstrated by the dismissive remark he is reputed to have made to Percival: "Well I expect you'll shove them off again."[13] He was equally dismissive of the need to construct air-raid shelters, drawing a comparison with the hardihood of the people in wartime Kent, where he had spent his vacation. At the first Legislative Council meeting on his return, he answered a question about shelters in words that convey his disdain for such measures or, worse, a facetious rejection. War was a subject he knew little about and would have preferred not to confront. Until this unwelcome "disruption" he had managed the affairs of his province with some success, overseeing the expansion of its manufacturing and industrial base and leading Malaya to become the world's major producer of tin and rubber. He was well past retirement age and had spent the previous seven years in Singapore, following a comfortable, well-ordered

---

[10] Appendix to Vlieland Memoir. Vlieland papers. LHCMA.

[11] See Chapter 4.

[12] Ibid., p. 65.

[13] See Chapter 5.

routine; in the words of Clifford Kinvig in his book *Scapegoat: General Percival of Singapore* (1996):

> He seems to have been initially opposed to any defence build-up in Malaya, was ill-disposed to upsetting his bureaucratic routine which war preparations required and ill-prepared for the hard decisions which war itself brought .... Shenton Thomas was not the man for the tempest that broke on all their heads. He and his officials seemed wedded to the pace and routine of peace. Even Percival, who seldom offered public criticism of his superiors, was forced to admit ... Thomas's seven years in Singapore were "a long time in that trying climate."[14]

The evidence exposing Thomas' ineffectual and half-hearted preparations for the onslaught and his indecisive management of civil affairs during the campaign is conclusive. However, the role of the military is equally shameful. The crisis required a strong, determined military leader with the foresight to impress upon the civil authorities the mayhem and destruction that loomed ahead. Neither the civil population nor the administration had any experience or understanding of war and its consequences. They needed a rude awakening. In a letter that Thomas received after the war from (then Field Marshal) Wavell, he said, rather pedantically and smacking of hindsight:

> It was the duty of the chief military authorities in the Far Eastern Command to accentuate or accelerate the civilian effort if it did not meet adequately the possibilities attendant on a Japanese landing.[15]

Thomas had a rigid focus about meeting the demands of his colonial authorities: he believed he had to set a tone of calm and reassurance. More than anyone else, Thomas needed to be ruthlessly and relentlessly harassed into confronting the reality of the circumstances and to galvanize his staff. Nevertheless, it should also be remembered that during his leave in 1940 he found time to attend a meeting in London of the sub-committee of the Joint Planning Committee. Here, he made a spirited follow-up appeal of his earlier memorandum, asking for the air force in Singapore to be reinforced to compensate for the missing fleet.

---

[14] Kinvig, *Scapegoat*, p. 125.
[15] Letter dated 1 Jan 48. Quoted in Thomas private papers.

Interestingly, the formal refusal came not from this committee but from the Overseas Defence Committee, dominated by FO officials. Giving the impression that this issue was a tiresome distraction, they stuck to the line that there were no forces to spare for areas not under immediate threat and that Malaya's prime duty was to produce as much rubber and tin as it could.[16]

The key question here is why it did not occur to Thomas to negotiate compromise. A study of the debates relating to these matters, as recorded in the later minutes of the war committee meetings, convey no sense of urgency or passion; all the senior figures seemed more concerned with simply making their point than forcing the issue to an unpopular conclusion. It was this lack of rigorous and concerted effort to reach an agreement between the administration and the military that forced the British government to send a minister, Duff Cooper, to Singapore.

In the event, most historians agree that the contribution made by Duff Cooper was at best minimal, at worst damaging.[17] After only three months in post, during which period he was away from Singapore for some weeks, travelling extensively around his "parish" of Southeast Asia, Duff Cooper wrote a formal, damning indictment of Thomas' administration. He corresponded privately with Churchill and although some of his observations about the poor relations between military and civilians were perceptive, his judgement on Malayan administrative affairs showed little understanding of the complicated governance in place.[18] He also broadcast an embarrassing statement about the rescue of all the civilians from Penang during the Japanese aerial attack on the island when, in fact, the only civilians rescued were Europeans. This insensitivity highlighted his ignorance of the complexities of Malayan society.

His appointment to Minister Resident in the Far East was a convenient means of finding Duff Cooper something in the way of gainful employment while removing his intrusive presence from the London scene. In his book, somewhat fittingly titled *Old Men Forget: The Autobiography of Duff Cooper (Viscount Norwich)* (1988), he openly presents himself as a

---

[16] See Chapter 3.

[17] See, for example, an assessment in Callahan's *The Worst Disaster*, pp. 247–50. Also, Gilchrist, *Malaya 1941*, p. 26. Hack and Blackburn, *Did Singapore have to Fall?*, p. 85.

[18] Ibid.

licentious and frustrated figure. He returned to London when Singapore was at the height of the crisis. His first remark on hearing of the surrender was not one of despondency or statesmanlike reflection on the impact of the loss, but rather what bearing it would have on his career:

> In politics it is damaging to be associated, however distantly, with failure. Singapore signified failure, and I had been out on a special mission to Singapore. The surrender which took place there coincided with my return. The most malevolent of critics, knowing the facts, could not with justice have accused me of any responsibility for what happened. It was primarily a naval and military disaster and I had no connection whatever with naval or military affairs.[19]

On 10 December 1941, Duff Cooper took over the chairmanship of the War Council in Singapore. The meetings, from this point on, were almost entirely concerned with the progress of the Japanese invasion and the military tactics deployed to meet it, and notably, following the early British reverses at the hands of the Japanese, Duff Cooper suggested at one of these meetings (13 December) that he considered the situation so serious that he proposed a radical change of strategy to the military commanders.[20] This is not the action of a man "having no connection with military affairs". He was dismissive of nearly everyone and everything in Malaya: he did not get on with either Brooke-Popham or Thomas, had a low regard for Percival and was instrumental in the dismissal of the Colonial Secretary. In early January he cabled the CO that, in his opinion, the MCS had failed lamentably in making adequate preparations for war. This judgement was made after nearly five weeks of war; none of his pre-war reports made mention of any inadequacy.[21]

Duff Cooper added yet another level to an already over-heavy command structure; as Callahan has written: "[he] was a failed politician, exiled to Singapore with great responsibilities of the vaguest kind, no precise terms of reference and no authority".[22] Shenton Thomas considered his behaviour as nothing more than an attempt to ingratiate

---

[19] Viscount Norwich Duff Cooper, *Old Men Forget*, p. 310.

[20] See Chapter 5.

[21] Duff Cooper reports and correspondence, except his private letters to Churchill, are filed in the CAB 66 series. He makes no mention of poor pre-war preparations.

[22] Callahan, *The Worst Disaster*, p. 248.

himself with Churchill by magnifying the responsibilities entrusted to him.[23] His brief tenure left no memorable legacy with the exception that he recognized the fundamental need for a supreme commander.

Directly after his release from prison at the end of the war, Thomas launched into a defence of his personal role and that of his administration before and during the war. Public accusations of incompetence had been levelled at both the civil and military authorities for the gross mismanagement of the whole affair. Churchill, while declaring that the loss of Singapore "was the worst disaster and largest capitulation in British history",[24] nevertheless rejected the call for an inquiry on the grounds that it was inappropriate while the nation's energies were consumed with a major war; in any case, he claimed that the key personalities could not be spared from their vital tasks.[25] In parliament, he admitted:

> I will, however, say this: Singapore was, of course, a naval base rather than a fortress. It depended upon command of the sea, which again depends upon command of the air. Its permanent fortifications and batteries were constructed from a naval point of view. The various defence lines which had been constructed in Johore were not successfully held. The field works constructed upon the island itself to defend the fortress were not upon a sufficiently large scale.[26]

Nevertheless, condemnation continued unabated until well after the war. Thomas set about putting the record straight and spent the rest of his life in this unrewarded mission. He wrote three major works, none of which were published.[27] He argued passionately that the role played by the Singapore government was distorted to accommodate military failings, and went to great trouble to retrieve retrospective records supporting his assertion that he had fulfilled his obligations to the CO

---

[23] Thomas Papers.

[24] Churchill, Speech, Caxton Hall, London, 26 Mar. 1942. Montgomery, *Shenton of Singapore*, p.189.

[25] Churchill, *History of the Second World War: Volume 4*, p. 81.

[26] Hansard 1941–42 Vol. 377, cols 1674, 1676.

[27] "What Malaya Did", "Malaya's War Effort" and a lengthy "Comment on the draft History of the *War against Japan*". All documents are held by RHL, Oxford. Vide, Shenton Thomas private papers.

and, within the restrictions this imposed on him, had met the demands of the military. There is no acknowledgement in these writings that many of his responses were tardy and made only because of persistent demands from both the military and the civilian population and at some considerable period into the crisis.

His civil servants in upcountry Malaya had no clear instructions about what to do as the Japanese approached. In nearly every case, senior government officials had to make up their own minds whether to remain at their posts or abandon their responsibilities. It has been said that it was the inherent capability of the British to improvise that resulted in many of the problems arising from the invasion being solved locally. District commissioners, officers of the PWD, the FMS Railways and the post and telegraph services kept the civil administration in being in the various states under circumstances of the greatest difficulty.[28] In a report after the war, the British government decided to make sure that, in future, civil servants were quite clear about their responsibility in such events:

> European officers of the civil government in areas of military operations should remain at their posts as long as they can serve a useful purpose and assist the military; but that, if and when they can no longer render such service and enemy occupation of their districts is imminent, they should (after completing the duties allotted to them) withdraw by arrangement with the military commander ...[29]

There was total confusion about the policy of evacuation and the management of refugees. Passive defence measures, on the other hand, after an initial muddle, responded well to the call. Additionally Thomas had the misguided belief that military setbacks and bad news generally should not be made public. Inevitably, this led to a serious breakdown of trust between the people and the authorities.

In April 1942, the editor of *The Straits Times*, G.W. Seabridge, compiled a secret report for the War Cabinet in London. He had been editor of this newspaper since 1928 until his escape to Batavia on 11 February 1942, so he wrote with some authority and experience of Singapore's affairs.

[28] Kirby, *Singapore*. p. 188.
[29] CAB/68/9/17 dated 25 Mar. 1942, NA.

He had been highly critical of Thomas and the Singapore government throughout the campaign. In his report, among many harsh comments, he said:

> Singapore itself was in a state of almost complete chaos from the end of December. Civil Servants who had evacuated from the Malay States sought to set up temporary departments in Singapore for no other apparent reason than the preservation of their jobs. Even the FMS Income Tax Department set itself up in Singapore after the last Federated State had fallen into Japanese hands. The Civil administration cracked badly and broke completely at some points. There was little co-operation with the Services, and many indications of jealousy and fear that outsiders might poach on the preserves of the Civil Servant ... The extent to which obstructionists flourished was staggering.[30]

As an example of Thomas' vacillation, Seabridge described the passing of a War Courts Ordinance to expedite the trial of persons charged with treachery, an ordinance the Governor felt was forced upon him and with which he was not comfortable. However, before anyone had been brought to trial the Chief Justice, "who also disliked the idea intensely, discovered a statement by *James I or II* (!) that the whole procedure was unconstitutional—and the War Court was stillborn".[31]

From a military point of view, I endorse the findings of most eminent military historians—that it would almost certainly have made no difference to the outcome of the campaign had there been a change of commanders at the very top, both military and civilian. Without the vital tools, the task was impossible. A more energetic and ruthless military leader might have delayed the Japanese advance for a longer period, and perhaps created time for more reinforcements to arrive. However, unless those reinforcements included essential aircraft, ships, tanks and other vital equipment, there was little hope of preventing an eventual collapse. At the end of the first week of the campaign, the army was without any effective air support and remained unprotected for the remainder of the battle. The seas around Malaya were unguarded and clear for the Japanese to use as supplementary resupply routes for their

---

[30] War Cabinet Paper W.P. (42) 177, 25 Apr. 1942. "Report on the Fall of Singapore" by G.W. Seabridge, NA.

[31] Ibid.

advancing forces and to insert troops behind the retreating British. Denuded of the support of the other two services, the army, in effect, fought a solitary campaign.

Taking up his post in May 1941, Percival, the Army Commander, inherited a strategy compiled and refined over many years but based upon mythical forces and equipment. The planners, who were encouraged in the belief that their demands for a garrison of the size needed for the task would in time be forthcoming, designed tactics based on this assumption, which inexorably led to the wrong conclusions. The RAF made itself responsible for the defence of Malaya. Moreover, the Air Commander, without consulting the other services, designed airfields on the exposed east coast of Malaya ready for the fabled modern fighter aircraft to assault the approaching armada. The army was told it had to defend these new airfields as well as those in operation. The disagreement between the army and the RAF on this fundamental issue of protecting airfields, while simultaneously deploying the same meagre ground forces to defensive positions on the anticipated axes of enemy advance, led to open hostility between the two services. It blighted the formulation of a sensible and practicable solution.

In an attempt to compensate for the paucity of soldiers, the plan Operation Matador was prepared. A division-sized force would pre-empt a landing in southeast Thailand by rushing to the assumed landing beaches before the Imperial Japanese Army stepped ashore. Again, it was a plan which Percival inherited but the authority to launch it was so tightly controlled by London, for fear of upsetting the sensibilities of the Thais, that permission came too late for it to be carried out. In any case, it was a plan that also assumed that the RAF would have created havoc on the approaching Japanese flotilla before its attempted landing. Historians generally agree that, with these conditions imposed on its implementation, Matador could not have succeeded.[32] A thorough time appreciation would have revealed that the calculated 36-hour warning to launch an operation of this complexity was wholly inadequate.[33] The consequence was a serious diversion of resources and energy from the main aim of defending the Jitra

---

[32] See, for example, Gilchrist, *Malaya 1941*, passim, for a clear analysis.
[33] Kirby, *Singapore*. p. 110.

area which, in turn, led to this vital position being ill-prepared and overrun before any determined resistance could be offered.

Percival's command and the tactics of his retreat down the Malay Peninsula and defence of Singapore has been the subject of intense and endless scrutiny. Nearly all the authorities agree that, even taking account of the scandalous conditions under which he was forced to operate, his conduct was poor, without imagination and conviction. He lacked firmness and authority in managing his subordinates when it was time for a ruthless assertion of leadership.

> There is no evidence that he ever directed his commanders' minds towards any plan that might regain the initiative, or to any area in which a decisive battle might be fought. Instead the only plan in their minds was to hold on as long as possible .... In the record Percival gives of his conversations with his subordinate commanders it is noticeable that the suggestions always came from them. It was never that he told them what to do but that they told him what they must do.[34]

However, of all his questionable judgments, the one that draws the most opprobrium was his failure, indeed refusal, to have defensive fortifications erected on the north shore of the island. He refused to countenance the construction of such preparations on the extraordinary grounds that they would be bad for morale. His Chief Engineer, Brigadier Simson, pleaded passionately and ceaselessly for permission to go ahead and drew up a list of the ten most important things, both civil and military, which should be done in preparation for the defence of Singapore. The list eventually came before Churchill, who claimed it was the first document to reveal to him the total lack of defence installations on the northern coast of Singapore Island. The historians of this period, Donald and Joanna Moore, put it succinctly:

> Every military shortcoming in the fight for Malaya and Singapore is explicable in rational terms but this. The deplorable absence of intelligence, the catastrophic notions of superiority and security, the chronic shortage of equipment, the lack of forward planning, the breakdown of confidence, and every aspect of the retreat itself – the

---

[34] E.K.G. Sixsmith, *British Generalship in the Twentieth Century* (London: Arms and Armour Press, 1970).

confusion, the failure of leadership, the inefficiency – all these things can be explained, if not excused. But Gen. Percival's refusal to fortify the northern shore of the Island opposite the advancing Japanese army until it was far too late is explicable only in terms of irrationality.[35]

It is interesting to compare the reluctance of Percival and Thomas to prepare defences with the tactics of the Japanese in 1945, when in similar circumstances they expected the Allies to return and invade Malaya. They were ordered to resist the enemy fully, even under the worst conditions. Artillery and close combat trenches were to be prepared, and infantry positions, tunnel-type communication trenches, and dummy positions constructed using local labour. Working parties, by the hundreds, were taken across the causeway to Johor and made to build tunnels for weeks on end. They also drove bunkers 4 metres (13 feet) high into the hills to protect Japanese troops and provide ambush positions.[36]

Attitudes towards the war in the predominant native population of Malaya and Singapore—the Malays, Chinese and Indians—differed. What is firmly established is that there was no effective fifth column at work during this period. There were isolated incidents of local people helping the advancing Japanese by giving directions and confirming the location of Allied forces, but practically no formed and directed fifth column. Nevertheless, there were some instances of behind-the-lines espionage but they were few and of little significance. It was discovered later that some Japanese soldiers dressed in local costume and speaking Malay attempted to infiltrate British lines. The unfortunate outcome was that British soldiers, with little knowledge of the country and its people, took no risks and on occasion shot any Asian approaching their positions. To be so unaware of local nuance was a fundamental problem for a colonial force in its early deployment. At the final conference in Singapore before the surrender, the Inspector General of Police (Dickinson) asked all the senior officers present to what extent had fifth-column activity contributed to the military defeat. All senior commanders reassured him

---

[35] Donald Moore and Joanna Moore, *The First 150 Years of Singapore* (Singapore: Donald Moore Press, 1969), p. 607.

[36] Yoji and Yoshimura, *New Perspectives on the Japanese Occupation in Malaya and Singapore*, p. 220. Frei, *"Surrendering Syonan"*.

that they had experienced no fifth column activity at all.[37] This assessment was later confirmed by Major Fujiwara, when he was interrogated after the war about his *kikan* (agency), whose task was to organize sabotage and promote pro-Japanese propaganda. He admitted that [fifth column activity] had been "militarily of no use whatever before and during the actual fighting".[38]

The indigenous Malay suffered least at the hands of the Japanese. Sjovald Cunyngham-Brown, a senior MCS with over 20 years of service in Malaya, in a rather jaundiced summation, declared:

> [T]he Malays were not taking any great interest and can you blame them. It was their country that was being rolled over by two vast overseas giants ... smashing and destroying everything. The Malays had benefitted by joining western Civilisation and now they realised with horror that they were about to pay for it: this was what happened if you joined the west— so they stood by. The Indians were mostly rubber estate workers who had no contact with what was going on. They lay doggo, hearing nothing, saying nothing and doing nothing—and I don't blame them either. The Chinese on the other hand were already at war with Japan. Their mother country was fighting Japan, therefore so were they, and the more virile of them were busy getting arms to go into the jungle to die fighting against the Japanese—as indeed they did.[39]

Another senior government servant, Hugh Bryson, the long-serving clerk to the councils (legislative and federal), also believed that calling on the Asians of Malaya to fight for the survival of the British was pointless and impractical. He wrote: "[H]ad we been able to show clearly that our rule was ideal, and that an invading power would bring the place down in ruins without firm local support, we might have succeeded".[40] Bryson was convinced that the Malayans were not particularly interested in maintaining British prestige. In any case, he noted, how was the message to be promulgated?

> Could we expect Residents and Advisors to stump their territories preaching all out preparations for war against another 'foreign' power?

[37] Thomas Papers, op cit. Letter Dickinson to Thomas, 5 June 1947.
[38] Allen, *Singapore 1941–1942*, p. 254.
[39] Allen, *Tales from the South China Seas*, p. 255.
[40] BAM Collection. Correspondence Dickinson/Bryson. Jan 1969. CU.

Malaya was so divided with Malays, Chinese and Indians all with their own axes to grind, and no common loyalty to bind them together that a unity of purpose would have been almost impossible to develop. The Sultans too would have been of little avail. Malaya was either a country where men were seeking employment and security (Europeans, Chinese, and Indians) or looking for a life of comparative ease and comfort (Malays).[41]

Moreover, he pointed out that it was official British policy to advocate procedures that would keep down any (internal) movements that might have bred local loyalty on the grounds that such movements were, in part, the work of outside subversives. Inflexible adherence to this rule was, in the end, more divisive. In addition, before the war, the British authorities looked upon the Japanese as no more than another group of potential developers who would invest capital ultimately of great benefit to the Malayan government. In 1928, when the Japanese wanted a licence to open a big iron mine at Dungun, the local British adviser in Terengganu agreed to grant it, with Singapore's endorsement.[42] Even then, some Malays pointed out the danger of creating this foothold. However, Terengganu needed money and, as no British company was prepared to invest in the Dungun mine, there seemed no alternative.[43]

After an extensive and detailed study of the loss of Singapore in 1942, a pivotal event in the history of the British Empire, it is evident, considering all the circumstances prevailing at that time, there is no particular issue, particular person or crucial activity that would have altered the course of history. No change of action or avoidance would have made a difference. Singapore was a lost cause from the day the construction of the naval base was complete. If such a large, comprehensive, modern facility, positioned on a strategic naval crossroads, was judged vital, it required a dedicated resident fleet with modern fighter aircraft protection and a large ground force in properly constructed fortifications to ensure its security. None of these needs could be met by a bankrupt and exhausted nation, as Britain was in the 1930s.

---

[41] Ibid.

[42] ODC Paper No. 353, 18 Jan. 1929 "Japanese Interests in Malaya, with specific regard to the Vicinity of Singapore", NA.

[43] CAB 5/7. 31 July 1930, "Malaya: Application by Japanese for Prospecting Licences in Southeast Johore", NA. See also Robertson, *The Japanese File*, pp. 26–8.

The naval base was barely used throughout its pre-war life, certainly not nearly to the capacity for which it was designed. The region was, in any case, regarded as less volatile than other areas of the world. Indeed, the people of Malaya and Singapore regarded their territory as a peaceful backwater and, with commercial transport still in its infancy, it was a long way from the contamination of western excesses. The benevolent 150-year rule of the British had bred complacency and an unjustified belief in immunity from danger. Both the populace and its government were so immersed in their peaceful existence that even when the harbingers of war came knocking, they were unable to believe there was serious danger, and incapable of galvanizing themselves for the struggle. The colony fell to inertia.

The British government's insistence that every effort be made to avoid offending or provoking Japan reinforced Thomas' early belief that there would be no confrontation. He did not want people frightened by overt military defensive constructions. In Percival he had an army commander who was willing to oblige, as he too thought building defences was not good for the morale of his troops. Thomas carried his obsession of preserving an air of composure to the point of negligence. He failed to alert his staff in Malaya of the dangers ahead, nor did he advise them to prepare contingency plans, initiate precautions or instruct them about their role in relation to their administrative responsibilities in a crisis. No advice was given regarding evacuation, no plans prepared. In addition, he controlled the release of truthful information about the war so that people were in total ignorance of the actual state of affairs. In summary, he displayed a lack of leadership and was indecisive; he failed to coordinate the activities of vital government departments and to prioritize civil defence and refugee activities.

His early lack of knowledge of military matters is perfectly understandable. A diplomatic career in Africa did not prepare him for this arena. However, he does not appear to have made any great or urgent effort to come to grips with the essentials of military affairs. Some of his pronouncements at critical times convey disinterest or lack of realism or, as he sometimes claimed, he was not told what was happening. An egregious example: he planned to replace the British resident in Ipoh,

Marcus Rex, with another of his staff, H. Weisberg, only to be told that Ipoh had already fallen to the Japanese.[44]

Recently released official documents reinforced the legitimacy of the many highly censorial charges levelled at the British administration in Singapore before and during the campaign. In essence, the role that Thomas' government should have played in this fateful event was, first, to warn the people of the country of the serious danger which could come their way and second, to introduce measures to minimize the threat to life. He should have given assurances that the authorities were being proactive. On the strategic front, he should have provided the military with the practical support it dearly needed to prepare for the onslaught. As it turned out, the government made minimum effort to put in place basic civil defence and passive defence measures until it was too late. There was no attempt to place the country on a war footing. On the contrary, the Governor stood firm on avoiding such measures.

It is tempting to speculate on the outcome if Thomas and his administration had acknowledged the Japanese threat at an earlier stage and followed the advice of the military authorities. Certainly, it is reasonable to assume that many more civilian non-combatants would have been evacuated safely and in time, and many less would have ended up incarcerated in Changi Prison. More air-raid shelters would have saved many lives. Efficient and practised emergency services would have dealt with the injured and coped with the damaged infrastructure. A coordinated and properly directed scorched-earth policy would have deprived the Japanese army of valuable supplies, transport and propaganda facilities. Releasing a workforce from industry would have enabled the preparation of properly constructed fortifications. Of course, this would have been at the expense of tin and rubber production, but it would almost certainly have disrupted the momentum of the Japanese advance.

Crucially, we now know that when the Japanese army arrived in Johor Bahru, it was dangerously short of battle supplies particularly artillery and small arms ammunition.[45] Its administrative tail stretched back up

---

[44] BAM Collection. Correspondence Dickinson/Bryson. Jan. 1969. CU.

[45] Henry P. Frei, "The Island Battle", paper given at conference (Singapore: National University of Singapore), 2002. Some Japanese soldiers, when they learnt a white

the Malayan Peninsula for several hundred miles and the forward troops had outrun this supply chain. Yamashita is quoted as saying:

> My attack on Singapore was a bluff – a bluff that worked. I had 30,000 men and was outnumbered more than three to one. I knew that if I had to fight for long for Singapore I would be beaten. That was why the surrender had to be at once. I was very frightened all the time that the British would discover our numerical weakness and lack of supplies and force me into disastrous street fighting.[46]

If the Governor had allowed Simson to construct vital defences in South Johor, as the latter had proposed in January 1942, it could have imposed a delay of some consequence on the Japanese advance, but Thomas refused because Johor was a UMS. If Percival had not rejected the construction of defences on the northern shore of the island, these two barriers would have had a significant effect on the course of the battle.

Most importantly, the effect on the morale of the people and on the image of the British administration, as a proactive, realistic, honest government acting decisively, with determination and authority, would have been immeasurable.

---

surrender flag had been raised, thought it must be theirs because they had run out of ammunition.

[46] Christopher F. Shores, Bran Cull and Yasuho Izawa, *Bloody Shambles. Vol. 1, The Drift of War to the Fall of Singapore* (London: Grub Street, 1992).

BIBLIOGRAPHY

PRIMARY SOURCES

National Archives Kew

Admiralty

ADM 116	Admiralty and Secretariat Cases, 1919–45
ADM 199	Admiralty: War History Cases and Papers, Second World War
ADM 167	Admiralty Board Minutes and Memoranda, 1919–42
ADM 223	Naval Intelligence Papers, 1940–42

Air Ministry

AIR 2	General Correspondence, 1923–48
AIR 8	Chief of the Air Staff Papers, 1938–42
AIR 9	Directorate of Plans Papers, 1921–39
AIR 22	Periodical Returns, Summaries and Bulletins, 1939–42
AIR 23	Overseas Commands Papers, 1936–45
AIR 40	Directorate of Intelligence and other Intelligence Papers

Cabinet Office

CAB 4	Committee of Imperial Defence: Memoranda Series C (Colonial Defence), 1937–39
CAB 7	Committee of Imperial Defence: Overseas Defence Committee Minutes, 1921–30

CAB 8	Committee of Imperial Defence: Overseas Defence Committee Memoranda
CAB 23	Cabinet Minutes, 1925–39
CAB 29	International Conferences, 1939
CAB 32	Imperial Conferences, 1921–39
CAB 53	Committee of Imperial Defence: Chiefs of Staff Committee Minutes, 1923–39
CAB 65	War Cabinet: Minutes, 1939–45
CAB 66	War Cabinet: Memoranda, WP and CP Series, 1939–45
CAB 79	War Cabinet: Chiefs of Staff Committee Minutes, 1939–45
CAB 84	War Cabinet: Joint Planning Committees, 1939–45
CAB 94	War Cabinet: Overseas Defence Committee, 1939–45
CAB 96	War Cabinet: Committees on Far East, 1940–45

Colonial Office

CO 273	Straits Settlements Original Correspondence, 1932–46
CO 323	Colonies, General: Original Correspondence, 1939–41
CO 717	Colonial Office: Federated Malay States, Original Correspondence, 1920–51
CO 786	Colonial Office: Federated Malay States, Register of Correspondence, 1919–51
CO 825	Colonial Office: Eastern Original Correspondence, 1927–51
CO 828	Colonial Office: Federated Malay States: Acts, 1925–48
CO 850	Colonial Office: Personnel, Original Correspondence, 1932–52
CO 865	Far Eastern Reconstruction: Original Correspondence, 1942–45
CO 953	Colonial Office: Singapore Original Correspondence, 1936–51
CO 967	Colonial Office: Private Office Papers, 1873–1966
CO 968	Colonial Office and Commonwealth Office: Defence Department and Successors: Original Correspondence, 1941–67
CO 975	Colonial Office: Far Eastern Reconstruction: Register of Correspondence, 1942–44

Foreign Office

FO 371	Foreign Office: Political Departments; General Correspondence, 1937–45
FO 436	Confidential Print: Far Eastern Affairs, 1937–56
FCO 24	Commonwealth Office, Far East and Pacific Department and Foreign and Commonwealth Office, South West Pacific Department: Registered Files (H and FW Series), 1967–78

Prime Minister's Office

PREM 3	Prime Minister's Office: Operational Correspondence and Papers, 1937–46
PREM 4	Prime Minister's Office: Confidential Papers, 1939–46

War Office

WO 106	Directorate of Military Operations and Intelligence Papers, 1930–45
WO 172	War Diaries, Southeast Asia Command and Allied Land Forces, Southeast Asia, 1939–46
WO 203	Military Headquarters Papers, Far East Forces, 1941–45
WO 208	Directorate of Military Intelligence Papers, 1939–45
WO 216	Chief of the Imperial General Staff Papers, 1935–47
WO 252	Topographical and Economic Surveys,1941–46

PRIVATE MANUSCRIPT PAPERS

Cambridge University

Churchill College Archive Centre
Cooper, Alfred Duff. Minister Resident Singapore, 1942–94.
Noble, Admiral Sir Percy, Commander-in-Chief China Station, 1938–40.

Cambridge University Library
Royal Commonwealth Society Collections. British Association of Malaysia and Singapore.
Bryson, Hugh Patterson, Malayan Civil Service, 1921–45; clerk to the Council SS and FMS, 1938–41.

Dickinson, A.H., Inspector General of Police, SS, 1940–42.
Onraet, R.H., Police Officer, Malaya, 1907–38.

Oxford University

Rhodes House Library
Bleakley, R.J., Malayan Civil Service, 1937–41.
Blythe, W.C., Malayan Civil Service, 1921–45.
Dickinson, A.H., Inspector General of Police, SS, 1940–42.
Heussler, R. W., Malayan Civil Service History Papers, 1929–84.
Rodgers, H.K., Chairman Singapore Harbour Board, 1937–42.
Thomas Sir Shenton, Governor SS and High Commissioner Malaya, 1934–42.
Turner, R.N., Malayan Civil Service, 1935–45.

Imperial War Museum

Ashmore, Lieutenant Colonel B.H. Staff Officer, Malayan Campaign.
Bangs, Bill. Rubber Planter—Oral History.
Grimsdale, Colonel G.E. Far East Combined Bureau, 1939–41.
Heath, Lieutenant General Sir Lewis. Corps Commander Malaya, 1940–42.
Percival, Lieutenant General Arthur. GOC Malaya, 1941–42.
Reilly M.M., Cipher Clerk to Governor Thomas and Duff Cooper, 1939–42.
Ryves, Harvey, FMS Police Force.

King's College London

Liddell Hart Centre for Military Archives
Brooke-Popham Air Chief Marshal, Sir Robert, Commander-in Chief, Far East, 1940–41.
Haines, W.A., FMS Police Force.
Ismay, General, Lord, Deputy Secretary to the War Cabinet, 1940–45.
Simson, Brigadier Ivan, Chief Engineer, Malaya Command, 1941–42; Director General Civil Defence Singapore, 1941–42.
Spooner, Megan, wife of Rear Admiral E.J. Spooner, personal diaries.
Vlieland, Charles A., Secretary for Defence Malaya, 1938–41.

PUBLISHED OFFICIAL RECORDS
Australia

Australian War Memorial
AWM 73 Series. Official History, 1939–45 War. Records of Lionel Wigmore.

Malaysia

Arkib Negara
Proceedings of the Federal Council,1937–41.
High Commissioner's Despatches, 1939–41.

Singapore

National Archives Singapore
"Proceedings of Secretariat and Legislative Council of the Straits Settlements
1937–1941".
"Straits Settlements. Annual Departmental Reports of the Straits Settlements
1932–1938".

National University of Singapore
Unpublished MA dissertations.
Ho, Peng An. "Civil–Military Relations in the Defence of Singapore, 1937–1942".
Teoh, Chai Lean. "The Administration of Sir Shenton Thomas, 1934–1936".

US Army Centre for Military History, Japanese Monograph Series
No. 24: History of the Southern Army, 1941–1945.
No. 54: Malaya Operations Record, Nov. 1941–Mar. 1942.
No. 107: Malaya Invasion Naval Operations (rev. ed.).

Official Despatches

Supplement to *The London Gazette*, 20 Jan. 1948. No. 38183.Air Chief Marshal
Sir R. Brooke-Popham."Operations in the Far East, from 17 October 1940 to
27 December 1941".
Supplement to *The London Gazette*, 20 Feb. 1948. No. 38214. Vice-Admiral Sir G.
Layton. "Loss of H.M. Ships Prince of Wales and Repulse".
Third Supplement to *The London Gazette*, 26 February 1948. No.38216. Air Vice-
Marshal Sir P. Maltby. "Report on the Air Operations During Campaigns in
Malaya and Netherlands East Indies from 8 December 1941 to 12 March
1942".
Second Supplement to *The London Gazette*, 20 Feb. 1948. No. 38215.Lieutenant
General A. Percival. "Operations of Malaya Command from 8 December
1941 to 15 February 1942".
General Sir A. Wavell. London: Her Majesty's Stationer's Office, 1948. "Despatch
by the Supreme Commander of the ABDA Area to the Combined Chiefs
of Staff on the Operations in the Southeast Pacific, 15 January 1942 to 25
February 1942".

Official Histories

Butler, J.R. (ed.). *History of the Second World War, Grand Strategy*, 6 vols. London: Her Majesty's Stationer's Office, 1956–76.

Churchill, Sir W. *The Second World War*, 6 vols. London: Cassell, 1948–51.

Kirby, S. Woodburn. *The War Against Japan, Vol.1, The Loss of Singapore*. London: Her Majesty's Stationer's Office, 1957.

Richards, Dennis and Hilary St George Saunders. *Royal Air Force 1939–1945: Volume II: The Fight Avails*. London: Her Majesty's Stationer's Office, 1954.

Roskill, Captain S.W. *The War at Sea 1939–45, Vol. I, The Defensive*. London: Her Majesty's Stationer's Office, 1954.

———. *Naval Policy between the Wars*, 2 vols. London: Trustees of the National Maritime Museum, 1978.

Conference Papers

**National University of Singapore Conference*: February 1962*
"Sixty Years On: The Fall of Singapore Revisited"

Callahan, Raymond. "Churchill and Singapore".

Dennis, P. "Australia and the Singapore Strategy".

Fedorowich, K. "The Evacuation of Civilians From Hong Kong and Malaya/ Singapore, 1939–42".

Flower, Sybilla. "Allied Prisoners of War: The Malayan Campaign, 1941–42."

Kinvig, Clifford. "General Percival and the Fall of Singapore".

Murfett, Malcolm H. "An Enduring Theme: The Singapore Strategy".

Warren, Alan. "The Indian Army and the Fall of Singapore".

Yoji, Akashi. "General Yamashita Tomoyuki: Commander of the Twenty-Fifth Army".

Contemporary Newspapers

The Straits Times, 1930–42.

Singapore Free Press, 1934–41.

The Daily Telegraph, 1940–45.

The Times (London), 1939–45.

The Malay Mail, 1939–41.

Secondary Sources

Alanbrooke, Field Marshall Lord. *War Diaries, 1939–1945*. Ed. Alex Danchev and Dan Todman. London: Weidenfeld & Nicolson, 2001.

Aldrich, Richard. "A Question of Expediency: Britain, the United States and Thailand, 1941–42". *Journal of Southeast Asian Studies* 20, 2 (1988).

————. *Intelligence and the War against Japan: Britain, America and the Politics of Secret Service.* Cambridge and New York: Cambridge University Press, 2000.

Allen, Charles. *Tales from South China Seas: Images of the British in South-east Asia in the Twentieth Century.* Preston, Lancashire: Abacus, 1990.

Allen, Louis. "The Surrender of Singapore: The Official Japanese Version", *Durham University Journal* (new series) 29 (1967): 1–6.

————. *Singapore 1941–1942.* New Jersey: Associated University Press, 1977.

Andaya, Barbara Watson and Leonard Y. Andaya. *A History of Malaysia.* New York: St. Martin's Press, 1982.

Barber, Andrew. *Penang at War: A History of Penang during and between the First and Second World Wars, 1914–1945.* Kuala Lumpur: AB & A, 2010.

Barber, Noel. *Sinister Twilight: The Fall and Rise Again of Singapore.* London: Collins, 1969.

Barnett, Correlli. *The Collapse of British Power.* London: Eyre, Methuen, 1972.

————. *Engage the Enemy More Closely: The Royal Navy in the Second World War.* London: Norton, 1991.

Bastin, John Sturgus and Robin W. Winks. *Malaysia: Selected Historical Readings.* Kuala Lumpur and New York: Oxford University Press, 1966.

Bayly, Christopher and Timothy Harper. *Forgotten Armies: The Fall of British Asia, 1941–1945.* London: Penguin, 2005.

————. *Forgotten Wars: Freedom and Revolution in Southeast Asia.* Cambridge, MA: Belknap Press of Harvard University Press, 2007.

Beesly, Patrick. *Very Special Intelligence: The Story of the Admiralty's Operational Intelligence Centre, 1939–1945.* London: Chatham, 2006 (2000).

Bennett, Henry Gordon. *Why Singapore Fell.* Sydney: Angus & Robertson, 1944.

Best, Antony. *Britain, Japan and Pearl Harbor: Avoiding War in East Asia,1936–41.* London and New York: Routledge, 1995.

Bird, Isabella L. *The Golden Chersonese.* Singapore: Monsoon Books, 2010 (1884).

Blackburn,Kevin and Daniel Ju Ern Chew. "Dalforce at the Fall of Singapore in 1942". *Journal of Chinese Overseas* 1, 2 (2005): 233–59.

Bond, Brian. *Chief of Staff: Diaries of Lt Gen Sir Henry Pownall: Vol II.* London: Leo Cooper, 1974.

Braddon, Russell. *The Naked Island.* London: Pan Books, 1955.

Brendon, Piers. *The Decline and Fall of the British Empire, 1791–1997.*London: Jonathan Cape, 2007.

Brooke, Geoffrey. *Singapore's Dunkirk.* London: Cooper, 1989.

Brown, Cecil. *Suez to Singapore.* New York, NY: Random House, 1942.

Butler, James Ramsay Montagu. *Grand Strategy. Vol. 2, September 1939–June 1941*. London HMSO, 1957.

Caffrey, Kate. *Out in the Midday Sun: Singapore 1941–1945*. London: A. Deutsch, 1974.

Callahan, Raymond. *The Worst Disaster: The Fall of Singapore*. London: Associated University Press, 1977.

———. "The Illusion of Security: Singapore 1919–42". *Journal of Contemporary History* 9, 2 (1974): 69–92.

Chapman, F. Spencer. *The Jungle is Neutral*. London: Chatto & Windus, 1963 (1949).

Charmley, John. *Duff Cooper, The Authorized Biography*. London: Weidenfield & Nicolson, 1986.

Chew, Ernest C.T. and Edwin Lee. *A History of Singapore*. New York: Oxford University Press, 1991.

Clarke, Peter. *The Last Thousand Days of the British Empire: Churchill, Roosevelt, and the Birth of the Pax Americana*. London: Penguin Books, 2007.

Clisby, Mark. *Guilty or Innocent: The Gordon Bennett Case*. Sydney: Allen & Unwin, 1992.

Collier, Basil. *The War in the Far East 1941–1945. A Military History*. London: Heinemann, 1969.

Connell, John. *Wavell: Supreme Commander 1941–43*. London: Collins, 1969.

Corner, E.J.H. *The Marquis, a Tale of Syonan-to*. Singapore: Heinemann Asia, 1981.

Corr, Gerard H. *The War of the Springing Tigers*. London: Osprey, 1975.

Cowan, C.D. *Nineteenth Century Malaya: The Origins of British Political Control*. London: Oxford University Press, 1961.

Craig, William. *The Fall of Japan*. London: Pan Books, 1968.

Cunyngham-Brown, Sjovald. *The Traders*. London: Newman Neame, 1971.

Dixon, Norman F. *On the Psychology of Military Incompetence*. London: Pimlico, 1994.

Drabble, John H. *An Economic History of Malaysia, c. 1800–1990: The Transition to Modern Economic Growth*. Basingstoke: Macmillan, 2000.

Duff Cooper, Viscount Norwich. *Old Men Forget: The Autobiography of Duff Cooper (Viscount Norwich)*. London: Hart Davis, 1953.

Elphick, Peter. *Singapore: The Pregnable Fortress: A Study in Deception, Discord and Desertion*. London: Hodder & Stoughton, 1995.

———. *Far Eastern File: The Intelligence War in the Far East, 1930–1945*. London: Hodder & Stoughton, 1997.

Falk, Stanley L. *Seventy Days to Singapore: The Malayan Campaign, 1941–1942*. London: Hale, 1975.

Farrell, Brian P. *The Defence and Fall of Singapore 1940–1942*. Stroud, Gloucestershire: Tempus, 2005.

Farrell, Brian P. and Sandy Hunter. "A Great Betrayal: The Fall of Singapore Revisited". Paper given at conference. Singapore: National University of Singapore, 2002.

———. *A Great Betrayal: The Fall of Singapore Revisited*. Singapore: Marshall Cavendish, 2009.

Farrell, Brian P. and Garth Pratten. *Malaya 1942*. Canberra: Army History Unit, 2009.

Feis, Herbert. *The Road to Pearl Harbour: The Coming of the War between the United States and Japan*. Princeton, NJ: Princeton University Press, 1971 (1967).

Ferris, John Robert. *The Evolution of British Strategic Policy*. Basingstoke: Macmillan in association with King's College, London, 1989.

Ford, Douglas. *Britain's Secret War Against Japan, 1937–1945*. New York: Routledge, 2006.

———. *The Pacific War: Clash of Empires in World War II*. London and New York: Continuum, 2012.

Franklin, Alan and Gordon Franklin. *One Year of Life, Story of HMS Price of Wales*. London: Blackwood, 1944.

Frei, Henry P. "The Island Battle". Paper given at conference. Singapore: National University of Singapore, 2002.

———. *Guns of February: Ordinary Japanese Soldiers' Views of the Malayan Campaign and the Fall of Singapore, 1941–1942*. Singapore: Singapore University Press, 2004.

Fujiwara, Iwaichi. *F.Kikan: Japanese Intelligence Operations in Southeast Asia during World War II*. Translated by Akashi Yoji. Hong Kong: Heinemann Asia, 1983.

Furnivall, J.S. *Colonial Policy and Practice: A Comparative Study of Burma and Netherlands India*. New York: New York University Press, 1956.

Furse, Ralph Dolignon. *Aucuparius: Recollections of a Recruiting Officer*. London and New York: Oxford University Press, 1962.

Gallagher, O'Dowd. *Retreat in the East*. London: G.G. Harrap & Co., 1942.

Gilchrist, Andrew. *Malaya 1941: The Fall of a Fighting Empire*. London: Robert Hale, 1992.

Glover, Edwin Maurice. *In 70 Days: The Story of the Japanese Campaign in British Malaya*. London: F. Muller, 1946.

Ghosh, Kalyan Kumar. *Twentieth-century Malaysia: Politics of Decentralization of Power, 1920–1929*. Calcutta: Progressive Publishers, 1977.

Grenfell, Russell. *Main Fleet to Singapore*. London: Faber and Faber, 1961.

Gullick, John Michael. *Indigenous Political Systems of Western Malaya*. London: The Athlone Press, 1958.

Hack, Karl. *Defence and Decolonisation in Southeast Asia: Britain, Malaya and Singapore, 1941–68*. Richmond, Surrey: Curzon, 2001.

Hack, Karl and Kevin Blackburn. *Did Singapore have to Fall?: Churchill and the Impregnable Fortress*. London: Routledge, 2005.

Haggie, Paul. *Britannia at Bay: The Defence of the British Empire against Japan 1931–1941*. Oxford: Clarendon Press and New York: Oxford University Press, 1981.

Harrison, Cuthbert Woodville. *Some Notes on the Government Services in British Malaya*. London: Malayan Information Agency, 1929.

Hastings, Max. *Nemesis: The Battle for Japan, 1944–45*. London: Harper Press, 2007.

Heussler, Robert. *British Malaya: A Bibliographical and Biographical Compendium*. New York: Garland, 1981.

———. *British Rule in Malaya: The Malayan Civil Service and its Predecessors, 1867–1942*. Oxford: Clio Press, 1981.

———. *British Rule in Malaya, 1942–1957*. Singapore: Heinemann Asia, 1985.

Higham, Robin. *A Guide to the Sources of British Military History*. Berkeley, CA: University of California Press, 1971.

Holmes, Richard and Anthony Kemp. *The Bitter End*. Chichester: Antony Bird, 1982.

Howard, Michael. *Grand Strategy Vol IV, August 1942–September 1943*. London: Her Majesty's Stationery Office, 1972.

Ike, Nobutaka. *Japan's Decision for War: Records of the 1941 Policy Conferences*. Stanford, CA: Stanford University Press, 1967.

Ishimaru, Tota. *Japan Must Fight Britain*. Translated and edited by G.V. Rayment. London: Hurst & Blackett, 1937 (1936).

Jackson, Robert Nicholas. *Immigrant Labour and the Development of Malaya, 1786–1920: A Historical Monograph*. Kuala Lumpur: Government Press, 1961.

———. "Indian Immigration into Malaysia". In *Malaysia: Selected Historical Readings*, ed. John Sturgis Bastin and Robin W. Winks. Kuala Lumpur and New York: Oxford University Press, 1966.

James, David H. *The Rise and Fall of the Japanese Empire*. London: Allen & Unwin, 1951.

Jones, S.W. *Public Administration in Malaya*. New York and London: Royal Institute of International Affairs, 1953.

Kratoska, Paul H. (ed.). *Malaya and Singapore during the Japanese Occupation.* Singapore: Singapore University Press, 1995.

———. *Asian Labour in the Japanese Wartime Empire: Unknown Histories.* Singapore: Singapore University Press, 2006 (2005).

Keegan, John. *The Second World War.* New York: Viking, 1990 (1989).

———. *Churchill's Generals.* London: Warner Books, 1993.

Kennaway, Anne. *Journey by Candlelight: A Memoir.* Edinburgh, Pentland, 1999.

Kinvig, Clifford. *Scapegoat: General Percival of Singapore.* London and Washington, DC: Brassey's, 1996.

Kirby, Stanley Woodburn. *History of the Second World War: Vol. I: The War Against Japan.* London: HMSO, 1957.

———. *Singapore: The Chain of Disaster.* London: Cassell, 1971.

Kirk-Green, A.H.M. *Britain's Imperial Administrators, 1858–1966.* Basingstoke: Macmillan and Oxford: St Antony's College, 2000.

Kitching, Tom. *Life and Death in Changi: The War and Interment Diary of Thomas Kitching, 1942–1944.* Perth: Brian Kitching, 1999.

Knight, Nigell. *Churchill: The Greatest Briton Unmasked.* Cincinnati, OH: David & Charles, 2008.

Latimer, Jon. *Burma: The Forgotten War.* London: John Murray, 2004.

Leasor, James. *Singapore: The Battle that Changed the World.* London: House of Stratus, 2001 (1968).

Lee, Cecil. *Sunset of the Raj: The Fall of Singapore, 1942.* Edinburgh: Pentland Press, 1994.

Lee Ting Hui. "Singapore under the Japanese 1941–1945". *Journal of South Seas Society* 17, 1961.

———. "Japanese Racial Policies in Singapore". *Journal of South Seas Society* 17 (1961): 55–65.

Legg, Frank. *The Gordon Bennett Story.* Sydney: Angus & Robertson, 1965.

Leighton, Richard M. and Robert W. Coakley. *Global Logistics and Strategy.* Washington, DC: Office of the Chief of Military History, Department of the Army, 1995.

Lewin, Ronald. *The Other Ultra.* London: Hutchinson, 1982.

Lodge, A.B. *The Fall of General Gordon Bennett.* Sydney and Boston: Allen & Unwin, 1986.

Lyman, Robert. *The Generals: From Defeat to Victory, Leadership in Asia 1941–45.* London: Constable, 2008.

MacKenzie, Compton. *Eastern Epic.* London: Chatto & Windus, 1951.

Marder, Arthur Jacob. *Old Friends, New Enemies: The Royal Navy and the Imperial Japanese Navy.* Oxford: Clarendon Press and New York: Oxford University Press, 1981–90.

Marriot, Leo. *Treaty Cruisers: The World's First International Warship Building Competition*. Barnsley: Pen & Sword Maritime, 2005.

Marshall, Jonathan. *To Have and Have Not: Southeast Asian Raw Materials and the Origins of the Pacific War*. Berkeley, CA: University of California Press, 1995.

Mason, Philip. *A Matter of Honour: An Account of the Indian Army, its Officers and Men*. Harmondsworth: Penguin, 1976 (1975).

Masters, John. *The Road Past Mandalay, a Personal Narrative*. London: Corgi, 1973.

Matthews, Tony. *Shadows Dancing: Japanese Espionage against the West, 1939–1945*. London: Hale, 1993.

Maxwell, Sir William George. *The Civil Defence of Malaya: A Narrative of the Part taken in it by the Civilian Population of the Country in the Japanese Invasion*. New York: Hutchinson & Co., 1944.

McIntyre, W. David. *The Rise and Fall of the Singapore Naval Base, 1919–1942*. London: Macmillan, 1979.

Menzies, Robert. *Afternoon Light: Some Memories of Men and Events*. London: Cassell, 1968 (1967).

Michiko, N. "The Civilian Women's Internment Camp in Singapore: The World of *POW WOW*". In *New Perspectives on the Japanese Occupation in Malaya and Singapore 1941–1945*, ed. Akashi Yoji and Mako Yoshimura, pp. 186–216. Singapore: NUS Press, 2008.

Montgomery Hyde, H. and George Robert Falkiner Nuttall. *Air Defence and the Civil Population*. London: The Cresset Press, 1937.

Montgomery, Brian. *Shenton of Singapore: Governor and Prisoner of War*. London: Leo Cooper in association with Secker & Warburg, 1984.

Moore, Donald and Joanna Moore. *The First 150 Years of Singapore*. Singapore: Donald Moore Press, 1969.

Morrison, Ian. *Malayan Postscript*. London: Faber and Faber, 1942.

Morton, L. *Japan's Decision for War. United States Army in World War II: The War in the Pacific*. US Naval Institute Proceedings 80 (Dec. 1954). Washington, DC: Office of the Chief of Military History.

Murfett, Malcolm H. "Living in the Past: A Critical Re-examination of the Singapore Naval Strategy 1918–1941". *War and Society* 11, 1 (1993): 73–103.
———. *Between Two Oceans: A Military History of Singapore from the First Settlement to Final British Withdrawal*. Oxford: Oxford University Press, 1999.

Neidpath, James. *The Singapore Naval Base and the Defence of Britain's Eastern Empire, 1919–1942*. Oxford: Clarendon Press and New York: Oxford University Press, 1981.

Ong, Chit Chung. *Operation Matador: Britain's War Plans against the Japanese, 1918–1941*. Singapore: Times Academic Press, 1997.

———. *The Landward Defence of Singapore 1919–1938*. Singapore: Heinemann Asia, 1988.

Onraet, Rene Henry de Solminihac. *Singapore—A Police Background*. London: Dorothy Crisp, 1946.

Owen, Frank. *The Fall of Singapore*. London: M. Joseph, 1960.

Palit, D.K. *The Campaign in Malaya*. Dehra Dun: Palit & Dutt, 1960.

Parkinson, Roger. *The Auk: Biography of FM Auchinleck*. London: Granada Publishing, 1977.

Parris, Matthew and Andrew Bryson. *Parting Shots*. London: Viking, 2010.

Percival, A.E. *The War in Malaya*. London: Eyre & Spottiswood, 1949.

Probert, Henry. *The Forgotten Air Force: The Royal Air Force in the War against Japan 1941–1945*. London and Washington, DC: Brassey's, 1995.

Purcell, Victor. *The Chinese in Malaya*. London and New York: Oxford University Press, 1948.

———. *The Memoirs of a Malayan Official*. London: Cassell, 1965.

Richards, Dennis and Hilary St George Saunders. *Royal Air Force 1939–1945: Volume II: The Fight Avails*. London: Her Majesty's Stationer's Office, 1954.

Robertson, Eric. *The Japanese File: Pre-war Penetration of Southeast Asia*. Hong Kong: Heinemann Asia, 1979.

Robertson, John. *Australia at War 1939–1945*. Melbourne: Heinemann, 1981.

Roff, William R. *The Origins of Malay Nationalism*. New Haven, CT: Yale University Press, 1967.

Royle, Trevor. *The Last Days of the Raj*. London: M. Joseph, 1989.

Russell, Edward Frederick Langley. *The Knights of Bushido*. London: Cassell, 1958.

Sansom, George Bailey. "The Story of Singapore". *Foreign Affairs: An American Quarterly Review* 2, 2 (1944).

Shennan, Margaret. *Out in the Midday Sun: The British in Malaya, 1880–1960*. London: John Murray, 2000.

Shores, Christopher F., Bran Cull and Yasuho Izawa. *Bloody Shambles. Vol. 1, The Drift of War to the Fall of Singapore*. London: Grub Street, 1992.

Silcock, Thomas and Ungku Abdul Aziz. "Nationalism in Malaya". In *Asian Nationalism and the West: A Symposium Based on Documents and Reports of the Eleventh Conference Institute of Pacific Relations*, ed. William Holland. New York: Octogon, 1953.

Simson, Ivan. *Singapore: Too Little, Too Late; Some Aspects of the Malayan Disaster in 1942*. London: Leo Cooper, 1970.

Stewart, Adrian. *The Underrated Enemy*. London: William Kimber, 1987.

Sixsmith, E.K.G. *British Generalship in the Twentieth Century*. London: Arms and Armour Press, 1970.

Stockwell, A.J. "British Imperial Policy and Decolonization in Malaya 1942–1952". *Journal of Imperial and Commonwealth History* 13 (1948).

Strabogli, Joseph Montague Kenworthy. *Singapore and After: A Study of the Pacific Campaign*. London: Hutchinson & Co., 1942.

Swettenham, Frank Athelstane. *British Malaya: An Account of the Origin and Progress of British Influence in Malaya*. London: John Lane, 1929 (1907).

Tamayama, Kazuo and John Nunneley. *Tales by Japanese Soldiers of the Burma Campaign 1942–1945*. London: Cassell, 2000.

Tarling, Nicholas. *The Fall of Imperial Britain in South-East Asia*. Singapore and New York: Oxford University Press, 1993.

———. *A Sudden Rampage: The Japanese Occupation of Southeast Asia 1941–1945*. London: Hurst, 2001.

Thomas, Mary. *In the Shadow of the Rising Sun*. Singapore: Marshall Cavendish, 2009 (1983).

Thompson, Peter. *The Battle for Singapore*. London: Portrait, 2005.

Thompson, Virginia. *Postmortem on Malaya*. New York: The Macmillan Company, 1943.

Thorne, Christopher. *Allies of a Kind: The United States, Britain, and the War against Japan, 1941–1945*. Oxford: Oxford University Press, 1979.

Toland, John. *The Rising Sun: The Decline and Fall of the Japanese Empire, 1936–1945*. New York: Random House, 1982 (1970).

Towle, Philip, Yōichi Kibata and Margaret Kosuge (eds). *Japanese Prisoners of War*. London and New York: Hambledon and London, 2000.

Towle, Philip. *From Ally to Enemy: Anglo-Japanese Military Relations 1900–45*. Folkestone, Global Oriental, 2006.

Trotter, Ann. *Britain and East Asia 1933–1937*. London and New York: Cambridge University Press, 1975.

Tsuji, Masanobu. *Singapore: The Japanese Version*. New York: St Martin's Press, 1960.

Wang Gungwu. "Malayan Nationalism". *Royal Central Asian Society Journal* 49, 3–4 (1962): 317–28.

Warren, Alan. *Singapore, 1942: Britain's Greatest Defeat*. London and New York: Hambledon and London, 2002.

Wavell, Archibald Percival. *Speaking Generally: Broadcasts, Orders and Addresses in Time of War (1939–43)*. London: Macmillan, 1946.

Wigmore, Lionel. *The Japanese Thrust*. Canberra: Australian War Memorial, 1957.

Wilmott, H.P. *Empires in the Balance: Japanese and Allied Pacific Strategies to April 1942*. London: Orbis, 1982.

Winstedt, Sir Richard. *The Campaign in the Malay States*. British Malaya, February 1942.

———. *Malaya and its History*. London: Anchor Press, 1950.

Yoji, Akashi. "Japanese Research Activities in Occupied Malaya/Syonan, 1943–45". In *New Perspectives on the Japanese Occupation in Malaya and Singapore 1941–1945*, ed. Akashi Yoji and Mako Yoshimura, pp. 158–185. Singapore: NUS Press, 2008.

———. "Colonel Watanabe Wataru: The Architect of the Malayan Military Administration, December 1941–March 1943". In *New Perspectives on the Japanese Occupation in Malaya and Singapore 1941–1945*, ed. Akashi Yoji and Mako Yoshimura, pp. 33–64. Singapore: NUS Press, 2008.

———. "General Yamashita Tomoyuki: Commander of the Twenty Fifth Army". In *A Great Betrayal: The Fall of Singapore Revisited*, ed. Brian P. Farrell and Sandy Hunter. Singapore: Marshall Cavendish, 2009.

Yoji, Akashi and Mako Yoshimura. *New Perspectives on Japanese Occupation, Malaya and Singapore 1941–1945*. Singapore: NUS Press, 2008.

Ziegler, Philip. *Diana Cooper: The Biography of Lady Diana Cooper*. London: Hamish Hamilton, 1981.

INDEX